Idom Ministries

~Millstone~

If Only I Would Have Known

Linda Idom

Dedication

This book was written for the

Hurting

Abused

Rejected

Abandoned

Bullied

Tormented

Depressed

Neglected

Hopeless
and the Used.

I dedicate this book to all who are
wounded and wonder where God is.

Acknowledgements

First and foremost, I thank the Holy Spirit of God who guides when we feel lost, comforts when we feel overwhelmed, and answers the desperate cries of our hearts.

My most heartfelt admiration and gratitude to Travis Idom, who loves and forgives like no one I have ever met. His bravery in sharing his past, his steadfast concern for others, and his hopefulness in the midst of brutal realities is the second biggest reason this book is here.

To the others whose names have been changed but also shared their stories, I am in awe of your courage and your honesty. Children will be saved the horror of being molested because of you. Thank you for helping me shine a light on the darkness. No matter what the critics say, you are the heroes.

Thank you to all my family who were totally supportive, and a special word of appreciation to Theresa Black for her constant, unwavering belief in God's calling on this project. Her words set me back on track, time and time again. Thank you also to Robin Parkin who cried with me, cheered for me, and whose encouragements were life giving and renewing.

A hearty "what would I do without you!" to many friends who critiqued my book. A special thanks to Hal Rhodes, Anita Graves, Marion Pietz, Misti Bullen, Angela Kenney, and Michael Chaney. Millstone is so much better than it would have been without you.

To my editor, Jeanette Morris, I just shake my head and wonder at God giving me such a gentle, patient spirit to work with on this project. Thank you. You taught me a lot.

To Alison, whose words of wisdom on one of my lowest days caused my heart to search God's heart at a deeper level.

I thank you for wiping the tears off my face and sharing His love with me.

There are many more, and God knows, as I do, who you are…Thank you.

Linda Idom

Contents

A Must-Read Introduction

Sunrise after sunrise slowly crept up on the black horizon as I lay awake and argued with a seed of an idea growing inside my heart. I agonized over the possibility that the stories begging to be told might hurt people I love. I didn't want to dig through a pile of pain or rub anyone's face in their sin. I certainly didn't want to ask questions that would cause loved ones to have to recall awful memories long buried and abandoned.

Travis and Suzie were certain that they wanted me to share their stories. But I wondered if they would one day regret speaking up about the childhood sexual molestation they had endured. What about their families? All precious, loved souls that might be shamed, harmed, or devastated by the painful truth. I dreaded the humiliation Travis and Suzie might feel, and I dreaded my own reactions to their pain. I worried and wondered if their stories would truly help others like them find healing. I worried that people would be so disgusted with the truth that they might over-focus on the deeply disturbing details and forget about the devastating physiological trauma experienced daily by abuse victims all around them.

Well, if you're reading this, you know I gave in to Travis, Suzie, and my heart. The doubts that tormented me faded bit by bit. Finally, I broke through the tangle of questions and could see a light at the end of a dense jungle. I worked hard to write Travis's and Suzie's stories as truthfully and realistically as possible. To do that, I had to share some of the awful realities. Granted, some critics will say that sexual predators may read these stories to get their sick kicks, so I shouldn't have included so much detail. In my defense, let me say that I thought long and hard about that. I tried to shed light on the circumstances in a way that is not salacious nor overly offensive. But omitting all the details would defeat the purpose of sharing their stories altogether, because I believe it is impossible to comprehend how someone feels unless you have a "reasonable" idea of what they went through.

There are wonderful Christian people who will say that Christians don't talk about such sordid things, and all this unpleasantness needs to be under the blood of Christ, forgiven and forgotten. To that point, I respond by saying that turning a light on something evil can be shocking, but how else can we change things or make our world a safer place if we won't even *try* to comprehend and confront the realities of our fallen world?

In Ephesians 5:11, Paul tells us not to participate in the unfruitful works of darkness, but instead to "expose" them. Paul then says in verse 12 that "it is a shame to even speak of the things evil people do in secret." (KJV)

I have thoughtfully considered this verse in reference to writing about what happens to sexual molestation victims and I have fully investigated this concern.

However, immediately following this verse, Paul again encourages us to expose evil deeds. (v. 13) *"For when anything is exposed to the light it becomes visible."* As these two admonishments to "expose" evil sandwich the statement that "it is a shame to even speak about their deeds," I assume that because Paul warned us in verse 4 to refrain from filthy, foolish conversation and joking about coarse, corrupt evil things, a reasonable conclusion is that He means for us not to speak about them in a way that is not productive, but rather to expose them in a way that will convict or condemn in the most productive, prudent way possible. I have tried to do that. You can read these verses now and decide for yourself. Please consider that we (as Christians) have covered over the raw reality about molestation under a beautiful umbrella of forgiveness and prudence for way too long. We do it because of our strong sense of decency, and it has gotten us nowhere fast. The perpetrators are protected, and the victims are left in their own private hell. We have got to try something different because our school hallways, our daycare playgrounds, our church pews, foster homes, our jail cells, our suicide watch hospitals, and our living rooms are filling with those injured. The truth is, we typically are not motivated to firm a resolve, make a difference, or effect change until we have experienced, up close and personally, the possible outcome of our being unaware of the devastation experienced by the victims.

When you get to a part of *Millstone* where your stomach turns and you want to throw the book across the room, understand that in that very instant of Travis's and Suzie's testimonies, I have left out the worst details. When you wonder, *how can a Christian writer even type this stuff,* try to remember that I protected you from the most disgusting acts and facts by leaving them out.

Unfortunately, no one was there to protect Travis and Suzie, or so many thousands like them. We owe it to the victims of sexual abuse to hear them, turn the lights on and start talking about the damage this does in an open and frank way. Travis's and Suzie's true stories are agonizing, but I believe their stories serve a great purpose for victims and their families who are trying to cope with the fallout from sexual abuse. I also believe there is a great benefit to those who are as yet unaffected by it. My hope is that Travis's and Suzie's stories will start a ball of "understanding the victim's loss" rolling downhill so fast and with so much momentum that it will knock a huge hole in the dead center of our current epidemic of ignorance. Their stories certainly changed me.

Nevertheless, if you are a victim or a victim's family member and you discern at any point that Travis's and Suzie's stories are too upsetting, too real, or too painful for you to bear on top of your own grief, then feel free to skip the even-numbered chapters. Move ahead to the odd- numbered chapters which contain life-healing truths. These chapters tackle hard impulses we have in our hearts as victims of any trauma, including death of a loved one, disability, or any tragedy that leaves you feeling hopeless. *Millstone* offers insight on the topics of anger toward God, blame, God's heart toward us, God's heart toward those who have hurt us, our hearts toward God, trust, justice, and judgement. If you read the odd-numbered chapters, you will gain a fresh perspective, which will bring healing to your heart and increase your trust in our Lord Jesus Christ.

Silence is the enemy. Satan wants to keep us all locked in our secret shame. *Shhh, don't tell. You'll hurt everyone. They'll think you're disgusting. They will see you differently. They'll despise you. They won't believe you. You need to hide it and never talk about it. They'll think you are sick. It's shameful to talk about these things.* Please don't believe those lies. What if "they" told you not to talk about some other traumatic event you endured, like a childhood disease, a hostage situation, a vicious dog attack, a fire or a brutal beating? Forbidding the telling of these situations seems ridiculous, right? It's the nature of sexual molestation that holds the victim and the perpetrator captive in a life- stealing silence. I say "and the perpetrator" because so many perpetrators are very young when they start offending.

Now don't get the impression that this book will be soft on any person abusing a child. It will not. That understood, we've got to stop this epidemic, and if we are going to make a difference, we have to look at these issues, talk about them, and try to figure out what will help.

For those of you who are victims of sexual abuse, let me ask you to please consider letting these stories act as a catalyst to walk you through the pain you've endured. As you feel the pain, go to God. Pay special attention to the even-numbered chapters as they are there to help you heal. Let these stories walk you through the journey needed for healing. That's what happened for me (also a victim of childhood abuse) as I wrote and experienced Travis's and Suzie's stories. I healed. Yes, it hurt, but it was worth it.

Millstone may also help you understand yourself and give you permission to mourn your devastating loss. No more stuffing your feelings in suffocating silence. If you are bound by habitual fear or other strongholds, you can have complete healing. However, it takes time and effort. *Millstone* may also help you understand that you are not alone in your journey.

Reading *Millstone,* you will discover a new view of God's heart toward you.

To those of you who have never been molested, let me say that Travis's and Suzie's stories spotlight the tremendous loss a victim endures. If you want to understand the victim, so you can help a victim you know, this is the book for you.

A note to all readers: If you feel overwhelmed by grief or anger as you read Travis's and Suzie's stories, stop and go straight to chapter 7: "If Only I Would Have Known." Read it several times if you need to. Go back to it if you find yourself struggling again. My objective is not to incite rage or hatred for abusers. My objective is to inform you about the psychological effects on these innocent children and to cause you to examine your own heart when it comes to blame, God, the perpetrator, suffering, trust, and judgement.

My hope is that *Millstone* serves as an eye-opening warning to parents to be proactive and aware of dangerous situations in their children's lives and surroundings. I also pray it's an encouragement to all who read it to evaluate all children's environments with a certain amount of suspicion and a more careful examination of the people our children are exposed to. I hope that by putting some real truth out on center stage, it will cause us all to lock arms and stand together using information, education, and wisdom to widen the circle around the children that we can protect in our lives. Lord God in Heaven, let us make a difference!

My deep desire is that people who have no idea how to relate to, talk to, or comfort a victim can read *Millstone* and come out filled with confident knowledge they can rely on to comfort, support, and protect the abused.

Anyone brave enough to take Travis's and Suzie's hands and walk through their experiences from a child's perspective will gain a unique and valuable understanding.

Millstone offers all people who have suffered at the hands of someone else the courage and renewed trust to forgive. It offers tools which will enable them to release the person or persons who hurt them. Not just the ones who hurt them in the past, but the ones who will hurt them in the future. *Millstone* paints a clear picture of God's plan and purpose for our existence, especially in the midst of devastating life events.

I have a great hope that victims of sexual abuse and their devastated family members will search their hearts as they experience Travis's and Suzie's pain to see if they too blame God. It certainly will bring them to a boiling point if they have their doubts about where God is and why He seems to remain silent in our suffering. I hope this book lays to rest nagging doubts about God's love for us. I hope that victims who read it will get a fresh, clear look at a holy God who hates sin and will one day serve a justice that only a holy God can serve.

Although I am not a pastor, preacher, seminary student, or teacher, I am a Holy-Spirit-filled, armor-covered child of the Most-High God. But I can still make mistakes. I learn from my mistakes, and so I tend to make them just as fast and furiously as I can. For me to entertain the thought that there might not be a single mistake in this book makes me laugh out loud. Please read my words knowing that I prayed and waited on the Holy Spirit before writing them. You and I are on the same road. I pray my words help and heal.

In addition, I have been an avid reader for years but can have a rather flawed memory at times. So, if you read anything I have written, and it seems you've heard it before, you probably have. I expect you to give full credit to whomever you heard it from first and understand that in no way did I purposely withhold credit from them or intend to plagiarize.

Also, the sixteenth chapter of this book deals with the pain and torment of suicide. If you are sensitive or have lost someone to suicide, please consider listening to your heart about whether to read those few pages. God is love and He is merciful. I believe He catches us when we fall. I believe He judges each case individually and considers the circumstance of every suicide through the Spirit of Love, because that is who He is.

Finally, most names and some details have been changed in Travis's and Suzie's stories to protect the innocent and respect their privacy. Our hope, (mine, Travis's, and Suzie's) is that this book brings healing, binds up the wounded, encourages the broken, and sets captives free.

CHAPTER 1

The Dream

In a dream, in a vision of the night; When deep
sleep falleth, in slumberings upon the bed; Then
He openeth the ears of men, and sealeth their
instruction.

(Job 33:15-16 KJV)

Have you ever just started thinking about something, and before you knew it, you had imagined some crazy story, some non-reality that had you upset to the point of paralyzing fear, severe anger, or tears? When my children were little, I sometimes imagined that something awful happened to them or someone broke into the house or that my mom had died. Before I knew it, I was upset. At some point, I would catch myself and talk myself back down. "What are you doing?" I would scold myself, "Why are you thinking about this? It's crazy. It's not even real, and here you are all upset. You're crying, and nothing has even happened."

So, this is what prompted me to question whether I was dreaming. I mean, could I have imagined it or hallucinated the horror I had just experienced? I'd have felt better if I had known I was hallucinating. Maybe you can decide.

Here are the facts:

I was lying in my bed. It was early in the morning and I had just awoken. I was aware of the room around me, yet I had not committed to opening my eyes. I know I saw everything in my mind as if it were happening. I snuggled into the down comforter and let my mind remember my deepest worries. Letting my thoughts wonder, I talked to God. I might have even dozed back off. I can't be sure.

The problem is, I was so present in this "dream" that calling it a dream doesn't seem real enough. For me, dreams are generally foggy, spotty, and unclear. This one was crystal clear and vivid with details not typical in my dreams. Nevertheless, I saw it all in my mind while my body was in the bed.

Once, many years ago, I dreamt that I was ice skating. It was a lucid dream (something I didn't even know existed until I looked it up on the Internet later that day). In this lucid dream, I could feel the wind on my face as I was gliding across the ice. I could feel every muscle in my body reacting to my thoughts as I pushed with each stroke of my legs, skating through the dimly lit arena. I could feel the tender skin on the inside of my forearms brush against the red velvet body suit I wore. I could feel myself breathe and could see the vapor of my breath. Gaining speed, I shifted my weight, turning and swinging my leg up, forcing the momentum of my speed to catapult me into the air. As I was twirling through the humid, cool mist, my arms were tucked tightly to my sides. I could feel the force of my spin whipping my hair through the frigid, damp air. I felt my arms carefully move away from my body as I slowed the spin in mid-air. Kicking my left leg out, I felt the blade of the skate gouging the ice as I landed. Gently and effortlessly, all my weight balanced on my left leg, my right leg up at a perfect 45-degree angle, I slid across the ice like I had done it a thousand times. When I awoke, I could have sworn I was able to put blades on and ice skate like a professional, even though I had never had a lesson in my life. It was without a doubt the coolest dream ever.

The dream I will soon share with you was just as lucid as the ice skating dream. It was like a Matrix download. Have you seen the movie *The Matrix*? Where Neo gets his fighting lessons? It was like that. So, because I have such a hard time deciding whether this was a lucid dream or my imagination on fire, (maybe half-dream, half-imagination), I'll just give up and call it a dream.

Before I share the dream with you, in order to help you understand its significance, you should first be aware of my mental and spiritual state leading up to the dream. So, in all fairness to you, dear reader, please bear with me as I explain the key circumstances and events that led up to that morning's vexing revelation.

Up until that season in my life, I had no concept of how many children were abused, hurting, molested, and victimized. The reason I didn't know was because up until the previous two years, I had lived in my own carefully orchestrated world. I hung around numerous, likeminded Christian homeschooling mothers. I visited with church families and I watched wholesome, carefully chosen TV programs. I really tried to keep the Scripture from Philippians in mind:

"Finally, brothers and sisters, whatever is true, whatever is noble, whatever is right, whatever is pure, whatever is lovely, whatever is admirable—if anything is excellent or praiseworthy— think about such things" (Phil.4:8 NIV).

I worked hard at doing what I thought was right. Looking back, it is painfully obvious that sometimes, despite my effort, I failed.

When my kids were ready for work and college, and I was on my own during the day, I decided to volunteer at Angel Reach, a center for young adults who have aged out of foster care. The term "aged out" simply means they turn eighteen and are no longer financially supported by the state. Whether they are in a state-run facility or a private home, their funds are cut off. If they happen to turn eighteen in the middle of their senior high school year, it's often too bad. The state gives them a map, so they know where the Salvation Army is, and turns them out on the street. Many foster care providers in private homes do the same. Sadly, some are only in it for the money.

At Angel Reach, I learned that within one year of aging out and trying to make it on their own, a whopping 50 percent of those youth in the Houston area become homeless. A mind-boggling 60 percent age out without completing high school. Fifty-five percent are seriously addicted to drugs (no surprise there). Twenty-six percent are incarcerated during the first year on their own. Shockingly, 67 percent of the females bear a child within the first year. What is really horrifying is that

70 percent of the children born to aged-out foster youth end up in foster care. Less than 10 percent ever complete any form of higher education or training; less than 2 percent ever finish a four-year college. I don't have a statistic for how many of them are turning tricks (selling their precious bodies) at the car wash or in the bathroom of the public library, but I know that they are. To further complicate matters, the state pays the facility or private home more money depending on how many psychotropic medications the foster child is on, a practice that encourages drug saturation.

During my time at Angel Reach, I was able to visit with and counsel several dozen of these young people. Since choosing to volunteer and eventually taking a paid position, I heard numerous broken-hearted friends and coworkers' hearts poured out over their experiences with these troubled young people. It truly was gut wrenching, especially because I had unknowingly secluded myself from many harsh realities. Except for an occasional astonishingly awful headline on the evening news, I was clueless.

The day I met Sandra Carpenter, the founder of Angel Reach, she impatiently glanced at me and said, "I had four volunteers quit this week, I lost an employee, and we had the police here twice. If you are dainty, soft, easily get your feelings hurt or are fragile, I don't need you here."

I stood there stunned. After all, I was there trying to help and do what I considered my Christian duty. I swallowed my joyful enthusiasm, tucked my shining benevolence into my back pocket, and a few awkward seconds later, I thoughtfully replied, "Well, in all honesty … I will probably get my feelings hurt and even cry. I get attached to people easily and I will grow to care about them. But I won't quit." The last four words were uttered with a steely determinedness that caused Sandra to stop and look me in the face with what seemed like serious consideration.

Sandra's large, round brown eyes almost flashed as she looked me over. She took less than three seconds to consider my countenance. Then without the slightest bit of hope in her voice she said, "We'll see, won't we?"

I have several times since then referred to Sandra as a

perfect cross between a pit bull and the Good Fairy. She's a petite brunette with a killer smile, but she can rain on a parade like a summer storm with multiple vortexes, flattening everything in her reach. I once saw her pick up a neatly duct-taped pup tent off the front porch of the assessment center and chuck it down at the feet of a young girl who was being let go from the program for drug abuse. This young girl was four months pregnant.

"You'll have to sleep in the woods," Sandra said to the girl. "You knew the rules, and this is your third offense. You can re-apply in three months."

It was November and cold. At that moment, I thought Sandra was about the most heartless woman I'd ever met. About five minutes later, however, I changed my tune as I walked into her office to give her a report and saw her weeping. I learned that Sandra believed in tough love, although she is one of the most compassionate people I know.

All statistics aside, it is my personal experience that brings me to believe that youth who have been raised in foster group homes are not ready for the world and can't thrive without help. They need cooking skills, which they have not received, as sharp knives and boiling water can be liabilities for the state. As is driver's education, so they can't drive. These young ones have almost all been on numerous hard-core psychotropic medications, and most all have been severely physically or mentally abused. The vast majority, sexually abused. Once dismissed from state-run foster homes or private foster homes, many end up in prostitution and on drugs.

In the course of my work, I spent one or two days a week driving these kids around town—to work, school, the doctor's office, or to just run errands. Because they needed a ride and were trapped in my car, we had lots of time to talk. We had conversations covering just about everything, including drugs, politics, and our favorite ice cream flavors. I enjoyed my time with them. I want to share one of these conversations with you. This subject came up often.

"I don't think there really is a God." Tristin's tight, choking throat was constricting his voice as tears filled his big, brown eyes. "I don't really believe in him. If there was a God, he would have helped when my foster parent was beating my little sister and me with a hanger over and over and over. Not a spanking, not a whipping, but beatings. Repeatedly."

He told me this while I was taking him to work one afternoon. Tristin's seventeen years on earth had not been a hayride. "I'm convinced that all these scientists who say we evolved must be right," he continued. "I mean, they would know, those scientists are way smarter than I am."

"So, you don't believe there is an intelligent designer?" I replied.

"No. They've studied all this stuff. I'm taking their word for it. We evolved over millions of years and it just happened by chance. We are a great big accident. Amazing, right?" he said, with absolutely no enthusiasm at all.

I asked him how the Grand Canyon got here. He replied that a lot of water must have flowed really fast through that area and caused the huge ruts (canyons) we see today. Then I asked him how the faces on Mount Rushmore got there?

His face twisted in a puzzled half-smile. "You mean where the presidents' faces are carved in the mountain?"

"Yes," I replied. "How did the visages of the presidents' faces get on the side of that mountain?"

He looked at me like I was stupid, and I guess that was an appropriate response.

"Did a huge amount of water rush over the mountain side and carve the faces in the rock just like the Grand Canyon?" I asked.

He put his hand up on the van door and shifted his body weight to turn his upper torso toward me, tilting his head while wrinkling his face. With one eyebrow raised, he said, "Mrs. Linda, now you're scaring me."

I smiled. "Well, how'd those faces get there?"

"Well, someone carved them of course," he replied. "They climbed up that sucker and used dynamite to blast the nose holes!" Then he laughed. "I don't know exactly," he shrugged his shoulders.

"Well, we at least agree that there was a sculptor? An

artist who carved it?"

"Well, sure," he concluded.

Just about then we arrived back at Angel Reach, and I stopped at the curb in front of the office. Turning toward him, I said, "Tristan, look at my face." I leaned toward him and closed my eyes.

"Mrs. Linda, you are beautiful."

I opened my eyes, as it was my turn to raise my eyebrow. "Tristin, look at me. I have a face just like the faces on Mount Rushmore, only I can think. I can see with eyes that turn the image upside down and back again for my brain to comprehend it. I can breathe the oxygen manufactured by living green plants all over this ball that is spinning through space. Even more incredibly, the plants and trees absorb the much-needed carbon dioxide I exhale. It's a system. It's a plan. It's a design. My tongue can form words to express feelings and ideas in my heart and mind. There are certain longings that I feel for love, acceptance, and being valued, and I have no idea how they got in me or why I feel them. They are just longings I can't shake off. You're telling me a rock image of the presidents' faces can't get on Mount Rushmore without a designer, a carver, or an artist, because that would be illogical. But, I, with all my complexities and designer details, I got here by accident? No artist for the details of my unique face? No engineer for my movements and body functions? No programmer for my exquisite mental ability?" I paused to grin at him. No personal entity who is responsible for fulfilling the longings and desires I feel yet can't escape?"

The look on Tristin's face was priceless. I could see a huge question walking its way across his beautifully rich, coffee-colored skin.

"They are wrong, Tristin. Don't let them confuse you with their scientific mumbo jumbo. Great scientific minds have been wrong lots of times before. This is pure logic and there is no way around its simplicity. There has to be a creator. You're right. The faces on Mount Rushmore can't get there by accident, and neither can I happen by mere chance. It's too farfetched to believe."

As my time serving at Angel Reach continued, I struggled

with how to explain to these injured young people that God exists or that He loves and cares about them when their pasts bore no proof of it. In fact, quite the contrary. Within that two-year period, I had a suitcase full of stories. They weren't just stories to me though. They were hurting, betrayed souls wondering and searching for acceptance and love. They were lashing out, they were crying out. They were completely and utterly lost, yet right there in front of me.

One young lady told me how her mother had traded her to a pimp for drugs. This man chained her to a bed. He poked her with needles, shot her full of drugs, and sold her to customers. She told me about the sounds of the outside world, the smells of their breath and the body odors, having only enough chain to get to the toilet that was a bucket.

The worst part about it was that she didn't know where her younger sister was, and she was constantly tormented by the thoughts and dreams that her sister was alone, terrified, and crying for help. The thought that her sister might have to wake up half-drugged with disgusting men raping her too was more than she could stand. As she spoke to me, she looked as if she was going to throw up any second. This child had been nine years old when this happened—a time when she should have been laughing and playing with friends on a playground.

This young lady's mother finally came and got her, only to turn around and abandon her again the next summer. Her mother had told her and her sister to wait by a dumpster behind a store while she ran an errand. She never returned. The bewildered young sisters lived on the streets for almost a week, and then ended up spending the rest of their youth in over twelve different foster centers. To make matters more awful, within a month of being picked up by CPS, she was separated from her sister.

It is hard to look these young adults in the face and say, "God loves you." It's like you're offering them the Water of Life, but they have nothing to put it in. Whatever vessel they once had has been broken to pieces, so the Water just spills onto the floor. They cannot believe the words "Jesus loves you."

I prayed for one particular young lady every time I thought of her and how she vehemently, in front of ten other girls at a mandatory Bible study in her group home, denied that there is a God who loves us.

"There is no God!" she shouted. "I know that for a fact. He doesn't exist. I'm certain ... because when I was begging, pleading, and crying out to him to get those men off of me, God did nothing. He didn't help me when I needed him." This last young lady's comment had been haunting me for several days.

I tried to move on, but this girl's comments felt like hooks in my back, hanging on me like dead weight. It wasn't the worst story or comment I'd ever heard. Not by a long shot. But, I couldn't shake it. This young lady was a victim of sex trafficking. I had learned, to my horror, that there was no shortage of devastating, mind-boggling, flat disgusting stories of abuse and depravity when I ventured outside my suburban, middle-class, homeschool, church family existence.

A few days after that last young ladies comment was made, I heard a story on the radio about a five-year-old boy who had been abducted from a school playground and sodomized in the nearby woods by a thirteen-year-old. Immediately, the thought popped into my mind: they should take that abusive kid, castrate him, and then throw him in prison for life.

I'm going to give you a second to let that sink in. Yes, that's exactly how I feel. Every time I hear some awful story like this on TV, radio, or from one of these precious young ones, I have to calm my anger toward the perpetrator and then reassure myself of God's love, as occasionally my next thought is: I know it's not okay with you, God, for this awful stuff to happen. But how can you watch this? I then set out to convince myself that even though God allowed this, God is still good.

This is how I sounded trying to convince myself: "I know God loves us. He cares about these wounded, weak ones. He doesn't want those things to happen. He's heartbroken when we hurt. He has to be.

The Bible says so. 1 John 4:8 says 'God is love.' Psalms 100:5 says, 'For the Lord is good and His love endures forever. His faithfulness continues through all generations.' And what about Psalm 86:15? 'But you, Lord, are a compassionate and gracious God, slow to anger, abounding in love and faithfulness.' I recalled a verse in Exodus 34:6 where God says the very same thing about himself.

That said, try and quote Jeremiah 29:11(KJV) (where God is speaking to the nation of Israel) to one of these young adults. "For I know the thoughts that I think towards you, saith the Lord, thoughts of peace and not of evil, to give you an expected end." Oh, they might nod, smile or make a joke. They might even have a cordial discussion with you, but they won't believe you.

It's hard to reconcile this God, whom the Scripture teaches us is love, with a God that will allow these atrocities. I believe in God. I know He cares. I could write several books about the amazing miracles He has done in my life. When I seek Him diligently, He answers me. No one can convince me He is not real. I know Him. I've really experienced God. But after all these heartbreaking stories that touched my life, something stirred in my soul. Did I doubt God's perfect love for us? From my perspective now, I'll whisper a soft, little "yes" right here. Did I realize it at the time? No, absolutely not. At least not consciously.

One more thing before sharing my dream. Just this morning, my husband told me a story a pastor told him. I want you to keep this story in your mind as you read my dream, which is coming soon, I promise.

The pastor found a cat. It was homeless, starving, and had a nasty cut. The pastor took the cat in and fed and nursed it back to health. The cut healed, the cat gained weight, and soon purred like the dickens every time the pastor came home. One day the pastor noticed the cat did not greet him. The cat was lethargic and not eating, so he took it to the vet.

"Well, here is the problem," the vet said as he pressed the old scar from the cut the cat had several weeks before. The pastor looked at it and told the doctor that the cat had a cut when he found it, but that he had cleaned it off and it healed. The doctor then squeezed the scar area. Nasty pus burst out of the side of the scar where the skin had torn open with the pressure. The cat was in great pain because the cut that had looked healed from the outside was infected. It could have caused the cat to die as the abscess was poisoning the cat from the inside out. The pastor was astonished to see that the cat had looked so healthy for so long, yet had this bad infection inside.

You see, I was just like this cat. I needed those verses about God's love to smear like an ointment over the pain I was feeling. Not that it's wrong to reassure yourself with the Word of God. Of course, we should do that, because it is true. But, I didn't realize that I was trying to take the encouraging verses (my head knowledge) and cover a deep, festering sore with them. The sore (my heart) needed to be cleaned out and healed. The depth of my mistrust was about to become apparent to me. It wasn't a little doubt, if there is such a thing. I not only didn't completely trust God, but I blamed Him and held Him accountable. This, my friend, is the difference between a completely healed wound and a disgusting, life-stealing, festering, but seemingly healed sore.

The morning of the dream, I believe that God opened my mind and let my heart go where I needed to go. I was fasting, and God often speaks to me when I'm fasting.

After a night of great sleep, I awoke. I could hear the wind chimes softly singing on my balcony. Suddenly, I was lifted out of my bed and flying over the neighboring houses. The early morning air was still and peaceful. I was gliding maybe thirty to forty feet high above the rooftops, but suddenly the houses had no shingles, and I could see clearly down into them.

Looking to my left and down into a house, I was suddenly looking at a man on top of a young girl. He wore a yellow, white, and brown plaid shirt and blue jeans that were pulled down around his upper thighs. He looked to be mostly clothed, but obviously raping the girl under him. My spirit cried out within me and I screamed at the top of my lungs, "Oh, my God! Someone stop him! Oh God! Someone please help!" I burst into tears, glancing up in a panic looking for help. I saw only a calm, peaceful and serene horizon. The quietness of the sky was shocking and disturbing, in a way. It was amazingly beautiful, yet the sky was still dark and lonely. The tranquil glory of the dawn was eerie. I looked to the left. Again, nothing but beauty and an absolute, silent loneliness.

My frantic cries for help soon turned into demands. "Just

kill him! Stop him! Oh God, someone kill him!" I was begging and pleading as loud as I could. "Please kill him, kill him, kill him!" I looked around desperately for someone to help, but again, I was alone.

I cannot describe how completely terrified and abandoned I felt. It was as if there was no one else in the universe except me, the victim, and the perpetrator. I was focused on the rapist with hatred, disgust, and horror. I felt something building within me. Now aware of this force of heat somewhere in my chest, I turned the hatred loose. All that rage went out of my stomach and flew toward the perpetrator.

With a ball of laser like light force, a kind of furious willpower, I shot him in the back. And I killed him! He fell to the side, his terrorized victim suddenly saved, but now only a vague shadow. Then she was gone. The release of vile hatred I felt when I shot him reverberated from the cheeks of my face to my knees. It was amazing.

Immediately, I was in the air again. Another shot was fired as I judged and sentenced the next perpetrator as viciously as my heart commanded. Again and again, my hatred growing, I killed them, one after the next. I felt more than justified in doing so; I felt righteous. The more I killed, the angrier I became. It was like a huge dose of gasoline being poured on a fire, and it felt incredible. I was shaking with hatred.

Just as hot liquid pours into a mold, vengeance filled every molecule of my being. Rage, Anger, Hate and I were newly born. The fierce disgust I felt toward the raping, selfish pigs was now itself the volume of my own voice turned up to the highest level. All I could hear was "Kill them!"

I was desperate to stop the perpetrator that I now focused on. A huge lump in my throat choked off my breath as outrageous pain flooded my heart and tears ran down my face. I could see him standing in a shower, his back to me. His victim on the opposite side was much smaller. It was a child. I couldn't tell if the victim was a young girl or a boy, but I think it was a boy. I tried to see around the perpetrator as I willfully released the shot of lethal power toward him.

Nothing happened. It was dead in the air. My power was suddenly gone without explanation. Somehow, in my mind

I understood it had been taken away permanently. But I was not even fazed by this abrupt change.

Aware of my sudden inability to shoot him, yet not even slightly swayed from my purpose, I went toward this man. Murderous hatred was fully aflame in my soul. "Fine," I said to myself. "I'll cut his throat if I can't shoot him. I'll just slit his throat and bleed him out." As I willed myself with fuming determination to drift toward him, I lifted my right arm. A blade appeared out of thin air. It was in my right hand, held twelve or so inches from my face and at eye level. It was curved and razor-sharp; the silver glistened, catching the light. As I came closer to him, my speed slowed. I put all my energy into getting close enough to cut his throat.

I screamed, "Where are you, God? Why don't you stop this man? How can you let this go on?" I gripped the knife tightly. Deliberately, I moved my arm back and out to the right. I steadied myself to grasp him from behind. "God!" I screamed furiously, "You're just letting this happen! Why don't you stop them? Why? Why? Why, don't you help us?"

Make It Personal

Have you ever had a dream you thought was from the Lord? Write a summary of it here:

_____

_____

_____

Can you relate to me (my state of mind) before I started volunteering at Angel Reach? If you feel like you are somewhat sheltered, list in what ways here:

_____

_____

_____

Can you relate to the youth at Angel Reach? In what ways?

_____

_____

_____

Have you ever wondered why God allows atrocities like child abuse? What other atrocities do you question as to why God allows them?

_____

_____

_____

What is your knee-jerk reaction to drunk drivers, murderers, thieves, rapists, or pedophiles? Write down three descriptive words.

_____

_____

_____

Do you ever blame God for the evil things others do because He doesn't stop them? What specific evil things come to your mind? How do you explain these things to yourself?

_____

_____

_____

Is there any possibility that, like the cat in the pastor's story, you have wounds that need healing? Or like me, you have questions deep inside that are causing you to be offended at God? Make a list of any you may be aware of.

_____

_____

_____

Notes

CHAPTER 2

Travis and Suzie
Rainy Saturdays and
Sunday Mornings

*"I have trust issues. I mean, if God allowed all those
awful things to happen to me as a child, what else
will He allow?"*

... Suzie

F ive-year-old Suzie sits in her quiet room on the edge of
the bed and stares at the closed door. *Why did it have to
rain on a Saturday? I wish it was a school day; then I wouldn't
be stuck inside with him.* Suzie glances out the rain-covered
windowpane. Huge, grey clouds push their way across the
tops of the tall pines. She tries to distract herself from the storm
and reaches for her Barbie doll. She straightens Barbie's silky,
blue ballgown then puffs Barbie's oversized sleeves. "Do you
want to put your boots and raincoat on?" Suzie asks in her
softest voice. Barbie doesn't seem to care, but like a concerned
mother, Suzie insists that Barbie...

BOOM! A clap of thunder hits so hard that Suzie jumps
straight up and darts to the door. She grabs the doorknob but
doesn't turn it. She doesn't know which she is more afraid
of—the lightning and thunder or her step-father, Ray.

Unable to stop herself, she starts to cry. Suzie cowers as
the thunder rumbles, shaking the old, rickety trailer where
she lives. As soon as she starts to cry, she feels the pain in
her face. Suzie squeezes her eyes tight together. *Your lip will
only hurt worse if you cry. You're okay. It's just thunder. He won't*

help you. He'll only hurt you worse. The tears flow. Continuing to hold the doorknob firmly, she reaches up with her other hand to feel her cheek. She runs the tips of her delicate fingers lightly over the tender, raised welts. *Why did he hit me? He is so mean. He hates me.* Her own thoughts viciously attack her and her fingers tremble. Suzie can't make sense of it.

Clenching her teeth and trying to keep her sobs quiet, she carefully surveys the room for the play makeup mirror set that Grams gave her for Christmas. She releases her grip on the doorknob and slowly walks over to the white wicker basket where her mother puts her toys. Suzie keeps her eyes glued on the window, watching the strobe-like lightning as the storm continues to rage outside. Wiping tears from her face, she reaches down for the tattered basket and rummages through it for the little mirror.

Crack! CRACK! Lightning strikes again, ripping through the air as the thunder rumbles. But this time, she is on a mission. She wants to see her face and that keeps her moving forward. Quickly tossing the other toys to the side, she digs for the mirror. "It's only thunder. It's only thunder," Suzie whispers to herself. "Ah! There it is!"

She grabs the pink, plastic rim of the mirror frame and lets the small basket drop to the floor. Lifting the toy mirror to her face, Suzie is horrified by what she sees. One, two, three lines. Perfectly outlined red fingers streak her soft white skin. Her bottom lip is swollen and bruised, and there's a tiny bit of dried blood on it. Suzie sticks her tongue out and touches the tip of it to her lip. She moistens the blood and reaches up to wipe it. A bitter, slightly metallic taste makes her salivate and swallow hard. Suzie's stopped-up nose is red and swollen from crying. Some of her light brown curls lie flat, sticking to her tear-soaked cheek. With her soft—pink-painted fingernails, she peels the hair off her wet face. Intently, she looks straight into her huge, greenish-blue eyes. Suzie watches as tears fill them up and then trickle down her cheeks. She feels even worse now that she's seen herself.

Turning her head as far as she can without losing sight of the raised imprint, she counts the lines again. *One, two, three... I hate him.* The tears flow as she wrinkles her face and gives in to the deep sorrow in her heart. She inhales deeply as she steadies herself against the pain in her lip. She can't control her crying anymore. Just like the storm outside, Suzie can't do a thing about it. Slowly, softly she lets go of the mirror and it thumps as it hits the floor. Fixing her eyes on the window, she walks to her bed. Suzie crawls in under the cheap, stiff comforter. "Momma, Momma," she whispers softly as she pictures her mother's face.

Remembering the walk that they had taken a few days ago makes Suzie miss her mom even more. Picking flowers had been a great excuse to get out of the trailer for a while. Her mom had picked some yellow buttercups and held the Texas-grown blossoms to her lips. "Suzie, can you see the yellow reflection under my chin?" she had said. Suzie had seen it, soft and glowing against her mother's flawless skin.

Then her mother had handed her a buttercup. Suzie remembers putting it under her own tiny nose and looking up at her mom. "Yes, there it is!" her mom had said excitedly. "There's a yellow glow on your nose." Her mom smiled and said, "You're my buttercup baby, and I'm your buttercup momma." Then she had leaned down and put her nose on Suzie's nose. Making her eyes big and smiling, she said, "Let's go pick some more flowers." Suzie had carefully chosen a handful of big buttercups and hurried home so she could step up on the stool in her bathroom. Stretching her short legs and standing tippy-toed, she had raised the buttercups to her neck. There it was…the yellow glow under her chin, just like her mom had said.

That happy memory made Suzie cry even harder. Wiping her tears, Suzie lifts her head off the pillow and looks across the room toward the buttercups she had left on her little white dresser. They are shriveled, drying out, and not pretty anymore. They remind her of the can of shriveled grass and weeds that Ray and her mom keep under the couch. They protect and fight over that red can of dried grass. *I wish I could get that red can and take it outside and dump it in the dirt and stomp all those dried weeds into the mud. Maybe then they would stop acting so stupid. Why does Mom always have to be gone working and him always home?*

Looking at the buttercups, she wonders if she would feel better if she put them in the thin white papers and smoked them, like Mom and Ray. Maybe Ray would like her more.

Staring at the worn carpet, she remembers a night last week when Ray was so mad at her mom about the can of weeds. Her mind slowly drifts back to the horror of it all …

While Ray was yelling about the can, someone knocked on the door. Ray had grabbed the handgun off the TV. Suzie looked at him from where she sat on the couch and wondered why he always got the gun when he answered the door, and why he was always so worried the police were coming. He looked out the window to see who it was.

"Who's there?" Ray demanded.

A man's voice answered. "It's me, Larry." The man sounded angry.

Ray lowered the gun and reached to open the door. BANG! The gun went off with a deafening blast.

Suzie starts to shake again as she recalls how terrified she was as she had jumped up and ran into the hall toward her room. Glancing back, she had seen Ray on the floor. There was blood. He had shot himself in the foot. Suzie could still hear her mother's voice crying out, "Oh my god! Oh my god!" as Ray cussed and screamed. She was sure Ray was going to shoot her mom.

Suzie cries even harder. She remembers other times when Ray pointed the gun at her Momma. As if some awful ghost was walking her back through the scenes, she sees herself throwing her arms up over her head and grasping her curly hair, holding handfuls of it in each hand. She remembers wanting to hide as Ray cried out in pain.

She had headed for her closet, but suddenly thought under the bed might be better. She couldn't decide. She wanted out of the house, but she was trapped.

Finally, she had run to the closet. Suzie hid herself, grabbing clothes and toys to cover up. "Please, Momma, don't fight, don't fight," she had moaned. Crouching down, making herself as small as she could, she prayed, "God, please, please help my momma. Don't let Ray shoot her."

The memory of herself rocking back and forth and crying plays in her mind like a movie. She wants to turn it off but can't. Suzie then remembers the front door slamming. Suzie had thrown her clothes and toys aside as she darted quickly out of the closet and ran to her window. She'd wiped the tears so she could focus, taking care not to be seen.

Suzie could see him in her mind as plain as day. There he was in his cut-off jeans and no shirt, just like always. His foot was wrapped in a towel. The movie played on in her mind. She could hear him cursing and threatening her mom as Larry got him into the car. As she recalls looking out the window at Ray's wrapped foot, she remembers how loud she was crying. He was leaving! She had been so relieved! She could see herself crawling up on her bed and burying her head in the pillow.

Suzie had then heard water running in the kitchen. A cupboard door opened and shut. The phone rang. She remembers her momma's frightened voice talking. Only then had Suzie mustered the courage to leave the safety of her bed to go to find her mom. She could see herself peeking around the corner. Her mother had been on the floor with a wash bucket and towels. Suzie had waited till her mother looked up at her. As soon as their eyes had met, her mom raised her hands, dropping the towel, and stood up to walk toward her. Suzie didn't wait. She had run into her mother's arms and buried her head against her thighs.

"Did Ray go to the doctor?" she had asked.

"Yes, honey, he went to the hospital." Her mom had then squatted so she could look Suzie right in the face. "Your Grams is coming tonight because I have to go to work." Her mother had tried to smile, but it was forced. She could almost hear her mother's words again as she remembered her saying "I'm so sorry that happened. I know it scared you, sweetie. It's going to be okay. You know how Ray is. He'll get over it."

Suzie recalls how hard she was crying when her mom wrapped her arms around her tightly, and while petting her head she had told her, "Don't cry, he is fine. He just shot his foot. Serves him right for being so stupid. Come on." She stood up and took Suzie's hand. "You should be in bed. You've got school tomorrow. Everything is going to be okay. Ray is just being an idiot. You know how he gets, honey." Suzie's mom led her down the hall. "It's alright. Tomorrow after school we will take a walk or something, okay, sweetie?"

"Momma, please stay home!" Suzie had begged.

"I can't, baby," her mother petted her head again. "Come on." Suzie's mom then took her hand and led her to the bathroom. "Let's brush your teeth." She had picked her up and placed Suzie on the stool. "Everything will be okay," she said as she stoked Suzie's soft, brown curls.

Suzie recalls how exhausted her mother's face had looked in the mirror as she stood behind her.

After Suzie's pajamas were on and she was tucked in bed, her mother had knelt down and picked Barbie up off the floor. Barbie was naked. Her mother wrinkled her face at the sight of naked Barbie and reached for the tiny, doll-sized slip that was lying on the floor. Suzie pictures her mom sliding the slip up over Barbie's torso and tucking her in under the covers. "You two get some sleep," she had told her. "We will get a sno-cone tomorrow," her mother had said as she walked toward the door.

As Suzie remembers her mother standing there ready to turn out the light, she longs for her and desperately wants to feel her mother's arms around her. *Why does she love him so much? Why doesn't she make him go away? He is always hurting us. He scares me.* She is so relieved that Ray didn't shoot her mother. But what if he does now that he's back?

Crack! Suzie is again jolted back to reality by another clap of thunder. She looks out the window and pulls the pillow close to her. She wishes Ray would have died in the hospital. But he didn't. He came home and now he is sitting in the big chair in the living room, smoking and yelling all the time. *Is that why he hit me? Maybe he's mad because he shot his foot. I didn't hurt his foot. I was just dancing and trying to make my skirt swirl. He is a pig. I hate him!*

The thoughts keep coming. *He always smells gross, like that stuff he drinks in the big bottles.* She remembers that Ray is just around the corner from her room in the tiny trailer. He's down the short hall and just to the right. She can feel his closeness as if he could reach right through the wall and grab her at any second. She whispers to Barbie, "I can't go out there till Momma gets home."

She looks longingly across the room at the dry buttercups on her dresser. She feels sorry for them. Scooting herself out of the bed, she tiptoes silently across the room. She cups one hand and carefully scrapes the flowers into it with the other. She walks back to her bed, being careful not to crush or drop the straw-like blooms. She tenderly rests the shriveled flowers on the bed and crawls in next to them. Suzie knows just how the flowers feel: dead and wounded and without hope. She reaches for her covers and pulls them up over her shoulder. Suzie puts her arm over the precious weeds to protect them. She will lie here with them and hold them. It's still raining, but the lightning and thunder are moving off in the distance. Carefully protecting the delicate, dying petals, Suzie watches the rain droplets roll down her windowpane until she falls asleep.

"As a small child, I remember being fearless. I thought I would grow up and be strong like Superman. I had no idea what kind of fear an dread would later torment me."

—Travis

Travis is a typical, happy, playful, three-year-old boy. He lives in a small Texas town. His father, a longshoreman at the ship channel, is a hardworking, honorably discharged, Navy/ Army man who started their large family at age twenty-eight. His mother is a stay-at-home mom who loves and adores Travis and his five older siblings.

Travis awakens this morning cuddled in his comfy, soft blankets, immediately aware of the smell of pancakes and sausage. *It must be a church day and Dad is cooking.* Travis crawls out of bed and rounds the corner. Rubbing his dark, green eyes he looks up to see his whole family, all seven of them, seated at the family breakfast table.

His mother turns to him, and, with a bright, loving smile says, "There's my little man! Come here, sweetie."

She holds out her arms and reaches for him to come to her. He yawns as he heads straight for his mother, his footed pajamas making a soft, patting sound. She picks him up and hugs him tightly, brushing the blond, almost white, curl from his forehead. She then offers him bites of her syrup-soaked pancake. Everyone greets him with "Morning, TV!" a nickname he earned by always begging for his favorite shows, mostly cartoons. Being the youngest definitely has its advantages.

His mother kisses his sun-bronzed cheek and says, "Travis, your face is getting so dark! You look like a beach baby." The family talks, laughs, and enjoys their Sunday breakfast together.

At twenty years of age, Micky is not just Travis's older brother, but also his hero. He is never too busy to joke, play, or take Travis fishing at the pond down the road. But Travis knows, even then, that something isn't right with Micky. He yells a lot and is sometimes sad, confused, or scared. Travis doesn't understand why. He just knows that as much as he adores his brother, sometimes Micky is not okay.

Travis's oldest sister, Rebekah, married at the tender age of seventeen. She lives next door with her husband, Kenny. She is spending her senior year of high school shuffling books and setting up their new trailer. Rebekah is a sweet girl and always treats Travis with a motherly love, welcoming his visits.

Adrian is twelve. She likes to cook, and Travis loves her bacon sandwiches.

Eight-year-old Cindy is the quiet one, and you hardly know she is there. Today at breakfast, Cindy has scratches on her freckled face from the swimming lesson that she and Adrian tried to give Travis at the community pool a few days ago. He begged and begged to learn how to swim, but he was so scared. When they tried to let him lay on his back and float by himself, he clawed frantically for his sister Cindy's arms and accidently scratched her cheek. He felt bad about that, but he had been terrified.

Travis looks at the red scratches. *I'll never be able to swim. It's just too hard.*

Theresa is just a year and a half older than Travis. At four-and-a-half, her blonde hair and huge, blue eyes are the perfect complements for her contagious smile and cheerful disposition. She doesn't know it now, but Theresa is going to be resilient when Travis is ready to quit. Theresa is going to be sure when Travis gets confused. Theresa is going to be positive and optimistic about life when Travis gets sick of living. Theresa is going to be his best friend. Her companionship and encouragement will help get him through the devastating, heart-wrenching years ahead.

After breakfast, Travis's mom dresses him for church and sends him to look for his shoes, but he gets distracted. He slides his little feet into his dad's huge, size twelve dress shoes and starts down the hall. "When will I be big, Daddy?" His dad reaches down and picks Travis up. He rubs his whiskers on Travis's neck and face. Travis laughs and turns his face away from his dad's scratchy chin. His dad sits him on the couch. Reaching in his pocket, he pulls out two quarters.

"This is for the offering plate, son. Put it in your pocket." As his dad puts Travis's little, brown dress shoes on his feet, he gives him a stern warning about talking too much when his Sunday school teacher is giving her lesson. Travis understands that his dad means it when he says, "I will take you out on the porch and you will get a whuppin' if you interrupt."

His dad teaches Sunday school and today, like always, Travis will carry his dad's Bible into the church.

With Travis, his four older sisters, his brother-in-law Kenny, his mom, and older brother, Micky, seated on the front row, Travis's dad leads worship. The entire family loves to sing and are often called on to lead the singing with Dad. Travis can't wait for his turn to stand in front of the big, fuzzy mic, even if it does smell really yucky. He loves to hear his voice singing all over the church at once.

Returning home after the service, the family eats fried

chicken, mashed potatoes, coleslaw, biscuits, and sweet tea. Today, Travis follows his dad out to the garden. He tries to hold the bucket that his dad is putting the tomatoes in, but it soon gets too heavy for him. He runs quickly across several rows when he spies a cantaloupe. "Look how big it's getting, Daddy!"

His dad points to his left. "Look at the watermelons, son. They're huge. They'll be ready in a week or two." He smiles at Travis. They carry the vegetables in the house. Travis cautiously steadies the biggest tomato in his hands as he steps through the squeaky back door.

"Be careful, son, if you drop it, it's going to roll down the hill and crush someone's house," his father says with a wink. Everyone looks to see the huge tomato that Travis holds up for them to admire.

"Wow, TV, you going to share that with us?" asks Adrian.

While the girls set the table, Travis's mom starts to sing one of her favorite choruses, "Prayer Bells of Heaven." The girls quickly join in. When the song is finished, Travis calls out to the group, "I want to sing! Momma, I want to sing!" His mother quiets all the girls and says, "Okay, Travis is going to sing now." The girls glance knowingly at each other, half-smiling, and wait patiently so Travis can have all the attention. He belts out:

"Jesus loves the little children, All the children of the world.

Red and yellow black and white they are precious in His sight,

Jesus loves the little children of the world".

"Good job, little man!" his mother says. The girls follow their mother's lead.

"Very nice, TV," Adrian says as she sneaks a look at Cindy, rolling her eyes where no one else could see her.

Cindy chimes in, "Yeah, good job, TV." Then she snickers to her sister.

"Just a closer walk with Thee…." Momma starts singing again and the girls join in. They enjoy lunch together and then spend the rest of the day resting and visiting.

Little Travis could never have known how different life would be for all of them in two, five, ten, or twenty years. Not one of them could have guessed the secrets that would be kept in the future or the cover-ups that would take place under their happy family façade.

Sometimes things are not what they seem. And sometimes, all that has to happen is for a string or two to be yanked out of the family tapestry. When it starts to unravel, the nightmare begins.

Make It Personal

Were your early years like Suzie's–fearful and tormented? Or more like Travis'–nurturing and safe? Or, were they a combination of both? List three of your childhood memories that relate to either one or the other of these situations.

_____

_____

_____

What factors do you think would make a family more likely to have sexual offenders operating without anyone noticing? Make a list of these factors.

_____

_____

_____

As you consider the children you know: Are you aware that the NAASCA statistics show that 1 in 4 girls will be molested by the time they are eighteen, and 1 in 6 boys? These are conservative statistics as many agree that it is higher: 1 in 3 girls. I believe that many people, boys especially, never report it. Do these statistics surprise you? Why or why not?

_____

_____

_____

What steps have you taken so far in your family to ensure that the children are protected from sexual predators? List them here.

_____

_____

_____

If you have been abused or molested, have you ever considered telling your story? Why? Why not?

_____

_____

_____

If you have never been molested, do you think abuse victims should remain silent? Why?

_____

_____

_____

Please stop now and pray that God will help you process Travis's and Suzie's stories, focusing on awareness, general understanding, and growth related to protecting children around you.

_____

_____

_____

Notes

CHAPTER 3

Barely Getting a Clue

Jesus wept.
(John 11:35 KJV)

C an you feel the heat of the steam? Can you smell the
soap and hear the water beating down onto his skin
and the tile floor? Can you hear the child whimpering
behind the domineering, naked man in the shower? Can
you see the blade clenched in my right hand? If so, then you
understand how vivid my waking "dream" was.

Still dreaming, I questioned God and told Him how I
would have done things. I made suggestions, yelling things
like: "You could have made men much smaller than women.
You could have thought of a way to keep this from happening.
You're the stand-alone genius of creation! You really couldn't
think of a way to do this without all the pain and suffering?
Couldn't You have engineered our body parts differently
so that if someone was being forced sexually they could
inflict severe misery? You could have made it impossible for
someone to take sex without permission. You can choose not
to let this go on. You can stop this! Why don't you?"

I said the stupidest things in my anger. I can't even tell you
everything I said here because it was too graphic and just flat
yucky. Honestly, I'm too ashamed. The last thing I said to God
was, "You could have made us like spiders. Women could just
eat men if they hurt or abuse us." Yes, that's ridiculous, but it
sounds just like me. I must have recognized the sound of my
own voice because I awoke at the violent thought of eating
men after copulating, and just seconds before grabbing the
back of the showering man's head and slitting his throat.

Right now, you might be thinking, "I'm so glad she's not God!" Or some of you might be thinking, "Yeah! That's what I'm talking about! Kill every last abuser!" I certainly wouldn't condemn anyone who came upon an adult molesting a child and out of shock, horror, and rage, killed them. I don't know how someone could be expected to control themselves at such a sight.

Nevertheless, as I sat up, crying and frightened in my bed, I immediately realized the depth of mistrust I had in my heart toward a holy, pure God. I was sick at how disrespectfully I'd addressed my Savior and the lover of my soul. I understood already that He is a mighty God and does not have to tolerate my judgmental accusations. I had just ridiculed my Jesus, who has spoken to me through His Word and comforted me so tenderly when I was distraught and crying out to Him. I had howled so rashly at the Jesus I believe died for my sins, the one who always answered me during my deepest, darkest hours.

I felt trapped and exposed, like a person caught in the act of stealing or lying. The guilt of my railing at God and blaming Him for those perpetrators' disgusting, cruel sins was in the air around me, and I felt oppressed. I sat there knowing full well that I held God responsible for these awful acts of sick molestation because He didn't stop them. My mind screamed, "But God can't be okay with this abuse! He can't!" I thought about how I would never have spoken to God like that in my conscious mind—not while I was awake. I remembered all the encouraging verses I had reassured myself with in the days before. I considered the "everyday" me that would never doubt, accuse, or talk to God that way. As I cried, I asked God to forgive me for what I now acknowledged was in my heart. It's true. It was exactly how I felt, although I'd never let myself admit it, and I would certainly never ever have said it out loud.

You know why? Because He is God. I fear Him; I understand that He made me and I am His creation. I also have this huge hope that He really is good and is doing what is best. Up until that moment, somehow, I had kept my deep, festering feelings at bay. As I sat crying, I picked up my Bible and asked God to speak to me. Most earnestly I pleaded, "God, please. I need to hear from you so desperately. I need you to talk to me this morning. How can you stand for these things to happen?"

I opened my Bible and looked down at the heading, hoping there would be a magic verse that would heal my soul. The heading read: "Lazarus raised from the dead." Disappointed, I thought, *I have read this story at least a hundred times.* Of course, that was an exaggeration, but something in the back of my head said to read it again. So I did.

When I finished the story, I was frustrated. Looking back, I honestly think that I was just too upset to be reasonable. I took out my pen and wrote this in the margin of my Bible: *God, I don't get you. First, you tarry and wait when you know if you don't come, Laz will die. Then, you weep when, first, you knew he would die, and second, you knew you were going to raise him from the dead. Why cry? I don't understand you. I needed you this morning and I asked for your help. I turned to your Word, and now I have more questions than when I first started reading.*

I put down my pen and closed my Bible. With tears running down my face, I thought, *I don't have time for this.* I shook my head, put my Bible on the bed, wiped my tears, got up and got ready for the day. For any of you unfamiliar with the story of Lazarus, please take a moment to read it in the Gospel of John, chapter 11. It's a short story, just one chapter. And its importance will be revealed soon.

This all happened on a Tuesday, and I was volunteering at a Birthright center for young women in crisis pregnancies. When I arrived, I was in a different frame of mind and had totally put the dream and that morning's frustrations behind me. I was working with Alison that day, a sweet woman who adored her grandbaby. To say that she was an incredibly talented knitter would not do her justice. I loved the color of Alison's thick, red hair (even after she pointed out her gray roots).

All the necessary chores were done, so while we were waiting on the next young lady to arrive, I decided to show her a short video about the kids at Angel Reach, the center for aged-out foster youth I mentioned in chapter one. The short video I shared with her can be found easily by searching You tube for: "If I could have my childhood back by Children's rights." Please watch this video now. In it you will hear firsthand the hardships and heartaches shared by many foster kids. These kids are the very kids I worked with on a daily basis. Please pray for these youth and consider getting involved in any local effort to help them, if at all possible. There are children and young adults like them in every city, and they're desperate for mentors, especially male mentors. If you are looking for a place to serve, please pray about this.

Alison watched the video with me, and I noticed she was visibly upset at the end. I asked her what was wrong. Through tears, she explained that she could have been one of those youth. She then told me that she had a very troubled childhood and that she had attempted suicide at the age of fifteen. Alison explained that when she attempted to end her life, it was illegal in the state of Texas. I did not know that suicide had ever been illegal or would land you in court. She said that she had to appear before a judge and in front of a whole courtroom full of strangers. With her mother and father standing right next to her, the judge publicly reprimanded her for trying to end her life. He was very angry and yelled at her for being so selfish. The judge continued humiliating and degrading her for trying to do such a thoughtless, mean, self-centered thing, and for not considering the pain and anguish she would cause her parents and siblings, who were all seated in the courtroom. The judge portrayed her as the worst sort of villain. She cried as she recalled the pain.

I asked her why she had tried to commit suicide.

"Linda," she replied, "my older brother was raping me on an almost daily basis, and I just wanted to die." I was horrified and immediately remembered the dream that morning. She continued. "My brother was sitting in the courtroom, right next to my other brothers and sisters, as the judge was yelling at me."

When the judge had finished verbally stripping her naked, exposing her inconsiderate, selfish, deplorable nature in public, the family got back into their station wagon to return home. Alison had no idea that the assault on her soul wasn't nearly over.

Her confused and bewildered mother turned to her from the front seat. "How could you do this to me?" she screamed.

"How could you? Do you want them to take your sisters and brothers away from me because they think your dad and I are bad parents? Do you want them to split our family up? How can you be so selfish?"

Alison had felt her heart breaking and wanted to escape. Anywhere but there. Anything but that. *Make it stop. God please, please make this all go away,* Alison had prayed.

Her brother was sitting right next to her in the back seat of the car, but she couldn't tell her family what he was doing to her every day in secret. Why? Because she didn't want to hurt her parents and, just like her mother accused her of not caring, the truth was she desperately didn't want the family to be split up. It was bad enough to endure her brother's abuse every single day, knowing full well that if she told it would be devastating. She knew her mother idolized her brother and would be heartbroken to learn what he was doing. So, Alison endured his abuse—the full burden of fear of her family breaking up squarely on Alison's young shoulders.

At this point in the conversation, I was crying. Alison stopped and apologized for upsetting me, but I couldn't control my tears. Alison didn't know about the sex- trafficked little girl who rejects God or the boy I was praying for who had been pulled off a playground and traumatized for life by being raped in the woods. She didn't know about the dream that I had that morning. Alison didn't know that I had just come to realize that I blamed and held God responsible at some level.

I looked at her eyes and surmised that she probably thought I was nuts for crying so hard over a stranger's story, but I couldn't say anything. Tears were streaming down my face. I tried to speak but could not. The huge lump in my throat felt like a bowling ball. I could barely catch my breath. My heart was broken. I felt like I was at the rock bottom of my understanding. She reached up to move my hands away from my face. I was unable to handle the weight of my feelings at that moment. I had fallen off my own map. I was lost in anguish.

After waving my hands in the air several times to motion that I would speak when I could catch my breath, all I managed to squeak out was, "Where is God? Where is He?" Really? Stop the bus! What a stupid thing to say to someone I barely knew and who had been victimized! Was I trying to make her angry at God too? Swallowing hard and gasping for air, I thought, *That is so not like me. I can't believe what I just said. I'm always the one saying "God is good and He loves us, even in the face of horrible stories." I've spent years trying to convince abused, neglected children (myself included) that God loves them and that He really cares.*

I gasped for air as if I had just run a marathon. Alison smiled through her tears as she took my right hand in hers and said, "I know exactly where He was." (I bet she didn't expect to be consoling me, right?) I looked directly into her eyes. Alison seemed so certain. I thought, *For heaven's sake, girl, please tell me!* I was still unable to speak. I just stared at her with a look on my face that probably demanded, SPIT IT OUT! I NEED TO KNOW!

Alison asked, "You know the shortest verse in the Bible, John 11:35, says, 'Jesus wept.'"

I knew exactly what she was fixin' to say. I had just read that story that morning. But it didn't make me feel any better.

She went on, "He was there. His heart was breaking for me when my brother was raping me."

I took a deep breath, nodded, and said, "I know, I know.

Everybody knows that. Of course, He cares."

I pressed the tissue she handed me to my face and it stuck. It just hung there on my face. We laughed through the tears. I assured her that I believed that God's heart hurts for us when we are hurt, but I still didn't understand why God doesn't just ... well ... how He just ... you know. How can He just ... well, why He doesn't ...?

I couldn't even form a question. I think it's because I was so sure that I had no business questioning God, especially in front of another Christian. But she interrupted me, and what she said next is something that I will never forget as long as I live.

"Linda," she said, "I don't think you get it. I don't think you really understand. God's heart was breaking twice. His heart was breaking for me and the trauma and pain I was going through, and, yes, of course, everyone knows that. But His heart breaks just the same, just as bad, a second time. God's heart was breaking and in anguish for the choice my brother made and the sin in his heart. My brother is His child, too. He loves my brother too."

My mind just froze on that thought. His heart was breaking twice. What? Long silence. No, I'm sorry that silence was not long enough. Wait, wait for it....

Let me be very transparent about my feelings, friends. Let's pretend that my cute little Chihuahua just looked up and said in perfect Spanglish, "Leenda, Leenda. Listen to me. God loves all de world, everyone. He created all of j'you. J'you are all His creation. How would j'you feel if j'your precious child–YOUR CHILD–chose to rape or murder?"

That's how I was feeling. I'm not trying to make light of this. I know those last four sentences may seem highly inappropriate, but I was that bewildered. As Alison was speaking, thoughts like *but I hate the perpetrator; I spent the whole morning shooting the perpetrators; I am fully prepared to slit their throats* were ricocheting through my mind. I was judging God because I would stop them if I could, and God just lets them do it. His heart is breaking for the perp? What? I despise the perp. She thinks God's heart is breaking twice. Let that sink in. I had to. I had my doubts. Is it possible that He loves them so much He cries for them too? Yeah, I know Jesus loves the little children, all the children of the world. But not those who grow up and molest innocent kids. Surely not pimps who recklessly destroy, beat, and manipulate young men and women in the sex trade. Not those drunks who shatter lives on the highways. Not those women who sleep with a married man and destroy families. Surely not those men who pay money to have sex with the young, often underage girls whom I have counseled. Those awful men have wives and kids at home.

I know this because when the girls come in from the streets, disgusted with their lives and so ashamed of what they have done to make ends meet, but are trying to clean up, they share stories, fondly a lot of times, about their johns.

They have shown me pictures of their regular clients and their client's families. These girls talk about their customers' wives and kids like they actually know them first hand. They refer to the wives and children by their first names. Not just birthdays, family squabbles, and stories about family vacations, but all kinds of personal details. Intimate details. How sick is that? God loves those lying cheats? How are these young girls used by them ever supposed to trust any man ever again as long as they live?

At this point, the thoughts were coming rapid fire. *Remember the thirteen-year-old boy who raped the innocent five-year-old?* Okay, on second thought, really? Just give that kid a lethal injection. He's only going to cost the taxpayers a ton of money and he'll do it (rape) again. Yes, I still felt the anger, nothing had changed. I was barely getting a clue. I despised that kid. I was grasping for how God could feel the same love and heartbreak for that kid. Yeah, yeah, I know He loves them, but not like He loves the innocent five- year-old victim. Surely not.

Then I thought of my grandson, Stephen. I thought about how I would feel if some older kid took him off a playground and raped him in the woods. A sick, desperate pain grasped my heart. I would want to die and I would want to hurt that kid. I'd want him to rot in jail or have a lethal injection. Then a thought occurred to me with the force of a smack in the face. What if my sweet grandchild, Stephen, my chubby- cheeked, curly-headed, black-haired, blue-eyed, adorable bundle of giggles, ever grew up to drag a child off the playground and rape them when he was thirteen years old? What? God, no! But sweet Stephen would never do that! But what if he did? Well, we raised him better. Again, the question came, but what if he did?'

A terrible realization gripped me. I sat there with a picture in my imagination of my precious grandson at thirteen, a rapist. I was slowly shaking my head from side to side. I'd want to die. I'd still love him. I can't *not* love Stevey, as I call him. That's not even an option. But I'd wish I were dead. I'd rather just be dead. It would kill me. And then the thought came, *but I wouldn't want to kill him.* I would never want to kill Stevey. How could I stand losing him? I love him. Not my precious grandchild. Holy God, is that how you feel? Oh please, you who are reading this, feel free to experience my dilemma with me. Jump right in.

You may be thinking if you raise your kids right they would never do that. Please do not be too hasty. I can point to family after family (including mine) that raised kids in the same loving, wholesome environment, and still, there is one who serves the Lord and one who chooses destruction.

What if it was your sweet older brother who always let you beat him to the mailbox so you could win the race for the mail, or your sister who baked brownies when you were sick, or Grandpa who always brought you maple syrup every time he visited? Maybe it was your dad who always played ball with you as a child? What if it was your own precious child? Someone you love and adore that suddenly commits some awful deed. Would you no longer love them?

Maybe, you say. It would depend on what they did.

Really? Are you sure? Oh, I know, your family member would never do that. But what if they did? Ugh! If your daughter cheated on her spouse with her best friend's husband, would you still love her? If your son stole a car or drove drunk and killed someone, would you stop loving him? If they got hooked on drugs, what then? If they lied, murdered, raped, or molested a child, would your love just evaporate? If they got hooked on pornography and spent hours a day obsessed with sex?

I don't want to know this, I argued to myself. I don't want to feel this.

I was exhausted. I could have lived forever and been fine not knowing this. I thought of the knife I had in the dream that morning. I could see that sharp, shining, silver justice there in my right hand, inches from my face. How could I, with the perpetrator in sight, lay that knife down?

Please don't get me wrong. I'm not suggesting that the offender shouldn't be punished, castrated, incarcerated, incinerated or worse, (yes, that last one is sarcasm and it really isn't funny. It's just the way I feel sometimes). I'm only facing the truth in my heart—that I don't love like God does. And

I was seeing for the first time a glimpse of how God might feel about His creation gone astray. Understand that I knew that God loves us all before I had my dream, and I am very familiar with verses that say that God isn't willing that any perish but that all have eternal life. In my everyday life, I would have said, "Yes, God loves the offender," but I would not have understood even a glimpse of how much until I put my precious, dearly loved child or grandchild in the offender's place. God wants us to forgive them and love them. Love? Love? Do I really understand what that word means?

That said, I also acknowledge that there is a balance between forgiving and justice. A huge gulf between letting go of an offense (freeing that person in your heart) and covering up a serious crime. Doing the latter will leave a perpetrator able to re-offend. Good, loving people often make mistakes here. We will take a look at the difference between forgiveness and justice in my next book. For now, I was just getting a clue, a tiny glimpse of how God might feel about His children. All of them.

Make It Personal

Right now, do you relate more to my journey (before the dream) toward the perpetrators (meaning, you want to kill them), or to Alison's (meaning you understand how someone could love an offender)? Explain why.

_____

_____

_____

Have you ever felt like me—overwhelmed with the suffering you see people you know going through? List those you know who are hurting, regardless of why they are hurting.

_____

_____

_____

Are you overwhelmed by your own suffering? How so? What things have you turned to in order to self-medicate or what steps have you taken to alleviate the suffering?

_____

_____

_____

Do you have questions for God about what you or others have suffered? Write them below.

_____

_____

_____

Like Alison, Travis and Suzie, did someone in your life, who should have loved and protected you, betray and hurt you? Who was it? What happened? Write it in code if you need to.

_____

_____

Will you stop right now and respectfully tell God how it makes you feel? Regardless of who or what hurt you or another, will you "cast your cares on Him?" (1 Peter 5:7a). It's the first step, and often we need to do it more than once.

_____

_____

_____

It's okay to vent to God.
Do you think God loves you? If you are not sure, write your feelings here.

_____

_____

_____

Notes

CHAPTER 4

Travis and Suzie Hot Wheels and Heaven Bubbles and Beatings

"When I was nineteen, I went back to the vacant home where my mom and dad had lived. I lay on the floor of the room they had shared and cried out, 'God, why did you let all this happen?'"

— *Travis*

Today at kindergarten recess, overactive, talkative little Travis plays under his favorite tree. The huge tree has amazingly big roots that sprawl across the ground like huge creeping legs, wrapping and curling around each other. Travis crawls over the roots, his faded, denim overalls protecting his skin from the rugged bark. He digs tunnels under them for his Hot Wheels cars.

Travis mumbles under his breath, "Mommy is in the hospital today cuz she's having a his-tore-ec-toe-mee. She'll be back home soon." His little fingers drive the cars over the knotted, crawling roots and then around and under through the tunnels he had carefully dug in the dirt. Travis hates to hear the bell ringing; that means he has to go back into the classroom. He quickly gathers his cars and shoves them in his pockets as he runs to get in line. No one wants to be last, especially Travis. He is getting used to kindergarten even though he gets in trouble for talking a lot. He likes his teachers and classmates, and they like him.

After school that day, Travis goes out into his front yard. Kicking a medium-sized rubber ball high into the air, he pretends the ball is the sun. It's hot and he has to pick it up quickly and kick it before it burns him. While he is playing, his sisters hatch a plan.

"Let's play a trick on TV," Rebekah says. "Let's fool Travis and make him think Mom is home!" All the girls grin. "Theresa," Rebekah continues, "you call Travis in as soon as you scoop up some ice cream for him."

Rebekah digs through her mother's collection of fashionable wigs and puts one of them on. She cleverly picks out a shirt their mom wears all the time. Rebekah then positions herself in the center of the living room in their mom's chair with her back to the large archway that Travis will see when he walks in the back door. Adrian and Cindy sit down on the couch across from Rebekah and face their sister. Rebekah cues Theresa to call Travis into the house.

"Travis!" she yells, "I've got some ice cream scooped. Come and get yours." As Travis comes through the back door to get the ice cream, Theresa points to it sitting in a bowl on the table.

"Where's yours?" Travis asks brightly.

Right then Adrian and Cindy yell, "Mom! Mom! You're home!" Both girls are looking toward their sister, Rebekah, seated in their mom's rocking chair down the hall in the living room.

Travis looks up and sees the staged scene. He forgets all about the chocolate ice cream that Theresa has set on the table and darts straight through the kitchen and down the short hall leading into the living room. He sees his sisters seated on the couch and the back of someone, whom he assumes is his mom. He recognizes her shirt and her hair. She's in her chair! He's so excited; she is home!

"Mom!" he yells as he runs down the hall. At about three feet away, he catches a glimpse of his sister Rebekah's reflection in the big mirror that's sitting on an end table opposite and to the side of his mother's chair. The look on his face changes from crazed excitement to confusion. As he slows his run and looks up toward his mother's face, he then realizes it is Rebekah wearing his mother's wig.

His eyebrows lower and disappointment fills his eyes.

Suddenly, his cheeks get red hot, and within seconds, he loses himself and lets the sobs come. The tears are flowing down his face so fast the girls stop laughing and glance at each other. They are all stunned and immediately sorry. They never intended to harm Travis; they didn't realize their trick would make him so sad.

Rebekah pulls the wig off her head and drops it on the wooden floor. She immediately puts her arms out as she stands to walk toward Travis.

"I'm sorry, TV. We thought you would laugh. I know you miss Momma. We didn't mean to upset you." She held Travis and petted his blond hair. "It's okay, TV," Rebekah says again and again. "Momma will be home soon. Come on. Let's go get some ice cream."

The next day there is a knock on the ABC-decorated door of Travis's kindergarten class. Travis's teacher is reading the children a storybook about bluebonnets. As Travis looks up, he sees Mr. Mack, the principal, standing there. Travis recognizes Sister Carpenter, the pastor's wife, right next to him.

"Travis, we need you to come with us, okay?" Travis follows them out of the classroom and down the long hall. As Travis gets into Sister Carpenter's VW Bug, he sees Theresa, his sister, sitting in the backseat.

Travis looks into his sister's big, confused eyes. "Is something wrong with Momma?" Travis whispers. Theresa shrugs her shoulders and looks away.

Rebekah is sitting in Momma's rocking chair again when they arrive home but this time with no wig on. Cindy and Adrian are there too. Rebekah looks up at her four younger siblings and says, "Momma is in heaven with Jesus. She's gone now and won't be coming home."

No one says a word. Travis looks around at his sisters. Everyone is staring off in different directions. Adrian sits down on the olive-green couch next to Cindy and looks down at her feet. Theresa looks out the living room window. Travis can tell Rebekah had been crying, but she is not crying now. Travis reaches over and touches Rebekah's arm. She wraps her arms around Travis and pulls him up on her lap, hugging him tenderly. Still, no one speaks.

Over the next few days, it was family, friends, and food. It seemed like the whole church was at the house day and night. "Wake up, Travis," Rebekah calls, "Come on, we need to get you ready. Today is momma's funeral." Rebekah lays the light blue suit that their mother had handmade for him just weeks before on the foot of his bed.

Travis looks down at the suit as he sits up. He remembers his mother trying it on him over and over as she pieced it together, making sure it would fit just right. He feels a sudden sense of nothing ever being the same again. No more hiding in the closet with Momma to trick his sisters. No more running errands and getting suckers at the bank. No more fried chicken or singing. He doesn't want to put the suit on. He wants to go back in time. He just wants to go back to before.

"Get up, TV. We gotta hurry," Rebekah says. Travis doesn't feel like getting out of bed. It feels like it's a going- to-the-doctor kind of day. He pulls the covers over his head and tries to block out the sound of knocking on the front door and more company and probably more food.

Travis is surprised when he sees all the people at the funeral. The nice bank lady who always gives him suckers rubs his head while lifting a tissue to her face to wipe her tears. Everyone he knows is here and they are all crying.

"We are going to miss her so bad, little man," says the lady who works as a cashier at the grocery store.

"You be strong for your daddy," says the pastor.

The librarian ruffles his hair. "You're going to be okay, sweet boy."

As his family all gather to sit in the front row, the music starts. Travis tugs on his dad's suit jacket sleeve.

His father leans down, "What is it, son?" "Can I talk?"

"Not now, it's Momma's funeral. We have to be quiet while the pastor is speaking."

As he sits quietly, he looks around and sees that people are looking at the floor, the ceiling, or the walls; but they aren't looking at each other. They are all sniffling. He feels a strong sense that this is all wrong. His dad has tears rolling down his face. *How come everyone is crying so bad?*

"Daddy," he touches his dad's arm, standing up this time. "Can I talk?" Little Travis points to the pulpit. His father looks surprised.

"You want to speak up there?" his dad says, gesturing toward the podium. "To everyone?" Travis nods his head up and down, his little face concerned and desperate.

"Can I?"

"Well, I don't ... I'm not sure ... I think..." "Please, Daddy," Travis begs.

"Um ..." His dad stalls and looks around. Caught off guard and stunned, he finally replies. "Let me ask, son." He lifts his hand to flag the pastor.

Minutes later, Travis climbs the three steps to the platform one step at a time. He walks over to the podium and turns to the audience in front of it. His soft, little boy features stick out like a lost puppy on a highway next to the large podium, the huge church, the endless crowd, and, of course, the casket his mother lies in covered with her favorite flower, pink carnations. The pastor looks like even he will cry as he leans down to hand Travis the mic.

Travis takes a few steps towards the edge of the stage and looks over at his four sisters, his brother, Micky, and his dad. He then glances slowly across the whole audience. Travis's voice is soft and tender.

"Please ... don't cry," he says. "My mom is in heaven. She wanted to go there. I know because she always told me. She is happy and only good things happen there." He sheepishly glances from person to person, focusing on the ones who were crying the most. "No bad things happen...nothing bad. She feels love and nothing can hurt her. She's with Jesus and Momma loves Him. She has a mansion there and she likes to walk through the silky grass with no shoes on."

Travis looks down at his mother's flower-covered casket. "I'm really sure, because she said she didn't want to come back after the first time she died."

"I often catch myself wondering what I would have been like if my step-dad had been a protective, loving man."

—Suzie

Suzie hears a familiar voice. *Is that Grams? Oh, good*! She jerks the covers off and scrambles to get out of her bed. Her door opens.

"Hello, sunshine! How's my sweet girl this afternoon? Did ya have a good nap?"

Suzie looks at Grams, putting her arms up for a hug, but Grams doesn't hug her like normal. Grams comes down on one knee to her level and stretches her neck to one side and then the other. Suzie can't understand at first what Grams is looking at, and she smiles at the thought of Grams looking her over like that. As soon as she smiles, she feels pain in her lip.

"Ouch," Suzie says out loud. Grams is still trying to move her head up and down, looking through her glasses as if she can't see right.

"My god, Suzie, what happened to your face? Is that a hand print? Oh, my god!"

Suzie had forgotten about the welts. She reaches up with her right hand and touches her right cheek. *It's much better now than it was before*. Gram's face tightens and she sets her jaw. Suzie knows that look.

"You know, it's stopped raining and the kids are out playing without you." Grams is breathing funny and looks like she is going to cry. "Get your shoes on." Grams points at her pink sneakers.

Suzie can just barely hear the kids laughing. She wants to go play. As she puts her shoes on, Grams stands up and heads down the hall. Listening carefully, she hears Grams say, "Have you seen her face?"

Suzie hears her mother's voice answering, "No, what's wrong?"

Then she hears muffled tones. She knows they are arguing, but she can't stand there cringing in the doorway all day. As bad as she doesn't want to go around the corner and draw attention to herself, she wants to go play more. Suzie steps out into the hall, and her mother walks toward her from the kitchen.

She looks down at her face. Her mother's eyebrows furrow as she takes Suzie's chin in her hand. Half-glancing back toward the bedroom, her mother says in a soft, sympathetic tone, "You're okay, hun. Listen, I've got to go back to work for a few hours. Go and play for a while, sweetie." The expression on her mother's face is a mixture of fear and anger. "First, give your Grams a hug."

Suzie runs down the hall, hugs her Grams, then runs back and wraps her arms around her mom's thighs. She squeezes tight and then takes off out the back door. As Suzie hurries down the steps, she thinks she hears her name. She stops and looks around. Again, she hears her name in a half-whisper. "Suzie! Under here." She looks back behind the steps.

It's Josh, who is ten, and several younger girls. She steps off the last step and bends slightly, looking at them under the trailer.

"Whatcha y'all doing under there?" she asks.

"Hey Suzie, we're going to make our own club. Only the really cool kids are allowed in it." Josh looks at the other girls knowingly and glances back to fix his brown, almost black, eyes on Suzie. "Come on."

Suzie crawls in on all fours, next to Mandy.

"To get in, ya have to pull your pants down and show us your girly parts." Josh smiles and lifts his eyebrows and looks around at the girls who are all crouching in a circle staring at her. "If you go first, we will like you even more, and I'll give you this." He holds out a Hostess cherry pie, still in its wrapper. She looks at the pie and can't stop the automatic salivation in her mouth. She wants it bad. She looks at Mandy. "What happened to your face?" Josh asked.

Suzie ignores him. "Let's go. He's going to get us in trouble." The other girls giggle. Suzie studies their faces for a moment. They look mean. She fixes her beautiful, intense eyes on Mandy and reaches for her hand. "Come on, let's go play," she urges her.

As she turns and scoots, pulling Mandy away from the group, Josh says, "We don't want you to be our friends anyways. You're both too ugly."

Suzie turns and sticks her tongue out at him. She can feel the pain in her lip again. She looks at Mandy. They both giggle. As they crawl out from under the trailer and walk away, Suzie notices that her Grams is leaving. She is sitting in her car and her mother is standing next to the car door. They are still arguing. Grams is crying. She knows both of them have to work tonight. Her mom is in her waitress uniform.

Suzie yells to them, "Bye, I love you!" Waving her hand and smiling, she then turns to Mandy and says, "I fell and hit my face on my toy box. That's why my lip's like this. Let's go catch some crawdads. It just rained—they'll be everywhere." On their way to the creek, they hear laughter.

It's coming from a nearby trailer. The two girls look at each other and then head straight for it. Suzie can see bubbles flying through the air about four trailers down from them. "Look, Mandy, bubbles! Let's go."

Billy's mom is blowing bubbles for the neighbor kids. The girls watch quietly for several minutes. Billy's mom soon notices the girls tucked just inside the tree line.

"Come on, girls," Billy's mother coaxes. "If you make a wish and then bite a bubble, your wish will come true." Billy's mom picks up her chair and moves it to the middle of the dirt road that's still a little damp from the rain. She tells the kids to circle around her. Suzie and Mandy move closer.

The other kids are clapping their hands and swinging wildly at the bubbles. Suzie sees them and wrinkles her face. *Are they crazy? They're doing it all wrong. You have to make a wish first. Then you bite the bubble. Not clap it in your hands.* That's okay, though. She will do it the right way and she will be the one with all her wishes coming true.

"I wish I had a kitten!" Suzie yells. She spies the closest bubble and runs toward it. Its big, blue, outer hue makes it so beautiful. She opens her mouth wide, baring her teeth. Smiling the whole time, she lungs up, high enough to bite it.

She tastes soap in her mouth. "I got it!" she giggled. Her lip hurts but she doesn't care. "Yippee! I wished for a kitten!" Suzie squeals. "I wish I had a bike!"

She sees a pinkish bubble, much smaller than the last, but closer, and who cares if it's tiny? Bite it. Bite it! *I wish I had a Barbie car for Barbie.* She chases the next bubble. She giggles and squeals. "Mandy!" Suzie yells, "Don't forget to make a wish! A pony, the big box of crayons, a real strawberry shortcake," she yells out to her friend, wanting Mandy to get some wishes too. The play goes on long enough for Suzie to start wishing for things like a new riding lawn mower for her Gramps and a dish washer for Grams, a new house for her mom and all new beds, covers and curtains!

Just then she hears her name. "Suzie!" Ray sounds angry. She stops dead in her tracks and looks toward their trailer. Suzie sees him there, leaning on his crutch. He's talking to the next-door-neighbor lady. A large, golden-hued bubble crosses slowly in front of her face and reminds her of the game. Frozen, she watches the bubble drift. *I wish I could get really small and climb in that bubble and float away. Far away. I wish I could disappear just like that bubble will.* Her eyes locked on the bubble as it drifts. Again, Ray yells,

"Suzie!"

The weight of her arms and legs feel as if they suddenly are filled with lead. She can't wish herself small and she can't float. She is stuck here and he is calling her. *I wish Ray would die.* The bubble teeters first to the right toward Ray and then to the left as it floats farther away from the group. Suzie glances down the road at Ray. He is looking straight at her. Knowing it will cost her, but not being able to help herself, she looks back at the bubble and, like a snake striking, decides she has to bite it no matter what happens. *I wish he'd die ... I wish he'd die,* she thinks to herself as she darts toward the bubble. Just then the bubble bursts, inches in front of her mouth. Suzie stops. She feels the tears well up in her eyes. A huge lump forms in her throat. She's too late.

"Suzie, get over here, now!"

Ray is really mad. She knows in her heart that this is the way things are. This is just her life and she can't do a thing about it. As she starts to turn her head toward Ray, she glances at Mandy jumping in the bubbles. She feels her throat tighten and a tear run down her face. Ray opens the trailer door and waits. As soon as she is close enough, muffled and low so the others can't hear him, he growls, "Get your chubby rear in there."

She runs through the doorway, leaning as far away as she can from him and clutching the door frame. She barely squeezes through, terrified that he will kick her or swing at her as she scurries in.

He comes in behind her and shuts the door. As scared as she is to turn around and look at him, she is more scared of not seeing him coming. From a safe distance at the end of the hall, she looks back. He is shaking his head from side to side and limping toward her.

He points in the direction of his bedroom. "Get your butt in that room."

Suzie knows the look in his piercing blue eyes. A look of hatred and disgust. Turning her head quickly, her soft, brown curls bounce as she runs toward the round breakfast table. She can barely see over the table as she clutches the side of it.

He is right behind her, already on the other side leaning over the table and yelling, "Get your butt in that room!"

She's afraid to run. She knows he will kick her if he gets the chance, and she hates that. He points again. His face ablaze with anger.

"What did I do? What's wrong? What!" Suzie cries. He snarls, "Don't act all innocent, you little brat."

She runs the opposite direction from his body to keep the table width between them. Suddenly Ray grabs the table as if to turn it over and she dashes away from him toward the bedroom. Suzie scrambles up onto the perfectly made bed and clutches the headboard. Again, she yells, "What did I do? What did I do?"

Ray heads for the belt that is hanging neatly on the closet door hook. Suzie cries "Mommy" out of habit but without any hope. She knows her mom has left for the day.

"I hear you've been a busy little girl today," Ray

sarcastically sneers. "Aren't you precious?" He makes a face as if he's trying to be cute. "Sandra next door says you've been under the trailer showing your 'little girl parts' to Josh." He raises his eyebrows and then nods his head in disgust. "Well, Suzie, that's just what we need. You showin' it off to all the boys in the park." He circles her around the bed.

"I didn't. I didn't. I left with Mandy. We didn't do it!" Suzie pleads.

"It's free, free. Come and look, it's the Suzie show," Ray taunts.

"Daddy, I didn't, I promise!" Suzie's hands shoot up to stop the belt as the loose end of it flies through the air toward her body. The belt strikes her chest and arms. She jerks her face back and away from the belt, letting out a high-pitched scream. She scrambles to the other side of the bed and he circles her, limping as he makes his way around. He reaches for her right leg with his left hand and jerks her off her feet as he yanks her small body toward him. She flips to her stomach, grasping at the bed in an attempt to crawl but unable to get away.

"Suzie, you're going to be a worthless tramp!" He swings again and again, hitting her across her backside. The pain is awful. She screams, crying out in terror. "You're going to be just like your momma!" He swings again. She rolls, kicking frantically and frees her foot from his grasp. Like an animal, she scampers across the bed and grabs the headboard. He circles her and keeps swinging, striking the bed as hard as he can. He leans forward and swings as she crawls to the other side of the bed. This time, the belt hits her across the front of both her thighs. She involuntarily reaches down with both hands and grasps her legs as she rolls away from him and hurls her body in the opposite direction.

Again, he limps around the bed. At this point, her hands are red and hurting so severely that she can't put them up to protect her body anymore. The belt strikes her across the back. "If you're going to act like a woman," he half- whispers, "maybe I'll just treat you like one. What do you think of that idea? Wanna show me your privates?" He swings again. "Show *me* whatcha got, Suzie!"

Make it Personal

What is your most painful childhood memory?

_____

_____

_____

What is your first childhood memory?

_____

_____

_____

What is your happiest childhood memory?

_____

_____

_____

As a child, did you feel like God cared about you? Why did you feel this way?

_____

_____

_____

Do all the children in your life know God cares about them? How often do you remind them and how?

_____

_____

_____

Have you lost a loved one? Who, when, and how?

_____

_____

Do you think you are holding on to resentment toward God regarding the death of your loved one? If you could ask God about his or her death, how would you phrase the questions? Write these questions below.

_____

_____

_____

Notes

CHAPTER 5

The Blame Game

*And the man said, "The woman whom you gave
to be with me—she gave me [fruit] from the tree,
and I ate." And the Lord God said to the woman,
"What is this you have done?" And the woman
said, "The serpent beguiled (cheated, outwitted,
and deceived) me, and I ate."*

(Genesis 3:12-13 AMP)

D id I still have questions about Lazarus and why Jesus
waited to go to him, knowing Laz would die, only
to be moved to tears before he raised him from the
dead? Oh, yes, I did, and I can't wait to tell you about them.
Because what I found upon prayerfully researching it was not
at all what I'd been taught for years or what I expected.

But, right now, my mind is scrambling for answers to a
number of questions, and here is a good one: Did Adam and
Eve (Gen.1:3) blame God when their firstborn son, Cain, killed
his younger brother, Abel? (Gen. 4) For those of you who might
be unfamiliar with this story, God created them. He gave them
a paradise to live in and walked with them through the garden
every day. And He gave them a choice. It was so simple. But
they didn't trust God. They didn't choose God.

I once bought some peacocks and I faced a dilemma.
I wanted them to stay and meander on my property, but I
didn't want to cage them. I wanted them to be free. My family
could not understand my unhappiness at the thought of my
birds in a cage because "people cage animals all the time." The
problem was, I had fantasized about having peacocks since I
was five, and I never once pictured them caged up. Picturing

them penned just took all the fun out of it. So, we hatched a plan, built a cage, and I bought three females and one male. As unhappy as it made me, they went straight into the cage.

I would sit on the ground by the side of the cage and throw their food to them, coaxing them closer and closer to me. Then I stapled a glove to my boot and put food on the glove, getting them used to me sitting on the ground in their cage with my leg stretched toward them. I tossed food all around my foot, and after weeks of tempting them, they finally started trusting me enough to eat out of the gloved foot. You cannot imagine my happiness when one day I approached the cage, and they ate out of my gloved hand.

Then we let just the male out of the cage, banking on the fact that the male wouldn't want to leave the three females that were still caged. I didn't like this plan. It scared me. I worried that the male would run away. He was the prettiest one and the most expensive. I didn't want to lose him.

To my happy surprise, the next morning when I looked out my sliding-glass door into the backyard, there was the strutting male. His tail feathers were spread as he shook them vigorously and circled the cage. He wasn't going anywhere, not without those females! After a month, when the male was used to perching in the trees at night and eating out of my gloved hand in the daytime, we let one of the females out, leaving the other two caged. A month later, we set the next female loose and then the next the following month. By the time the third female got out of the cage, the male and the other two females were trained. Within one summer I had peacocks that stayed on my property without the wire cage. We took that ugly thing down and I enjoyed those peacocks for over ten years.

Because of my deep disturbance at the thought of caging the peacocks, I can relate, in a way, to God. I would have rather not had the peacocks at all than have to keep them in a pen. God wanted Adam and Eve, His creation, to want to be His. He wanted them to choose Him. He did not want to cage them. He didn't want to force them. And He doesn't want to hypnotize us or make us a controlled-by-design species like the Borg on Star Trek.

I remember watching a scene from one of those TV episodes years ago when I was in my early twenties. I was terrified at the thought of that kind of control over me by a forced authority. I remember a Borg had one of the Starfleet crew pinned up against the side of the Enterprise. Without any feeling, the Borg said, "You must be assimilated. Resistance is futile." The Borg repeated the confining, smothering, lifeless sentence over and over as he slowly approached his prospective captive. Seriously scary stuff right there!

God isn't interested in puppets on strings. He never pictured Himself with a remote control in His hand, just pushing buttons to get us to obey His every command like drones or remote-controlled cars. I respect and admire that about God. When He created mankind, He wanted us to be free to choose where we go, what we think, and what we do. And He wants us to choose Him. He wants us to love Him.

These are small examples of a bigger point. We don't want a friend we have to bribe to spend time with us. If you have to sit your friend down and explain that they are avoiding you or not making your friendship a priority, it's just not worth having, because you have to beg for their time and attention. That really hurts and is especially painful if you truly care for that friend. The next time you got together, how would you know that they were there because they cared? Maybe they are just there because you hounded them. You'd suspect they were watching the clock till they could get away to go do what they want. Same with a spouse that never smiles at you, never says I love you, and never tells you that you look nice or just flat never makes a fuss over your wonderfulness. How many of us know that if we have to demand something, it's not worth having? It takes all the joy out of it. To have a good relationship, you have to have a willing partner, someone who freely chooses you.

Adam and Eve, being able to think for themselves, were not forced to love or trust God. When confronted with Satan's lies, they considered that God (their Creator) was holding out on them, and there was some serious blaming that went on in the garden as a result of their choices. Adam blamed Eve and Eve blamed the serpent. Everyone who reads this in Genesis will admit that every single one of us would have done the exact same thing. No matter what it was that God told us not to do, we would, at some point, toss God's will and take what we want. They chose to disobey, which showed their lack of love for God. We show the same lack of love every time we knowingly choose sin. Then God (for their own good) forced them out of the garden so that they and their children wouldn't be able to live forever in this willful, sinful state. Yes, that's rough. They now faced a new reality that God explains to them. I see it as not simply a punishment but also an explanation of what life will be like from then on because of their choice.

These are the consequences: Adam has to work and sweat and toil under the sun because the land was now cursed, and Eve will be ruled over by Adam and will have pain in childbirth. There will be an ongoing fight between her children and the serpent, but Adam and Eve are still alive, and they have each other. They know they are dying (that's actually God's mercy) and life was nothing like it was in the garden. But still, things could be worse, right?

So, Eve has two boys and what's the first thing that happens? Seriously? Brother kills brother. That's right. Their firstborn, Cain, kills his younger brother, Abel. Our very first innocent victim and our first perpetrator/offender arrive on the scene. Sure, there was an anger/jealousy thing going on and we are going to think about that in a bit, but now let's consider how Adam and Eve must have felt. They had two boys who no doubt they loved with all their hearts. They were Eve's babies. She took care of them from infancy. She raised them, wiped their tears, and kept them safe. When Eve bears her first son she is overjoyed and says, "God has given me a son." That woman was crazy excited. The Amplified version says in Genesis 4:1, "And Adam knew Eve as his wife and she became pregnant and bore Cain; and she said, 'I have gotten (and gained) a man with the help of the Lord.'" She saw Cain as a gift, her first son. Cain was something that she considered gain and she had gained him (Cain) with God's help. She thanks God and gives Him the credit.

I experienced that exact feeling when I held my son

Gentry in my arms for the first time. To this day, I remember the promises I made him as I held him. I knew I would always love and protect him. I would always be there for him and never turn my back on him. As I lay there in the hospital bed, I could see the next eighteen years stretched out before me, and I knew I would choose to do what was best for him. Promises and protection flowed out of my heart toward him like they were being drained out of me by some mysterious, unseen sinkhole located in my sons' being... I was in love.

Eve, like me, must have been smitten when she looked at her children. She taught her boys to walk and talk. After nursing, she chewed food and pushed it into their mouths to sustain them. Just like us, Eve must have comforted them when they hurt. There were giggles and tickle fights and they must have played games. How much joy did watching her sons grow up bring her? I sure enjoyed mine.

Adam must have spent countless hours teaching them to garden and tend the livestock. Laughing at them as he discovered his boys growing and learning new things. They didn't have distractions like TV, video games, or social media to keep them occupied; they just had each other. Adam taught them to work alongside him. He must have stopped their arguments and watched as they discovered, played, and wrestled.

I often reflect on my two sons who are ten months apart (yes, that's a story in itself) and how many times I broke up an argument and encouraged them to work things out and be kind to one another. How did Adam and Eve teach their kids to treat each other? I'm sure it didn't sound anything like what I said to mine, but Adam had to have encouraged them to get along. Was Adam proud of his sons? Was Eve disappointed when she saw her children fighting? I hated to see my sons fight. I still can barely handle them disagreeing, criticizing, or fussing with each other. I just want them to love each other like I love them. Of course, Adam and Eve wanted their sons to care about one another. All good parents want that for their children.

How Eve must have cried for her dead son, Abel. How did she find out that he was dead? Did Adam tell her? What words did he use? Do you think they looked for Abel for several days, not knowing where he was? Adam and Eve had seen death in the animals they had raised. They must have been familiar with the smell of death and even seen vultures circling in the sky. Is that how they found Abel's body being torn apart by scavengers? When Eve realized Abel was gone and she would never ever see his smile again, did she cry her heart out until the tears that fell down her face burned like ice water on her red-hot cheeks? Did Adam hold her and rock her as she wept and asked God why? Could she even be consoled?

How did Adam feel about his boys after this tragedy? Was his heart crushed? Did he yell out in anguish for his dead son, Abel? What thoughts were going through Adam's mind when he looked at his son's lifeless body? Did Adam lift and carry his son down to the creek and slowly submerge his body to wash the blood from his head as tears ran down his cheeks and into his beard? Was Adam the first one to dig a grave and put his own flesh and blood in it? I don't know how they handled Abel's body. Maybe they just decided to burn his body or put it in the river and let it float away.

How horrible that first human death had to be for both Adam and Eve. At that moment, did it cause Adam to recognize and regret his sin in the Garden and the high cost of that choice? Did Adam stop and feel the weight of every choice that people might make to do evil from that point on into the future? How horrifying! Did he still blame Eve? Did he blame God?

Did Eve reach up and grab handfuls of her hair and try to rip it out of her head in anguish? Did she run to the place where she thought God was most likely to hear her and scream? Did she rage at God from the top of her lungs, demanding an answer as to why God didn't stop Cain? Or did she just sit slumped and staring at the ground, forced to look at her own free will and her choice to disobey God? Did Eve recognize that Abel's death was a result of both free will and the knowledge of good and evil? (Cain wanted to be good enough for God on his terms.) I'll bet she did. It wasn't Eve's choice to kill Abel; she didn't hit him with a rock. Cain made that awful decision, but, like Eve, and all of us, Cain wanted what he wanted.

None of us would prefer to be a robot. To not have a choice feels scary, confining, and demented. If we didn't have our free will, every one of us would yearn for it, beg for it, howl and rally for it.

Curious how we get mad at God when He doesn't stop the drunk driver before he gets in the car, yet most of us don't think alcohol should be illegal. We don't want a higher power controlling us, not even on a much smaller level. We want people to take personal responsibility. We get mad at God for not jamming the gun, but we don't want gun control. We don't want to step in gum, but we also don't want to be told there will be a two-hundred-dollar fine if we get caught chewing gum.

You want to know what makes it even worse? Cain was angry at Abel because of his knowledge of good and evil. Cain wanted desperately to be good. He wanted to earn God's approval by being good enough, and he was furious at Abel when Abel seemed to do it easily. We are all exactly like Cain. We want to be good enough for God by ourselves and in our own power. You may be thinking, no, I don't. I trust in Jesus Christ and His shed blood. Really? Do you never feel you have to jump through a single hoop to please God? Cain hated his brother because Cain worked that cursed land so hard and his brother only brought a lamb that God created, provided, and sustained. The lamb Abel brought was a picture of Jesus Christ. It was to show us today that the only "first fruit" that God cares about is the shed blood of Jesus Christ. There is nothing else He wants from us. Not one thing. The only "first fruit" there is, is the Lamb of God, Jesus Christ, provided for by God and sustained by God. The enemy wants you to think that all your "good" doings are going to make you right with God. And, here is the kicker— we are just like Cain. We want a hoop to jump through and we desperately want to earn it ourselves because deep down inside we want and love the idea (knowledge) of being "good enough" for God. Does that sound familiar?

There's one problem. Only God decides what is acceptable. I suggest that Abel's burden was light and he rested in God's provision. He had no pride caught up in his sacrifice as he couldn't create a lamb and he couldn't sustain the lamb. Only God's provision can do that. Cain fought against the weeds, the thorns, briers, and the thistles. He worked the curse. We all do it, and that's why our world is upside down. But that won't change the fact that when we stand before the Throne of God, only the Lamb, Jesus Christ, will be acceptable for our approval from God. I've included a note at the end of this book to remind you to visit our website and click the link "Good enough for God."

Can you imagine Eve knowing that her first born killed her second child over the knowledge of being "good enough" to please God? How horrific to know that you wanted the fruit and the knowledge of good and evil, and now both your sons are lost because of it.

Now, please picture Eve looking into Cain's eyes after he murdered his brother. I have three sons and I (crazy) love them. I'd be so angry at my murdering son, but I wouldn't want to flick him off the planet like a troublesome bug that just landed on my pizza. I can't. I love him. When I imagine looking into the eyes of my murdering son, all I feel is sorrow. Heartbreaking, deep, dead, empty, ugly, gut- wrenching sorrow. I'd still want to raise my arms and reach out in love to my wayward, jealous son. Can you believe that?

I'd probably also want to swing at him with both of my fists. But then I'd still want to take him in my arms and hold him. Yes, both those feelings at the very same time. That's right, even if he murdered his brother. Why? Because he's mine. Because he came from me; because I love him with all my heart.

My heart would break and yearn for my dead son (Abel) whom I could never see again, who would never play another trick on me or sneak up behind me and scare me. My precious baby whom I could never see walk up to my house for a visit or hold his own sons in his arms. I would be furious for the harm done to him, but the pain of one son lost could not be fixed by hating or killing the other son. It would just be twice as bad.

Is this how God feels when one of His created souls harms

the other? My heart can see God's heart right here. I see it, even if it's just a tiny glimpse.

While I was working on this chapter, I asked my husband how he would feel if one of his children got jealous and killed or harmed the other. He was driving and I could see tears wet his eyes. He said, "Hopeless, crushed, angry…confused."

I asked, "Could you hate them?"

He answered abruptly (and I mean fast), "No." He had a far away, fearful look in his eyes. He shook his head from side to side. Again, he said, "No."

As I put myself in Eve's place, I knew my heart would be broken and never the same, but I would love both my sons. The pain would be doubled. Do you remember when Eve was so excited about having Cain? She thanked God for the gift that was Cain. Now how does she feel? Can she hate Cain? Does she blame God in the same way she thanked Him before? She can't blame God because she knows the tragedy was a consequence of the exercise of her free will. Eve was the one person who walked the face of the earth who saw free will from a truly unique perspective.

How does this relate to our suffering? If you really love two people and one hurts or destroys the other, you are going to suffer. Because they are yours. They belong to you. So, does it not stand to reason that God's heart is broken over the condition of his creation? I wonder why we never stop to think how much the sin and pain in this world (caused by our free will) hurts or breaks the heart of our Heavenly Father.

God loving both the victim and the perpetrator doesn't mean that He isn't a God of justice. He certainly *is* a God of justice, and you see this in so many places in the Bible. For example, check out His punishment for sin with King David (2 Samuel 12:9-18). David had also killed a man. He did it to cover his sin of adultery. Here too, God's punishment is severe, yet He is merciful. But, consider God's approach with Cain in Genesis 4:10-16 AMP:

And [the Lord] said, what have you done? The voice of your brother's blood is crying to Me from the ground. And now you are cursed by reason of the earth, which has opened its mouth to receive your brother's [shed] blood from your hand. When you till the ground it shall no longer yield to you its strength; you shall be a fugitive and a vagabond on the earth [in perpetual exile, a degraded outcast]. Then Cain said to the Lord, My punishment is greater than I can bear.

Behold, you have driven me out this day from the face of the land, and from your Face I will be hidden; and I will be a fugitive and a vagabond and a wanderer on the earth and whosoever finds me will kill me. And the Lord said to him, Therefore if anyone kills Cain, vengeance shall be taken on him sevenfold. And the Lord set a mark on Cain, lest any finding him should kill him. And Cain went away from the presence of the Lord and dwelt in the land of Nod [wandering] east of Eden.

It cannot escape anyone reading this that God was punishing Cain big time and being merciful at the same exact moment.

Cain cries out, "My punishment is greater than I can bear!" Now Cain feared for his life, the very thing he took from his brother. But God was merciful and gave him his life, putting a mark on him so that he wouldn't be killed. God allowed him to have a wife and children, the very things he took from his brother Abel. I wonder if Cain ever thought about Abel when he looked at his own sons growing up. Did he feel sorrow that Abel would never have these moments? Did he wonder if one of his own children might kill the others? Did he regret what he had done? Only God knows Cain's heart, but it is obvious to me that God loved and protected Cain (Eve's precious son) even after he murdered his own brother. What does that tell us? It tells me that I don't love the way God does. I cannot fully comprehend God's heart, and it tells me that something in my heart definitely needs to acknowledge this and change.

It doesn't mean we should let the perpetrators go or be the least bit lenient with their consequences. I'm not suggesting that anyone who murders or rapes should ever be let into the general population again, even if it is my own son. Perpetrators should be in prison where they can't hurt people. But if God can punish Cain until he cries out, "My punishment is more than I can bear," and still love Cain and have mercy, maybe

I can try to see Cain, or the next perpetrator I encounter, through God's eyes.

This is especially hard for a victim and the victim's family, unless of course you are like Alison (whose brother was raping her almost daily) and the heartbreak was perpetrated by someone you loved dearly. In some of those situations, it brings an understanding about our collective brokenness. In other cases, the wound inflicted by someone who should have loved and protected you is so deep that it fills you with a relentless fear of the future and what else God might allow while fueling a fierce bitterness. This is exactly why we need to understand God's heart concerning these situations.

In 2 Samuel chapters 13-19 we read a tragic story about King David and his son Absalom who was chasing him and trying to kill him. You may ask yourself why a child would try to kill his own father. I'm certain there were numerous reasons, but one possibility is that Absalom had lost all respect for his father after his half-brother, Amnon, had raped his beloved sister, Tamar, and King David had left that heinous act unpunished for two years. Absalom decided to take revenge, and so he killed Amnon.

I wonder if that family upheaval caused by Absalom's hatred for his brother could have been avoided if King David would have disciplined Amnon and required a hearty restitution. Nathan the prophet had previously warned David that the sword would never leave his house after his sin with Bathsheba and the selfish, ruthless murder of her husband, and so it didn't. When King David and his other sons heard that Amnon had been killed by Absalom, they lifted up their voices and wept bitterly.

Can you imagine? King David still loved his son Amnon enough to weep bitterly, even after he tricked him and raped his own sister, David's daughter. Think about that. David's heart is breaking because he still loves his son Amnon, but it gets worse. Absalom runs to his mother's house and stays there for three years. Eventually, King David (who misses his son Absalom) sends a message that Absalom can return to his own home, but also warns that Absalom is not to come into his sight or presence. Yes, King David was still very angry.

Millstone

Absalom then turns against his father, going after David's life, wives, and the throne.

This is where the tragic family drama gets even more heartbreaking. Absalom, after chasing King David off his throne and out of town, sleeps with the king's women in plain sight of all of Israel and begins trekking thru the countryside on his father's heels. Twenty thousand men are killed between the two armies in one of the battles, and the Bible says even more died that day because of the terrain. Finally, when Absalom is running from his father's men, his mule runs under a great oak tree and Absalom's head is caught in the fork of the tree, which yanks him off his mule and leaves him dangling—stuck between heaven and earth. Joab, whom the king put in charge of a third of his army, then orders ten young men to surround Absalom and kill him.

What is so interesting is that the one man who witnessed Absalom getting his head stuck in the tree could have killed him right there on the spot, but instead he ran and told Joab because the man knew that King David had warned people not to harm Absalom. What? Does that make any sense? Your son is turning the people against you, he's killed his brother, raised an army, chased you off of your throne, killed thousands of your men and slept with your wives, yet you warn people not to harm him. Let's see how King David responds to the news that Absalom has been killed.

"And the king was deeply moved and went up to the chamber over the gate and wept. And as he went, he said, 'O my son Absalom, my son Absalom! Would to God I had died for you, O Absalom, my son, my son!'" (2 Samuel 18:33 AMP)

Again, in Samuel 19:4 (AMP): "But the king covered his face, and the king cried with a loud voice, 'O Absalom, my son, my son!'"

Wow! Can you hear a father's heart for his child there? When the news about how upset the king was spread, the people started mourning. David's display of grief escalated to the point where Joab, his men, and the army were getting miffed. Oh yeah, they were getting flat ticked! David carried on so much that Joab decided to go talk to David and warn him that the men who fought to save his life felt like David would have rather they all had died fighting and Absalom would have lived. Joab warned him that he was on the verge of turning his whole army against him. That's how heartbroken a father can be, even when his child betrays and attacks him personally.

If David loved his sons like this in their sin, then how does God feel when we take revenge on each other, doubt Him, disobey Him, resent Him, and take advantage of Him? There are those of us who even plot against Him and would try to destroy Him. How does it feel to God when we harm each other and defy and despise Him? David is an amazing picture of the heartbreak of our Heavenly Father toward His sin- filled children. Could this have anything to do with God saying that David has a heart after God's own heart? I can't be certain, but I truly suspect that is the case.

Do we blame God, reject God, or hate God because we can't control other people's free will and He won't? Why won't God, just for us, just this once, step in? If He really loves me, then why was I abused? Why was I raped? Does He want my life to be ruined? Satan lies to us as children and as adults and says, "God abandoned you. He doesn't care." Do you think that God abandoned Abel? No, you think his brother knocked him in the head with a huge rock because that is exactly what Cain did. Why don't we see our personal situation from that perspective? "But, God, this is my child who died, my parent who's suffered, my future that's ruined. Why wouldn't you step in and (take their free will) to help me?"

I recently read *Terror by Night*, the true story of Terry Caffey. His Texas home was invaded and his family attacked. Terry was shot five times, once in the face. He awoke to find his house engulfed in flames. He tried to save his wife, but she had been shot dead by the assailants. Terry barely escaped the fire. When he awoke in the hospital, Terry was told that his two young sons had been brutally murdered. The only ray of hope was that his daughter Erin, sixteen, had survived the attack. Unfortunately, the good news was not so good after all. Terry was then faced with the reality that his daughter had inspired the killing spree, talking openly with her boyfriend about it at school in front of others. She was aware of it and was being charged with murder.

This was not a home of violence and abuse, but a God-fearing, loving home. What his daughter had done was more than Terry could understand or explain. I walked through the depths of Terry's despair as I read the pages of his painful story and know that if that had been my daughter, I would have been so confused, yet I would still love her. Terry, in my mind, is a wonderful human example of how God loves us and sticks with us even when we don't deserve it.

If you doubt God's love for you because of something you have done in your past, ask yourself if Terry, who still loves his daughter Erin, can be capable of loving her more than our Heavenly Father loves His children. Could it be that God is a less loving father? Can we as humans have the capacity to love more than the God who created us? It's not likely. If we as humans have the capacity to love our kids in their brokenness, being made in His image, then God loves us in our brokenness. Yes, even the pedophile. Even the rapist, the robber, the drug addict, and the murderer. Even the person who has horrible disgusting thoughts about God.

This does not mean that some of them shouldn't face the death penalty or be locked up forever where they can never hurt someone again, but it does mean that God can still love them like we still love our children. We may hate that thought, but if my own child was a pedophile, I would agree for him to be locked up, and I would pray desperately that he come to a humble, sincerely contrite place of surrender and broken heartedness over his disgusting actions.

Terry Caffey has made the necessary sacrifices to visit his daughter regularly in prison, just like I would do everything I could to be able to visit one of my children if they were incarcerated. Think about how many people are walking out a punishment or difficult circumstances in their life. God is there with them. He cares and holds them in their suffering as a result of their bad decisions. He even tells us to visit the criminal in prison. God knows they deserve to be there but He asks us to care about them. God walks through our consequences with us, just like Terry suffers with Erin—not because he was at fault in any way—but because Terry loves his daughter. The Holy Spirit of God endures our circumstances and consequences along with us, never leaving us. He is with us as we walk through the messes we've made. We often want God to deliver or save us from the consequences of our or others' bad decisions. Sometimes He does, but sometimes He allows us to walk through them. When that happens, He chooses to never leave us or forsake us. Sometimes walking out our circumstances or consequences is what is best for us, because in it we come to see Him more clearly. If you would like to see what God has taught Terry through this horrific ordeal, search for Terry Caffey on Youtube.

Many will say that not everyone is a child of God and that some are the children of the enemy and that we shouldn't have mercy on them. We as a society know that there are sociopaths who have absolutely no feelings of remorse or compassion. These people should be swiftly and sternly handled by our justice system. But what of our hearts? I tell you that I can't muster the slightest feeling of love for them, but I can purpose in my heart to ask God how He feels about them, because they are His creation and He will one day punish those who don't eventually repent, regret and despise what they did. I can at least pray that they come to a complete knowledge of their evil, abusive actions and broken heartedly loathe the sin they have committed. I will try to do that for God's sake. You see, if I can desperately love my children and be furiously angry at them also, so can God.

We cannot decide or know who will eventually come to a full saving knowledge of Jesus Christ. We have to treat everyone as a potential child of God. You may say, "Well, what about the terrorist who kills innocent people in a zeal for his religion?" Isn't that exactly what Paul the apostle did? Only God can change a heart. We can't know for sure who will cry out to God or respond to God.

I'm intrigued that free will is so precious to our Creator. I like that He doesn't want Siri for a companion. Yet free will is so very painful...even for God. Free will is also how we know truth. I once said to someone who was hurting me that their actions were speaking so loudly, I couldn't hear a word they were saying! You see, someone can tell you they love you all day long, but their free-will choices will never lie. You can't have love without free will, and you can't know the truth about yourself, others, or God without it either. For instance, if God had to act within certain specific outside perimeters, how would we know the true character of God? Ditto for us. If God set boundaries on our treatment of each other or we did it ourselves, how could we ever know the truth about ourselves or others? How would we know what was in our hearts? Yet we don't respect or appreciate the beauty of His plan, and so we blame each other, and we blame God.

When Abel was murdered, I wonder if Adam ever looked over at Eve with anger and disgust in his eyes and said, "You are the one who wanted to eat that fruit. Cain would still be here if you had left it alone. It's your fault Abel is dead and Cain is gone." After all, he blamed her in the garden. He also blamed God. He was standing right there when Eve ate it. He didn't try to stop her and then he did it too ... because, of course, he wanted to. Have you ever seen anyone being forced to eat something they really don't want to eat? Yeah, even if the "someone" is a baby, it's really hard to get their mouth to open when they refuse. I remember trying to force medicine into my infant's mouth and ending up changing my shirt and pants, totally out maneuvered by a one-year-old. Yet, when confronted in the garden, Adam blames God and Eve, "The woman whom 'you' gave to be with me—"she" gave me fruit from the tree and I ate." (Genesis 3:12)

We are all lined up behind Adam and Eve, absolutely grasping with both hands at our own free will and our knowledge of good and evil, yet devastated by the effects of it in our lives as we blame and question whether God is really good. Yesterday a young lady sat across from me on my couch and said, "What kind of 'loving' god forces you to love him?" "He doesn't," I responded. She immediately snapped back. "Oh, yes he does. He threatens you with hell...so love him or burn forever! That's not free will...that's not even a choice!"

I explained to her that I believe God is being merciful when He gives us examples using pain-filled adjectives we can relate to that describe hell. She tilted her head and looked at me questioningly.

I continued to explain that God often gives us words

we can relate to so that we have the best understanding. God told Adam and Eve they would surely die if they ate the fruit, but did they physically die right away? No, and that must have been a big shocker! Nevertheless, God had given them free will and a warning. What they suffered was spiritual death. His plan obviously was bigger than they had anticipated. They couldn't understand the words "You will surely die" (as they had never seen death) any more than we can comprehend "hell" as we have never been separated from the goodness of God's glorious nature. I do believe that God created Hell and that in some sense He is present there. As David wrote, "If I make my bed in hell, you are there" (Psalm 139:8 KJV). I'm sure God explains it to the best of our ability to comprehend it. Just the same, God gives us free will, a choice, and a warning today.

I encouraged her to look around at what God created. He is the genius of creation. He is the mastermind behind geometry and every science we know. He created mountains, ocean ecosystems and kitten fur. Does that tell us anything about Him? If God knows that the people who choose to reject Him are willingly going out of His grace and mercy forever to a place where there is nothing good from Himself, nothing of His glory or beauty, none of the wonderful things He created—no blue skies, no lakes, no puppies, no breeze, no light, no love—do you think it could be merciful for Him to warn us using the worst things we can imagine? He is just and righteous, so He has to punish evil. What kind of God would let murderers, pedophiles and rapists enjoy eternity? God going as far as actually making hell awful so that we might seriously stop and consider our eternity would be appropriate for a merciful Creator.

Have you ever considered that His warning could be purely merciful and truly a freewill choice?

Not just that, but many, including myself, believe there is a good chance that the souls of those who reject Jesus will be destroyed in the second death (Gehenna) after the torment of Hades ends. If you die in the second death, I think there is at least a good possibility your soul will be just that, destroyed and therefore dead, yet your eternal "dead" body may be an eternal warning or monument to those who defy God. (See Matt. 10:28.) This subject deserves a book of its own as some of the words for hell are translated in a way that's a little confusing. Here again, we need to trust God.

You know, it was a trust issue from the beginning. Eve didn't trust God. She thought He was holding out on her, and we are no different. Many of us, like Lisa, are suspicious of God. I was; that's why I blamed Him, and I didn't even realize it. Many of us struggle to trust God today, especially in the wake of someone else's devastating free-will choices from the past.

You know what's funny: the answer to my trust issues— the ones my pride-filled heart demanded in my dream (Where are you, God? Don't you even care? Why don't you help us?) are all treasures found in the story of Lazarus. The answers were right there, in a story I had read a hundred times before.

Make it Personal

Have you ever felt frustrated because you desperately wanted something from another person but felt if you had to repeatedly ask for it then it wasn't worth having? What was it that you wanted?

Have you ever blamed or been super angry at God for something someone else chose to do? Write about the situation below.

If you had the power, is there a time you would have changed someone else's free will to suit your own needs? Please describe.

Would you be willing to totally give up your free will to choose a spouse, where you live, where you work, what you listen to, what you eat, etc., in exchange for eliminating the suffering caused by other humans?

How would you feel if someone you dearly loved hurt someone else that you also dearly loved? Use three descriptive words in your response.

Why do you think God was merciful to Cain after He punished him?

_____

_____

_____

If it were your child who was an offender or a perpetrator, would you want others to pray for his or her salvation?

_____

_____

_____

Notes

CHAPTER 6

Travis and Suzie Foot Rubs and Pine Trees

*"I can't even describe how much I loved or missed
my mom as a child. There just aren't words. I ached
for her."*

— Travis

E veryone in the audience knew exactly what little Travis was talking about. Years before Travis was born, his mother had suffered a miscarriage at the hospital that left her hemorrhaging so badly she had bled out before the doctors could give her enough blood to save her. The doctors had pronounced Evelyn dead and left the room. Travis's dad and some church family were then allowed to go in to say good- bye. Travis's father gently took Evelyn's hand and started asking God for a miracle. "Please, God, please let her stay longer." Within a few minutes, Evelyn moved her hand and the doctors and nurses excitedly rushed back in. To everyone's shock and amazement, she was alive.

Evelyn had to work hard to regain her ability to walk and talk. She had to learn a lot of things over, but she was alive. In six months or so, she was back to 100 percent. After that, she talked about heaven to anyone who would listen.

Little Travis continued, "Mom says that everyone has a 'p-pacific' time to die, and Jesus wanted her to come back because she had work to do here on earth. She told Jesus she didn't wanna come back, but He said she had to. Mommy says that God wanted Cindy, Theresa, and me to be born." Travis glanced at his sisters. "When all of us finish our work, it will be our time to go to heaven too. We will get to see her then. Now it's Momma's time to go. Maybe Jesus needs her to do some work there." Travis looked down at his feet. "I miss Mom. I want Momma back." His voice tightened and Travis looked up and straight at his dad. "But I know she is so excited to be with Jesus instead of here." He glanced at the audience. "So you can stop crying. Don't cry anymore. It's okay. Really, it is."

Travis holds the mic up for the pastor. The pastor's cheeks are bright red and his usually happy blue eyes drop huge tears down his face as he blinks. Travis turns to walk off the stage, but before he takes a step, he feels his dad's arms lifting him as his father picks him up and squeezes him tightly. Travis doesn't understand why his dad and others are crying even more.

"We are just sad because we will miss her, son," his dad says to him. "Sometimes tears are okay. Some tears are even good." His father looks Travis right in the eyes, "Thank you, son, for reminding us. You are right. Mommy is okay." He hugs Travis again very tightly.

Travis lays his head on his dad's shoulder and hears a strange noise, a sorrowful, pain-filled moan comes from his father's throat. He then feels a tight lump in his own. Then tears fill Travis's eyes and fall down his cheeks, but Travis is not crying for his mom. He's crying for his dad. Travis presses his face deep into his dad's neck and breathes in the faint, comforting, familiar smell of Old Spice. His dad pats his back and carries him back to their seats.

The first few weeks weren't too bad, except for the general feeling of things just not being right. But, very quickly, the reality of the situation sank in. As the dirty dishes and the dirty clothes piled up; everyone realized just how much Momma did for them. At age fourteen, Adrian wasn't prepared to be a mom. Rebekah, living next door, a newlywed, pregnant and going to school, was busy, so things just didn't get done. Nevertheless, months later they had managed to finish the school year and summer was a welcome break. No alarm, no hurrying, no homework.

Travis excitedly strips off his shirt, shorts, and underwear.

Dropping them where he stands, buck-naked he runs to the rain-filled ditch at the edge of the front yard. Knee-deep in mud, he turns around and grins at Adrian, then dives into the muddy water, face first, and rolls.

Theresa begs him to think about their mom and how sick she would be at the thought of him playing in the ditch. Travis looks up at Theresa and smiles wild and mischievously, raising and wiggling his eyebrows...and the summer rolls on.

One day after a busy few hours of outdoor play, Travis quietly creeps through the house. He finds all three girls are lying on their parent's queen-size bed for a nap. *Wow, they don't even care about me or what I'm doing.* He looks down at the banana peel in his hand. Not wanting to walk back to the kitchen, he decides to put it under the bed. The girls are all fast asleep. Travis realizes how tired he is and slowly crawls up onto the foot of the bed to join them.

As he tries to crawl in, the girls respond in protest.

"Go on," Adrian says sleepily, "you won't behave so you can go sleep somewhere else. Git!" She kicks at him and makes it impossible for him to snuggle in between them.

"Please," Travis begs, "please, I'm tired too." "Go lie in your own bed, you dirty brat!" "Come on, Adrian, please?"

"Okay," Adrian says. "You rub my feet and I'll let you in the bed."

Travis wrinkles his face in protest. "Yuck," he quips. "That's the deal, Travis. Take it or leave it."

Travis looks over at Adrian's sock-covered feet, drops his shoulders, and sighs. "Fine, I'll rub your stinky old feet."

Travis takes her toes in his hands and starts massaging. Adrian smiles as she lies comfortably sprawled out on the bed. Travis feels abused and angry, but he wants to crawl in the bed and sleep with them instead of having to take a nap alone. He often feels lonely since his momma died.

After several minutes, he asks, "There, is that enough?" He hops onto the foot of the bed again.

No," Adrian replies. "The deal is off because you called my feet stinky. You can just go sleep in the mud," she taunts. "I'm tired," Travis whines. "I rubbed your feet, but you lied."

"Yeah, and you disobey me all the time," Adrian reminds him.

Travis yawns as he stretches his neck and arms. "Please, Adrian."

"No way, Travis, beat it." Adrian determinedly shifts her body, sprawling her legs to block him from crawling up between them.

Travis sits on the end of the bed for several minutes. He waits till he gets so sleepy he doesn't care and relaxes onto the bed. He curls up at the girl's feet. He wishes he was under the covers. He shivers, but moments later, he is asleep.

Soon Travis can hear Cindy and Theresa talking, but he's too tired to wake up. He feels them get out of the bed and hears something about playing dress up. He awakens enough to feel the cool air and quietly crawls up to get under the covers next to Adrian. As soon as he gets comfortable, Adrian gets up. An intense feeling of loneliness comes over him. He misses sleeping with his mother. He misses cuddling. He needs to be held. He feels like he's going to cry, but Adrian doesn't leave. Instead of leaving, Adrian shuts and locks the door.

"I knew he would kill my mom if I told on him. There was no doubt in my mind."

—Suzie

Ray limps around the bed, focused on Suzie like she was his worst enemy. The belt catches Suzie across the right calf and she screams like a wild animal.

"Please, stop, stop, don't, no...no...no!" she begs. "I didn't do it!"

"Stop your lying," Ray yells, "or I'll beat your backside again."

As he takes one more swipe, the belt barely catches her

left foot as she runs across the bed. That one really stings and she buckles, falling and grabbing her foot with both her hands. Her crying moan rips through the air one more time as he swings wildly at the bed and wickedly hisses, "Knock off that screaming right now, or I swear I'll whip you again." Ray finally looks tired and throws the belt on the floor in the corner. He limps over and bends to pick up his crutch.

"Don't you dare go outside again today," he demands.

Suzie takes a deep breath, letting out a cry that sounds like a wounded animal howling. Several long, shaky breaths later she realizes the beating is over. She can feel her heart pounding. It stings. Her fingers sting. Her arms and legs sting. Everything stings. Her back feels like the skin has been ripped off. Painful, red, raised welts appear across her little body. She crawls to the corner of the bed, holding her swelling red hands out in front of her. Whimpering and shaking, she looks down at them. Her hands hurt so bad she doesn't want to set them in her lap, so she just holds them up. She heaves in huge breaths of air and cries them out. Suzie can barely hear the faint squeals and laughter of the kids outside, still frolicking as they play in the bubbles. Suzie's eyes are huge with shock and staring at the doorway, her tear-soaked face is cherry red. Suzie doesn't even try to move, everything hurts too bad. But her heart hurts too. Her mind won't let go of the words replaying over and over. *I didn't do it. I didn't do it.*

Sobbing for what seems like forever, she finally notices the TV. It's an episode of "The Dukes of Hazzard." She can hear Ray laughing. She loves that show, but there is no way she would ever go out there now. She is terrified to draw his attention. She will just stay in there and wait. "Momma," she quietly whimpers, "Momma, please come home."

Soon she hears Ray snoring. She is suddenly very alert; now is her chance. She carefully crawls off the edge of the bed and walks over to the door. She waits to hear him snore some more. Yes, she hears him again. He's out cold. She peeks out slowly and then she tiptoes across the small living room, through the kitchen, and down the hallway to her room. She softly puts her little hand on her bedroom doorknob and turns it. Her hand is slightly swollen and it hurts. She creeps through the doorway and carefully closes the door behind her, making sure to turn the knob hard and release it slowly so it doesn't make any noise. Suzie breathes in quietly, trembling as she tiptoes over to her bed.

Suzie cuddles in the corner of her bunk bed and cries some more. As she lies still, every sound startles her. "Momma will be home soon," she tells Barbie.

As the afternoon turns to night, her room gets dimmer until, finally, it's dark. She chooses to leave her light off so she won't draw her step-father's attention if he were to get up. Suzie pulls her Barbie up to her face and rubs her cheeks in Barbie's stiff, blonde hair. Her stomach growls. She hugs Barbie tightly and tells her, "It's okay. That's just my tummy growling."

After many long hours, Suzie hears a noise in the living room. Her heart pounds and her stomach aches. Instantly, she's awake. That's his recliner. She is used to listening for the sounds. He's getting up. Suzie hears the now-familiar sound of Ray's cast hitting the floor … thump, thump, thump as he limps through the kitchen, down the hall, and finally past her room, and out the front door. She is relieved.

As he goes out the door, she thinks again about how hungry she is. When she hears him talking to Larry, she knows he will talk for a few minutes. Suzie creeps out into the kitchen and quickly opens the refrigerator. She is so hungry and there is nothing to eat. No lunch meat, no cheese, or leftovers. *I sure wish Mom was home.* All she can find is ketchup. Suzie takes two pieces of bread out and lays them on the table. She opens the bottle of ketchup as fast as she can, struggling to turn it over and dump it out. She squeezes a generous amount of ketchup onto the two pieces of bread and then carefully turns the bottle back up and sets it on the table, licking the ketchup that dripped on her pinky finger. It feels good to lick her sore finger. Suzie picks up one of the pieces of bread and carefully sets it on the other piece. She pats it, then puts the lid on the ketchup and puts it back in the refrigerator so she won't get in trouble.

Suzie runs back to her bedroom with her sandwich. As she gets to her door, she can hear Ray out on the porch talking to Larry about picking up some stuff. More grass for their can of weeds. She licks the side of her sandwich to catch the drip before it runs onto her hand as she gently closes her bedroom door.

Soon she is sleepy, but she can't relax. Her body still hurts and she can feel the small but painful welts on her legs, back, and arms. Ray laughs loudly on the porch, and she hates the sound of it. *I wish he would die.* A raindrop hits her window and she looks up. There's another and another. She can hear the rough splat of rain on the window as the wind starts blowing. The rain is now freely falling. The door opens and Ray is yelling, "Okay, man, see ya tomorrow."

She feels terror grip her body as he limps down the hall toward her room. Thump, thump, thump. He limps past and goes to the living room. She listens like a deer in the woods, but the rain is loud now, and she can't tell where he is. She wants to get up to crack her door open—to figure out what he's doing so she can relax—but she is too scared to draw attention to herself. She huddles in the far corner of her bunk bed and waits for sleep. Finally, it comes.

Later that same night, Suzie hears Ray's voice close to her ear. "Suzie," he whispers, "wake up."

Suzie rouses just enough to realize that Ray is kneeling next to the bed. She feels pain on her arm. *Ouch, ouch! Why is he pinching me?*

"Wake up," he whispers again.

What's he doing? He lifts her up a little bit to try to rouse her, but she tucks her little legs up under her, tightening into a ball. He pinches her again. This time on the outside of her upper thigh.

"Wake up," Ray insists, his voice increasingly angry and commanding.

Suzie is so tired from crying, she can barely hold her eyes open. *What is he doing? Why is he touching me?* She's so sleepy. He pinches her again.

"Ouch!" she cries. "Wake up, I told you."

She feels his hands on her tiny body, but she is so exhausted she can't stay awake.

It is getting light in her room as Suzie opens her eyes the next morning and sees her rumpled sheet and blanket. She notices the stems and wilted, mashed petals of the dried-up buttercups that she had put in her bed yesterday. She had forgotten about them.

Suzie starts to reach for them but immediately is distracted by the position she is sleeping in. She suddenly remembers Ray lying next to her on the bed and touching her in the night. She realizes she is sleeping in the same position as when he was touching her, her legs still tucked up under her in a ball. As she pushes her torso up, she feels something on her ankles.

It's her panties. They are down around her feet. She rolls to her side and reaches down for her underwear. It didn't seem real. *What had happened? He pinched me!* She pulls her panties up as fast as she can. *Why was he trying to wake me up? Why did he touch me?*

Suzie is suddenly full of anxiety. Something was wrong. This feeling is new. It was like feeling scared and very alone but not the same. Suzie often felt alone, but this feeling was different. It was like she suddenly was sinking to the bottom of the deepest, darkest cave where it is pitch black and no one else is in sight. Only Ray is there. She is alone with him! She felt a horrible dread grip her. *Will he do that again?* Suzie's heart cries out...*Momma, please be home.*

She looks out the window of her small, cramped room at the tall, swaying trees. She usually loves watching the huge pines that encircle the trailer park. But it's not the same today. Normally, the trees make her feel lifted up and swept away to a strong place of peace and safety, but now her heart can't be comforted. The trees today feel like they have turned on her. As she looks at them, she feels small, helpless, and trapped. They surround her like a huge confining wall, creeping up on her, making her feel blocked in, just like he does. The sun is shining through the big pines and the wind is moving the thick trunks back and forth. The trees aren't going anywhere; they can't run away and neither can she.

Suzie breathes in slowly. It's so quiet in the house she can hear her own breath as she exhales. She glances back at the trees. *He's awful. I hate him.* Disgusted at the thought of his hands on her, she desperately wishes she was one of the trees so she could live outside and not have to live in this place with him. She pictures his face and hates the thought of it.

Huge brown leaves scamper like small creatures across the back yard. *I hate him.* She sees the neighbor's black and white cat come out of the dense underbrush. *He laid in my bed and touched me.* She hated the thought. *What else is going to happen?*

Suddenly a tree frog jumps on her window, landing a few feet from Suzie's face. Oh, hurry, hurry! she thinks, as she whips the covers out of her way and scampers out of the bed. She grabs her shorts and glances back at the window. She is sore and she sees bruises and red marks on her legs, but she can't waste time, not now. The little green visitor is clinging calmly to the glass window pane, his soft white belly moving against the window as it breathes. If she hurries, she can sneak outside and try to catch him.

Make it Personal

Do you believe God has abandoned Travis because his mom died? Why or why not?

_____

_____

_____

At times, has it seemed like God has abandoned you? If so, when?

_____

_____

_____

How do you feel about children being left alone for long periods to watch over other children?

_____

_____

_____

The Bible says, "Foolishness is bound up in the heart of a child" (Proverbs 22:15 KJV) .Were you ever hurt as a child by another child who was supposed to be watching you? Did you ever harm a child you were supposed to be watching? Were you ever tempted?

_____

_____

_____

What do you think might help Suzie get out of this abusive situation?

_____

_____

Do you blame God for what Ray is doing to Suzie? If not, who is to blame?

_____

_____

_____

How do you feel about Ray? Be truthful ... God already knows anyway.

_____

_____

_____

Notes

.

CHAPTER 7

If Only I Would Have Known
Millstone

All scripture is given by inspiration of God, and is profitable for doctrine, for reproof, for correction, for instruction in righteousness: That the man of God may be perfect, thoroughly furnished unto all good works.

(2 Timothy 3:16 KJV)

Did you know that Jesus Christ says that every child has an angel that stands in the presence of God and looks into His face over that child's treatment? Yes, It's true. Matthew 18:10 (AMP) says: "Beware that you do not despise or feel scornful toward or think little of one of these little ones, for I tell you that in heaven their angels always are in the presence of and look upon the face of My Father who is in heaven." Their angels stare or focus constantly on the face of God over the way children are treated by human beings.

As I ponder this, I picture my little Yorkie, Marco, sitting beneath me as I put my dinner plate on the table. Marco never takes his eyes off me. His big, shiny, dark brown beggarly boulders never lose sight of my face. He isn't even slightly distracted when my husband, Travis, gently scoots him aside so he can take his seat at the table. Marco means to get a response from me, and he will wait forever if he has to. He waits expectantly anticipating my next move. He is looking for a payoff. A piece of my roast beef is what he is after. His mouth salivates, and he trembles with excitement and the promise of what he knows is coming soon. The angels looking at the face of God over their children's treatment also know that what they expect from God will happen soon.

What do you think is going through the minds of these angels? How do they feel about the abuse that children suffer? Do they feel anguish? Anger? Do they long for justice? Are they outraged? Do their hearts break the way ours do? Regardless of how they feel, they trust God, they see His face, and they know, like my Marco, what is coming. I wish I knew God the way the angels do.

What a difference it would make if every child understood that an angel was standing before God on their behalf, looking into His face over the way they are treated. I didn't know. And I think if I had known it as a young girl, it would have made a big difference. I will share more about my personal experience with childhood abuse in a later book. But for now, just know that from the age of about four or five, I was touched inappropriately by an older neighborhood man. It had a devastating effect on me. Before I turned eighteen, a total of five different men made attempts to molest me. I know what it means to feel alone and terrified.

I'm sure some of you noted that the title of this book, *Millstone*, references a Scripture in the Bible. When Jesus was here on the earth, He told the disciples that it would be far better for a person who offended a little one to have a millstone tied around their neck and be thrown into the depths of the sea than what will happen to them on judgment day. This specific account about the punishment for offending a child, or any small one, is recorded in three of the four gospels: Matthew, Mark, and Luke.

But I want to ask some questions before we look at these encouraging verses. Please take some time and consider them. You may even think of some very good questions yourself. Jot them in the margin if you do. Here goes:

Would a perpetrator stimulating a child sexually and trying to elicit a response be considered "enticing wrong conduct or thought?" Could an offender having sexual conversations with a child or fondling a child cause that child to have unforgiveness, hatred, or resentment? Could it cause them to "entertain wrong thoughts?" Could heartlessly stealing a child's virginity, robbing them of a natural, wonderful, God-designed relationship, and totally undermining their sense of a normal sexual experience cause hate-filled or even murderous feelings toward the perpetrator? Would making a child look at porn or viewing an offender's nakedness be "leading them astray" or "enticing them to wrong thoughts or conduct?" Could a perpetrator exposing a child to an adult's sexual appetite cause a future broken or skewed view about what normal sexual desire should be? Can years of torment at the hands of a sexual deviant cause "a little one who relies on Him" to be filled with anger, shame, bitterness, fear, or unnatural sexual desires? Could these sexual acts cause them to sin or be "led astray?"

The answer to all these questions is yes. Any abuse toward a child could cause them to hate or harbor resentment. Sexual abuse can cause a child to be consumed with shame or lust and thus act out by covering their pain with alcohol, drugs, food, sex, cutting or some other painful vice that again might blind them to the love of God. It can also cause them to be tempted to abuse another child. I could think of a thousand different scenarios where a child or "weak innocent" might be "led astray" as a result of being molested. But the biggest, and certainly most grievous, is that every molested child inadvertently decides that there is no God, or if God exists, that God doesn't love or care about them. Sexual abuse drives a wedge between a child and our loving Father. That would definitely be "leading them astray."

You may have noticed strange language when I asked some of those questions like "enticing wrong conduct or thought," "leading them astray," "weak innocent," and "little ones who rely on Him." That's because those are the words used in the Scriptures we will be considering.

Let me start in Mark 9:33-34. Jesus's disciples had been walking to Capernaum. On the journey, they had been discussing (disputing, actually) who would be the greatest in the kingdom of heaven. When they arrived at Capernaum, Jesus asked them what they were having a dispute (a dignified word for arguing) about on the road. I think they may have been ashamed (been there, done that) since they didn't answer right away.

Mark then records that Jesus gathers the disciples to him and tells them that if "anyone desires to be the first he must be the last of all, and the servant of all" (Mark 9:35 AMP). Ouch! That was probably sobering and not at all what they wanted to hear, but He had answered their question. After Jesus answers, Mark records that Jesus calls a child to them and places that child in the midst of them. He puts his arms around the child and says, "Whoever in my name or for my sake accepts and receives and welcomes one such child also accepts, receives, and welcomes Me; and whoever so receives Me receives not only Me but Him who sent Me" (Mark 9:37 AMP).

In Mark's gospel, Jesus is asked a question about someone casting out a demon. After Jesus answers that question, the way Mark records the (Peter's eyewitness account) encounter, Jesus returns to the subject of children, warning about offenses and the "millstone." Remember, He has a child on His lap. Here is His warning:

"And whosoever shall offend one of these 'little ones who believes in me,' it is better for him that a millstone be hanged about his neck, and he were cast into the sea. And if thy hand offends thee cut it off: it is better for thee to enter into life maimed than having two hands to go into hell, *into the fire that never shall be quenched: Where their worm dieth not, and their fire is not quenched. And if thy foot offends thee, cut it off: it is better for them to enter maimed into life, than having two feet to be cast into hell, into the fire that never shall be quenched. Where their worm dieth not, and their fire is not quenched*: And if thy eye offends thee, pluck it out: it is better for thee to enter into the kingdom of God with one eye, than having two eyes to be *cast into hell fire: Where the worm dieth not, and the fire is not quenched* (Mark 9:42-47 KJV) [emphasis added].

Do you think that Mark was trying to stress any certain idea or point here that he felt Jesus was making? I made it bold for you in case you didn't notice the repeating pattern. Three times Jesus says it: "Into hell, the fire that never shall be quenched: Where the worn dieth not." This phrase stated three times is a huge warning to those who might hurt a child. Even more interesting is that the "cut your hand off, pluck your eye out" Scripture immediately follows the warning not to offend or lead astray a little one. Did you realize this? I didn't. What could you do with your eyes that would cause you to harm a child? The first and only other time I know of that the "pluck your eye out" phrase appears in the Bible is in Matthew 5:29 where Jesus says it immediately after talking about looking upon and lusting after a woman who is not your wife being the sin of adultery. So, it stands to reason (if we follow that same pattern) that in Matthew 18:6- 10, and then in Mark 9, child molestation is definitely a possible identifiable act that Jesus is warning about along with many other kinds of child abuse. We certainly can't rule it out.

For a moment, please look back at the phrase from Mark 9:42, *"little ones who believe in me."* This may be confusing at first glance and, because of that, sometimes even misconstrued to convince people to think that Jesus is talking about adults who have accepted Him and believe in Him as their Savior. The following is their argument: Jesus would consider all of us "God's children," right? He just told us (believers in Christ) to become like children. And how can a child believe in Jesus? Certainly, all children don't. A child raised in India may not even know who Jesus is. So maybe this is more universal and just means everyone who believes in Jesus and not specifically children? I don't think so, and in hopes to persuade you, I'd like to start by asking the same question backward. How can a child not believe in, rely on, and trust God? Keep in mind that Jesus is the physical manifestation of God and He created the child in His lap. Because it's important in this instance to establish that Jesus is God, we are going to camp here for a short bit, but please bear with me as this concept is so important and encouraging.

Consider the Old Testament Scripture, "For unto us a child is born, unto us a son is given: and the government shall be on His shoulders: and His name shall be called wonderful, counsellor, **Mighty God, the everlasting Father**, The Prince of Peace" (Isaiah 9:6 KJV) [emphasis added].

In this Old Testament Scripture, the "child" that is "born unto us" is "Mighty God and everlasting Father." The first chapter of Hebrews declares it: "But about the Son (the Father says to Him), your throne, O God, is forever and ever, and the scepter of (absolute) righteousness is the scepter of His Kingdom" (Hebrews 1:18 AMP). Here, God clearly refers to Jesus as God.

What about when Jesus says, "Destroy this temple and in three days I will rebuild it." John 2:19 Jesus says, He will rebuild it! Remember Thomas's words? "Thomas answered and said unto Him, 'My Lord and my God!'" (John 20:28 KJV). Here, the disciple who doubted "Jesus Christ resurrected" declares who Jesus really is, God. Jesus responds by immediately affirming to Thomas and all those present that He is God when He says, "Thomas, because thou hast seen me, thou hast believed: blessed are they that have not seen, and yet have believed" (John 20:29 KJV).

I've heard people say that Jesus never claimed to be God. I assume they are saying that because Jesus never spoke the English word-for-word translation "I am God," they believe there is no real proof. But Jesus did proclaim He was God and the Jews knew exactly what He was saying. You can see this clearly by their reactions to His words. For instance, in the gospel of John, Jesus says "I and the Father are one" (John 10:30 KJV). The Jews responded by trying to stone Him. They are recorded by John as having said, "You a mere man claim to be God" (John 10:33 KJV). They heard Jesus loud and clear.

In John 8, Jesus states, "Before Abraham, I am." Again, the Jews took up rocks and tried to stone Him. The Jewish people knew exactly what Jesus meant in their language.

I know a lot of people, including myself, have difficulty understanding the concept that Jesus is God, especially because He is often referred to as the "Son of God." It makes it a lot easier for me when I remember that the Greeks had more than one word for our word "son." Kind of like we have the word "bat," and it can mean a bat you hit a ball with or a bat you see flying through the twilight late in the evening looking for bugs. Or you can even bat at bugs with your hands. You might call a cranky old lady an "old bat". We know by the way it is used in the sentence which definition should be applied.

Years ago, while studying Jesus being God in the flesh,

I looked up the word "Son" in the Greek when it is used by God to describe Jesus, which is *huios* (pronounced hwee- os'). This word is used by God in Matthew 3:17 (KJV): "And lo a voice from heaven saying, This is My beloved Son in whom I am well pleased."

The Strong's expanded exhaustive concordance 2001, describes this word *huios* this way:

Primarily this word describes the quality and essence of one so resembling another that distinctions between the two are indiscernible.

This meaning is a little different than the word "son" used when referring to a biological male offspring. That Greek word is *teknon*, meaning child. No matter which word you look up in the Strong's you will find a contrast comparing it to the other word. When you look up *huios* in the Strong's, part of the definition reads: "*Teknon* gives prominence to the physical and outward aspects of parentage. *Huios* gives prominence to the inward, ethical aspects of parentage." When you look up *teknon* the Strong's it reads: "*Huios* gives prominence to the inward, ethical, legal aspects of parentage, the dignity and character of the relationship. *Teknon* denotes a child with respects to descent and age."

So, when Jesus is called "My Son" by God, it means he is the perfect and identical manifestation of the character or essence of God in a human body. Here is further proof:

"For in Him (Jesus) dwelleth the fullness of the Godhead bodily"

(Colossians 2:9 KJV).

"Before Me there was no God formed, nor shall there be after Me. I even I am the Lord, and besides Me there is no Savior"

(Isaiah 43:11 KJV).

"Indeed, before the day was, I am He"
(Isaiah 43:13KJV).

(Both of those passages from Isaiah were God speaking and referring to Himself as Savior and there at creation.)

"In the beginning was the Word, and the Word (Jesus) was with God and the Word was God. The same was in the beginning with God. All things were made by Him; and without Him was not any- thing made that was made"
(John 1:1-5 KJV).

In Isaiah 43, God says that there is no Savior beside Himself and that before the day was created, He was. Then in the first chapter of the book of John, Jesus is right there creating all things and nothing was created without Him. Because Jesus created all things, children are His creation. Mark said Jesus "placed a child in the midst of them and took that child in his arms." That child would, of course, be considered by Jesus to be one who "relied on Him" in the sense that a child isn't old enough or mentally capable of reasoning an argument for rejecting Him.

I'll keep in mind here the sin nature and acknowledge our human instinct to lie or steal. But God doesn't hold us accountable for willfully sinning or rejecting Him until we understand fully what we are doing. We assume that if a three-year-old dies, even if they have told a lie, they still go to heaven. We probably assume that if an eight-year-old dies, they also go to heaven. Would a nine-year-old go to heaven even after they have repeatedly sinned? I'd say yes. We could keep asking, but I don't know the age of accountability. Maybe it is different for every individual. Maybe it's forty. God is good, merciful, and righteous. We can trust Him with that.

My point is, I think God sees every soul He created as a "being" who relies on Him until they have reached the age of accountability and either acknowledges or rejects Him.

Another very interesting point is that there are many other places where we are warned about causing our brothers or fellow believers in Christ to stumble and thus causing them to sin. (See 1 Corinthians 8:9, 13 and Romans 14:1-23.) Yet, for these adults, there is no mention of a millstone. Jesus, in Matthew 5:44-45 (KJV) says to "love your enemies, bless them that curse you, do good to them that hate you, and pray for them which despitefully use you, and persecute you. That you may be the children of your father which is in heaven." This is Jesus telling adult believers to love and forgive those who offend us or wound us. As adult Christians, He expects us to handle it and not sin. Not just that, but to turn around and bless those that curse us. Yet here in Mark, when Jesus is speaking about children, He gives a fierce warning.

Now let's jump to Luke, who has the shortest account, only two verses. Luke 17:1 (AMP) records that "Jesus said to His disciples, 'Temptations (snares, traps set to entice to sin) are sure to come, but woe to him by or through whom they come!" We can stop and acknowledge free will right here, which is another thing I wished I would have understood (at a beginner's level) as a child. Luke then quotes what Jesus said when warning about hurting a child and the millstone in verse two. Please take the time to read that Scripture now.

Now let's take a look at Matthew.

"And Jesus called a little child unto Him and set him in the midst of them. And said, Verily I say unto you, except ye be converted, and become as little children, ye shall not enter into the kingdom of heaven. Whosoever therefore shall humble himself as this little child, the same is the greatest in the kingdom of heaven."

These Scriptures answer the arguments that the disciples were having as they walked along the road. Because these two verses are misinterpreted to mean that from this point in the Scripture forward, we are now talking only about "grown-ups" who humble themselves to be like "children" and not referring to actual children, like the child in Jesus's arms, we need to ask some questions: How could it be possible that in the verses following this, Jesus is still talking to grown-up Christians who are becoming child-like, considering that both

Matthew's and Mark's accounts repeatedly use the descriptive word in the Greek for "little one" *paidion* meaning "a half-grown boy or girl" or *mikroteros* meaning "small." Luke says "little one" interpreted "lowly in rank or influence." Remember, the whole while, Jesus has a child in his arms for an example, probably so we wouldn't try to rule out children or take the emphasis off of them. Unfortunately, many people do this.

Jesus starts by using the child as an example for us to become like them because of the disciples' questions, but then in the following verses he "adds" and "contrasts" information. Two times, Jesus ends His sentence with the words "the kingdom of heaven." Both of those sentences are answers about grown-ups becoming like little ones and address the argument the disciples were having about the kingdom of heaven, but that's as far as it goes. After that, Jesus is speaking about the child in his lap. Verse five offers additional information: "And whoever receives and accepts and welcomes one little child (small) like this (again referring to the *paidion*, half-grown boy or girl in his arms) for my sake and in my name receives and accepts and welcomes me" (Matthew 18:2-4 AMP). The word "and" at the beginning of verse five tells us this is additional information about the *paidion*. Not only do you need to become as a "child" (like the child in His lap) to enter the kingdom of God, but also if you receive a child, like the child in His lap, you receive Him as if you are doing it unto Him. When you read these Scriptures, do you see what I see? Jesus is talking about children here.

Matthew follows his account of Jesus's answers to the disciple's questions about the kingdom of heaven with the warning about offending a "little one" and the "millstone." The word "offend" here in all three of our earliest copies of the Gospels comes from a Greek word, *skandalizo*. It literally means "entrap, trip up, or entice to sin; to put a stumbling block or impediment in the way, upon which another may trip or fall." (Strong's Expanded Exhaustive Concordance, 2001).

Here is the verse from Matthew 18:6 (AMP): "But whoever causes one of these little ones [*paidion*: half-grown boy or girl] who believes in and acknowledge and cleaves to

Me to stumble and sin (this is, who entices him or hinders him in right conduct or thought), it would be better (more expedient or profitable or advantageous) for him to have a great millstone fastened around his neck and to be sunk in the depths of the sea."

Now could Jesus also mean any grown person who is small in faith? Well, I suppose He could, but not to the exclusion of the primary subject in his arms, a *paidion*, a half-grown boy or girl. Are there other ways besides molestation that you can lead a little one astray? Of course. Some people teach children to steal, lie, or to hate other people who are from a different race, culture, or religion. Some people teach children to have sex before they are supposed to. It's that simple. If you lead a little one astray, and into sin, you are, according to Jesus' words of warning, "in danger of being cast into everlasting fire" (Matt. 18:9).

The word "but" at the beginning of Matthew 18:6 tells us that Jesus is saying something that contrasts with the verse before it where he is commending those who receive, accept, and welcome a child. The opposite would be to offend a child. Jesus is, without a doubt, still talking about children here. My point is that you can't add information like Jesus does in Matthew 18:5 with the word "and" or contrast information like Jesus does in Matthew 18:6 with the word "but" unless you're still talking about the same subject, a child, in this case. Why did I spend so much time on this? Because so many people say Jesus is talking about grown- ups in these Scriptures, but that is simply not the case.

Matthew's and Luke's gospels agree that the "temptations or influences (free will, sin)" to do wrong must come but "woe to them that do these things." Jesus is talking about the perpetrators or offenders here. He says it as if free will is something that absolutely must happen. This is where it gets very interesting to me. Both in Matthew and in Mark, right on the heels of the "millstone" warning, and while he is still talking about children, is the verse we all know and recognize as the "cut off your hand" or "pluck out your eye if it causes you to sin" Scripture. When I read it in context here (just like in Mark), it again makes me stop and think about the fact that I always thought of this verse in the context of a man lusting after a grown woman or maybe a greedy person tempted to steal, but there it is immediately following the millstone warning.

Sure, I had often thought about it at a very assuming level, you know, about abuse in general, but not carefully. Probably because I heard the other reference from the beginning of Matthew 5:27-30 when Jesus is talking about the sin of adultery and lusting after a woman numerous times and exclusively in church.

Which begs the question: if I have heard this "pluck out your eye" verse from Matthew 5:27-30 that refers to lusting after women so many times (literally hundreds), why hadn't I heard the same "pluck out your eye" verse from Matthew 18 taught as many times, or even one single time, in its context about abusing, hurting or leading children astray? I've never once heard it taught in a Sunday school class, on the Internet, or at a home Bible study.

Wouldn't it be refreshing and amazing to hear a sermon about leading little ones astray and have it cover the actual ways that happens and the punishment for it? But we never hear that. Instead, we hear that Jesus is speaking about adults here because of the verse about "becoming like children." But, that is only meant to be answering the question about the kingdom of Heaven.

I also suggest that the context of the word "children" or "weak ones" here includes the mild or severely autistic, Down syndrome, or anyone mentally impaired or mentally ill. Anyone who couldn't (by argument) or physically (by fighting) defend themselves or decide not to sin, they (the ones who must rely on God as they are incapable of rejecting Him) are the ones Jesus is warning us not to lead astray or cause to sin.

Guess what verse immediately follows the "millstone warning" and the "pluck your eye out" Scripture in Matthew 18? That's right, *"See that you do not even despise one of these little ones. For I tell you that in heaven their angels always see the face of my Father who is in heaven."* [emphasis added].

The context of this last verse clearly indicates that Jesus

is referring to children in this Scripture. It is the big clincher for me that Jesus is still (since he put the child in the midst of them and answered the question about the kingdom of Heaven) talking about children here and not grown-ups. He is talking to the audience and says, "Don't even despise one of these little ones." He has just raised the bar to even despising a little one. He never stopped talking about children. When Jesus says "If your eye causes you to sin, pluck it out" and "If your hand causes you to sin cut it off" He is talking specifically about children. These children have "their" own angels who are actually looking at God's face. His face! Wow! Do you see God's heart for children? To think that God will not avenge these little ones that have angels looking at His face and expecting God to do something is preposterous! Yes, free will is running amuck and time is ticking by, but God will deal with the people who have offended these little ones.

I think Jesus was spelling it out for us, and somehow (because it is such an uncomfortable subject) we inadvertently avoid it, we don't deal with it. It is understandable for us to avoid the uncomfortable. But, think of the suffering that might be avoided if leaders taught this from the pulpit and we as parents taught and celebrated these Scriptures with our children and grandkids, eagerly focusing on these passages as they are, in context.

Think about it, if we taught our young ones all of these concepts before they started having sexual desire we could probably "slow the roll" immensely on the cases of children molesting children. When a ten-to-twelve-year-old, who has been adequately trained that hurting a younger one is such an offence to God that the "millstone" warning was His teaching to us, is tempted to hurt a child, he may think twice knowing how God will deal with us. These are super important Scriptures.

We have got to start teaching our children not only about their bodies being precious and not for others to take but also teaching them that touching someone else's body might not harm them physically but that it will harm them in their heart and their spirit. We need to teach children that damage can be done to people that you can't see on the outside. We need to start having some new conversations with our kids, but this should give you a great starting point.

Not only do our children need to understand free will, but we need to share the above Scriptures with them at age appropriate times. They need to be told that the Holy Spirit will never leave or forsake us, even while other people choose to do awful things to us like steal or lie, or worse. There are staggering opportunities to teach and protect our children using these Scriptures. Please be watching, as we are also planning an age-appropriate curriculum based on these Scriptures and the concept of free will, so sign up to be notified at www.IdomMinitries.com.

While visiting a friend of mine who is a youth pastor recently, we discussed these Scriptures. My concern was that so many Internet teachers explain away the child on Jesus's lap by using the quote, "unless you become like this little child" from Matthew 18:3 to mean that from that point on we are talking about grown-ups who humble themselves and become like children. From there on, they interpret and apply the Scriptures to a lot of different circumstances, but not specifically to children, abuse, or molestation. It worried me that we don't see or hear it taught from the perspective of Jesus's heart toward kids and abuse. The youth pastor explained that a lot of times people will take certain scriptures and they will apply them to their specific subject like mine (child molestation) to make their desired point and, in the process, limit the interpretation of the Scripture so that it can no longer be timeless and universal. In a sense, that you couldn't apply the Scriptures broadly and to a host of peoples and subjects but restrict it to their (my) particular point.

During our conversation, I questioned the possibility that just the opposite had happened here concerning this Scripture and that, in an attempt to make these Scriptures timeless, universal and broadly applicable, maybe we have taken the focus off of the children (child in Jesus's arms) to their detriment. He was open-minded and thoughtful about my concerns.

I think it robs children to reason away the child in Jesus's lap in an attempt to make these Scriptures "universal, timeless, and broadly applicable." These Scriptures are for the children and we need to give them back!

Hypothetically (I'm not being critical here, just noticing an opportunity to teach), I wish a grown-up had taken advantage of situations where I had lied or stolen something as a child and sat me down and explained to me that I had made a free will decision and that my decisions were mine alone. I chose to sin. I wish they had explained that lying or stealing was against God's will and then followed up with "now you be on the watch for when someone else makes a free will decision and it hurts you. Maybe someone will decide to steal from you. Maybe someone will choose to lie about you. That won't be God's fault. It will be because, just like you decided to steal that gum, they chose to lie or steal from you, and that will hurt you."

If I had realized when I was molested that the person doing it was making a free will decision to sin, and that God loved me to the extent of taking it personally by promising a severe (millstone) punishment, I wouldn't have felt so alienated and forsaken by God. If I had known how God felt about me as a child, regardless of the actions of the men who harmed me, I may have even been terrified for the perpetrator, knowing his probable fate. I may have even wanted to warn him to his face, out of fear for him. If I'd really believed that at the moment when people hurt me that my angel was sitting and waiting on God with me for God to (one day soon) administer justice, it would have made a difference.

Today, as I think back to the minute when my heart was breaking, that moment when I was so confused and terrified, realizing that God **knew** (designed free will so we would have love) and He **cared** (warned of a horrible punishment for offenders), it makes me ache. At that very minute when those tears were rolling down my face, what if I'd known that my angel was already certain, expecting, and anticipating that God would act on my behalf?

God is just. If that perpetrator isn't sincerely broken-hearted and repentant over his sin, then he will be punished, but I didn't know that either! How many people out there need to walk back through their memories and realize these things?

If you are one who needs healing from abuse, don't go back as the wounded victim picturing your abuse through a child's eyes. Go back as the (survivor) adult you are now who trusts in God's holiness. See the situation from an adult perspective and see your angel looking at the face of God, waiting and expectant with you. Explain to the child that was you what you know now about free will. Encourage that child in your mind. Understand the resolve in God's heart to punish that person, remember the millstone, trust God, and let go of the offense in your heart toward the perpetrator and God. God has got this, and He won't let you down.

I understand now that I wasn't alone. It makes it so much easier to bear. I'm never alone. Those facts changed me. God will deal with the perpetrators. He hasn't forgotten me. He hasn't forgotten Travis, Suzie, or the kids at Angel Reach. He hasn't forgotten you or your loved one. He hasn't forgotten anyone. Have you ever heard this expression? "You don't mess with a cub!" Well, God is no different than most of us when it comes to the little ones.

This is where forgiveness comes in. As hard as it is to forgive someone who has caused so much devastation, we can trust a holy God who has promised to hold the offender accountable. Either they will be brokenhearted and devastated over their sin, or they will have to answer to the Creator. God knows our hearts and no one fools Him. We can trust Him and forgive. Let it all go, let the pain, hurt, devastation and the perpetrator fall into God's capable hands.

Make It Personal

Before reading this, did you know that all children have angels who are looking at the face of God over their mistreatment?

_____

_____

_____

Did you realize that the "pluck your eye out" and "cut your hand off" Scriptures were directed at those who would harm children? Would you be willing to help children by sharing that with others?

_____

_____

_____

Take a minute to write out Matthew 18:6. Will you commit this verse to memory?

_____

_____

_____

Do you know any children who might benefit from or be comforted by a clear understanding of free will, God's fierce defense of them, and God's promised punishment for anyone who hurts them? List them, pray about it and talk to them.

_____

_____

_____

Is it easier to forgive as you trust God to judge the hearts of those who have harmed you and hold them accountable? What specific incidences are you waiting on God and trusting Him to handle?

_____

_____

Is it possible to forgive, feel mercy, and let the perpetrator off your hook but still expect God to require brokenhearted repentance or judgement concerning them?

_____

_____

Have you ever done something you are broken hearted over?

_____

_____

Do you need to repent for treating a child harshly, hurting a child, or even despising one? Do you need to ask that person for forgiveness?

_____

_____

_____

Notes

CHAPTER 8

Travis and Suzie
Blue Crabs and
Rolling in the Surf

*"Not very often, but every once in a while, I still
have nightmares."*

— *Travis*

I s she going to whip me?
Travis sits up and braces himself. Adrian slides back into the bed, lifting the covers, scooting next to him. She pulls Travis up on top of her, taking his hand and placing it under her shirt on her bra-covered breast.

Why did she lock the door? Is it bad what she's doing?

His sister pats his back and holds him, but something doesn't feel right. He finally rests his head on her chest. It feels so wonderful to be held. Five-year-old Travis falls asleep.

Adrian didn't say it was a secret, but Travis kept their secrets for years.

"Travis," Adrian would say, "it's time for your nap." "I'm seven," Travis replies, "Why do I have to?"

"You just do. If you're good, later I'll take you to the store."

Once locked in the room, Adrian, now sixteen, pulls the covers over both of their heads and removes her bra. Travis knows that seeing a girl's nakedness is a big no-no, but it had always been okay for him to touch her bra before. Travis thinks her breasts are interesting, and being a child, he is curious. There is nothing sexual about it. Still, something feels bad. Travis senses a presence in the room like someone else is there. But that's impossible. They are alone.

This must be how you love someone, he tells himself. *Does Adrian love me more than the other girls do? Will Theresa and Cindy love me and hold me like this?* Without a word, Adrian takes his hand and places it on her chest. He feels an overwhelming, uncontrollable urge to laugh. His feelings are mixed up—confused and disturbed along with the extreme comfort of being held. Almost as if Momma was still there.

When Travis is eight years old, his dad remarries. The family moves across town into his new mother's house. At first, Travis is very excited, but that changes quickly. He thinks his new mom is trying hard to be a good mother, but she is strict and controlling—not the loving, adoration-filled mother he had lost. But he does have hot meals and clean clothes to wear now. He knows his dad is happier and that makes him more tolerant of what he perceives as her shortcomings. The way she treats him often leaves him asking himself questions like: Does she hate me? What did I do wrong? Why doesn't she like me? *Momma, why did you have to leave me?* Adrian no longer put him down for naps, and Travis never thinks about what happened before. Months go by and everyone adjusts to the new routine.

The heavy, black rotary-dial phone rings and Travis and Theresa race to answer it. Theresa wins and uses her body to block Travis's attempts to grab the phone from her hand.

"Stop it, Travis! I can't hear!" Theresa howls. "Guess what?" Theresa quickly yells, "Rebekah and Kenny want to take us crabbing tomorrow in Galveston." She finally looks at him.

"Oh, man, we're going crabbing!" Travis shouts.

Travis is so excited about going to Galveston with his oldest sister and brother-in-law that he doesn't sleep well that night. The next morning, they pack bologna sandwiches, Fritos, and a Twinkie for lunch and then pile into Kenny and Rebekah's car to take off for the bay.

"Hey, Rebekah, are you going to hold a crab?" Travis asks.

"No, and neither are you. I don't want anyone getting pinched. Kenny can do that part," Rebekah replies.

"Travis, those big crabs can pinch your fingers right off," says Kenny. "I'll use the net, okay?"

"I'm squished back here," Travis complains.

"We could always leave you home," Cindy teases, as she tilts her head and lifts her eyebrows in a questioning, suggestive manner. Travis flashes her a fake smile and mimics Cindy in a taunting way.

"Maybe we could tie him on the top of the car?" Theresa suggests.

Travis shoots her a sinister smile, squinting as he reaches over to tickle her knee.

Kenny adjusts the rearview mirror and looks Travis in the face. "Hey, Travis, you gonna help me catch some blue crabs today?" Kenny smiles at him.

"You betcha, I am," Travis replies.

"Okay then, it's the girls against the boys," Kenny announces. "Alright?"

Travis grins and nods his head at Theresa, lifting his left eyebrow high and wiggling it as he shouts, "It's on!"

"There are more of us girls," warns Adrian. "Yeah, we'll see," says Cindy.

Rebekah interrupts and changes the subject. "Y'all need to practice your song for church tomorrow."

"What are you singing?" Kenny asks.

Theresa answers excitedly, "I'm Going Home Where I Belong."

"Let's hear it," Rebekah encourages.

Adrian starts the song and Theresa and Cindy harmonize. Travis joins in, his voice powerful and right on tune. After they are finished, Theresa claps and flashes an approving smile at Travis. Rebekah turns toward the kids in the back seat and smiles too, her blue-green eyes sparkling as she says, "Great job, y'all sound amazing singing that!

When they finally gather on the dock in Galveston, Kenny carefully shows the kids how to tie a chicken neck onto a string and throw it in the water for bait. "Wait until you feel the crab tugging on the bait, and then slowly, carefully pull the crab up," Kenny encourages. "Then I'll scoop it into the net."

"Oh man, this is awesome!" Travis says, lifting his hand to meet Theresa's as they high five.

The day was full of laughs, sunshine, and smelly crabs. As Travis eats his lunch, he thinks about his older brother, Micky, who went away to a mental hospital about six weeks ago. He wishes Micky was there. Micky was a tormented young man, but he had always been very kind to Travis.

The ride home was full of crabbing stories and talk of how good the crab feast would taste. Once home, Rebekah realizes she had forgotten to stop and get ice. "Who wants to run to the store with me?" she asks.

Adrian, Cindy, and Theresa all respond at once, "Me!" "I want to go, too," says Travis.

"Travis, you stay here with Kenny and watch TV," says Adrian.

"What's new," grumbles Travis as he clicks the TV on and sits on the couch, settling in to watch "Tom and Jerry."

A few moments later, Travis hears Kenny calling his name.

"Travis, come here for a second. I want to show you something."

Travis gets up and heads into the bedroom. He sits down on the bed and looks around his sister Rebekah's room. Kenny steps out of the bathroom, naked.

"Look. Look what I've got." Kenny approaches Travis, placing himself directly in front of Travis's face. "Open your mouth, Travis," he commands.

What? Is he kidding me? Travis hesitates and looks at him, his eyes wide, fearful and questioning.

"Open it," Kenny says more forcefully, thrusting himself closer to Travis.

Travis, confused and terrified, clamps his mouth shut. Again, Kenny orders, "Open your mouth."

Travis now knows that Kenny is not asking him, he's telling him, so he tries to obey. Travis gags and pushes Kenny's privates away from his face. He tells Kenny that it stinks and that it's nasty.

Kenny looks impatient. "Wait there," Kenny warns as he hurries three or four steps into the bathroom and washes himself.

During these brief minutes, Travis prays desperately, "God, please, please God, let my sisters come home. Please, let someone walk in."

Kenny returned, "Now open your mouth."

Travis knew that tone in Kenny's voice. He didn't have a choice.

A long minute later, Kenny pulls out a five-dollar bill. Travis gags, chokes and spits into his own hand, looking away from Kenny, ignoring his offer. Kenny tucks the crisp, green bill into Travis's shirt and tosses a small towel at him. "This is our secret, okay, buddy?

Kenny's voice softens. "Now go back to the living room."

Travis wipes his face and hands and spits repeatedly into the towel, knowing he would never tell a soul what just happened.

"Go on," Kenny says.

As Travis walks, he reaches up and pulls the money out of his shirt. He looks at the five-dollar bill. *What if someone sees this? I'll get in big trouble.* He knows he has to hide it, so he shoves the money down into the pocket of his shorts. He decides to stash it in the back of his stereo speaker when he gets home. No one will ever find it there.

Moments later, his sisters walk in. Travis is so relieved to see them, but is so angry at them. It's their fault he had to stay home. He wants to yell, "Look what happened to me because you made me stay!" But he can't say it. He wants to scream at them, "You gotta get me out of here!" But at eight years old, he can't find the words. They just won't come out. *Just pretend nothing happened. Just fake that you're okay. Smile, just smile.*

Travis avoids looking directly at Kenny. The girls make a salad and cook the crab. Travis helps and listens to his older sisters talk about how good crab is and what a treat it was going to be. There is a familiar sense of family togetherness as they set the table, but Travis now has an agitated nervousness in his chest. Fear, Shame, and Hopelessness are with him in the kitchen, but no one can see them.

Everyone gathers around Kenny at the kitchen sink. Kenny light-heartedly and without a care tells them how to crack the crabs and get the meat out. "Careful," he says, "if they come back to life, they'll pinch you and we will have to take you to the hospital and have your fingers sewn back on." Kenny teases the kids as Travis's new invisible companions circle around him. Travis looks at his sisters who are smiling at Kenny. There is so much excitement and anticipation on their faces. Travis feels terrified inside, but he copies his sisters, joining in as they work together to clean all the crabs and pile the meat on a platter. As they sit down to eat, Travis finally musters the courage to glance at Kenny's face. Kenny's blue eyes are bright and cheer- filled as he continues to tease about the dead crabs coming back as ghosts and haunting them in their sleep.

"They are going to crawl up on your beds with their little crab feet and pinch your nose off in the middle of the night," Kenny jokes.

Shame moves in closer to Travis and whispers, "Kenny is bad and so are you." Travis dips his crab in the melted butter. "Kenny doesn't care about you at all. None of them do." Travis feels a lump in his throat. Hopelessness comes around the other side and laughs. Travis swallows, but it's hard. "The girls wouldn't let you go with them, they really don't care about you. You wanted to be just like Kenny." Fear swoops in from above. "You're all alone. Just you and the secret." He hovers over Travis. Travis feels Fear's hot breath on the back of his neck. "You can't ever tell. No one will believe you. You can't stop him. He'll do it again."

Ghost crabs are the least of Travis's worries.

Later that night, Theresa and Cindy are asleep on the pull-out couch in the living room. Rebekah has left for her regular night shift at the hospital and Travis awakens abruptly. He can see Kenny standing over him, balancing on the bottom bunk so he can reach Travis.

What's Kenny doing? Why is he taking my underwear off? What's happening? Travis starts to cry. *What else will he do? Travis's heart pounds. God, please, help me! No, no!* "Don't cry, sweetie," Kenny whispers in a babyish voice. "Awl lidoo boys luv dis. It's what all lidoo boys want." Kenny leans in close to Travis and groans. Kenny whispers, "You mustn't tell your sister. She will be vewy mad wif you.

Vewy mad. She will hate you. Come on, now, pull youwr pants up."

Finally, after what seemed like forever, Kenny steps down off the bottom bunk and turns to leave. Travis pulls the blankets up and wraps himself tight in them. Tears roll across his face as he lies stiffly, not moving at all.

I gotta get out of here! What if he comes back? What will he do? Momma, why did you die? Momma, I need you.

Momma. Momma, please. Momma, please...

"Looking back, I realize that there were signs that people should have noticed.
It hurts to understand that they didn't care enough to save me."

—Suzie

Suzie sneaks around the side of the trailer, but the little green tree frog is not there. The neighbor's black and white cat comes over to greet her. Suzie turns and picks her up. "Hey, Kitty," she says. Kitty is purring loudly. Suzie thinks that her whole body might vibrate with the sound. She rubs her face into Kitty's cuddly, soft fur. "I love you, Kitty," she says as she tenderly sets Kitty down.

The cat walks four or five steps away before stopping suddenly and crouching low. Kitty shifts her weight back and forth between her two back legs. Both Suzie and Kitty spy the tiny frog as it jumps from the safe green jungle up to the bottom edge of the trailer.

"No, no!" Suzie shouts. "Don't get it!"

Suzie quickly hops to the spot and raises her net. Slowly, she eases the small net toward the frog and it leaps again. She runs after it, hopping through the wet grass, and raises her net just as Kitty pounces on the frog with both her front feet. Suzie smacks the cat's behind with the net, but Kitty doesn't even notice. Suzie drops her net and snatches Kitty up with both hands, slinging Kitty out into the grass.

"Stop!" she yells. Suzie grabs her net and drops it squarely over the stunned little captive. Suzie smiles with delight and bites her bottom lip. Kitty is coming around to her side, watching intensely for movement. "Go away, Kitty," she demands, but Kitty's isn't going anywhere. Suzie carefully slips her tiny hand under the edge of the net and cups the little frog under her palm. She slowly and tenderly closes her grasp and feels the frog crawl up onto her fingers. Satisfied, she removes the net. Gripping the frog gently but firmly, she stands up and walks quickly to the front steps of the trailer. Suzie opens the front door, cradling the frog close to her body, careful not to drop it. Her mother is standing at the kitchen sink.

"Look, Mom, I caught a frog. It jumped on my window and Kitty tried to eat it, but I saved him. Can I keep it a while?" Suzie smiles and tilts her head to one side, looking up into her mother's face. "Please, Mom?"

"Okay, but don't let that thing loose in the house, you hear me?"

"Yes, ma'am."

"Go get your bathing suit on. We are going the beach."
"Oh, wow!" Suzie yells.

"Hurry, you need to eat some breakfast before we go. I'm going to sleep on the drive there and I'm going to nap on the beach," her mother adds. "I have to put a bag and some duct tape on Daddy's cast so he won't get sand in it. Hurry now." The April breeze is still cool, but the warm sun on her skin feels wonderful. Suzie lifts her head and faces the wind. She breathes in through her nose so she can smell the sand under her feet, the green water, the seagulls that are flying straight into the wind about thirty feet from her, and the bright blue sky. She thinks she can smell it all, even the seaweed.

Suzie gets her green beach bucket from her mom and

combs the sand for shells. She looks over at her mother, who's now taking off the blue-jean cutoff shorts and black leather vest that she wore over her yellow bikini. Her mother is so beautiful. Suzie looks at her step father, Ray, and wonders why her mother likes him. He is only twenty-five but looks much older. His tall, drastically skinny, tattooed body now lies next to her mom. She wishes he would go out into the water swimming and never come back. Only he can't swim because he shot his foot.

Suzie turns away from them and looks out onto the horizon. As she studies the beauty in front of her, she wonders about the little blue pills Ray was crushing this morning and how he yelled at her to get away when she walked near him in the living room. Ray had a red band wrapped tightly around his arm. He was clutching it in his teeth to pull it tighter. Suzie looks down the shoreline at the cars and trucks parked along the beach. The blue step-side that Momma drove was right there. Suzie's mom was now lying face down on a towel in front of it and Ray was rubbing her with lotion. Her mother smiles at Ray and laughs. Suzie feels fire in her stomach at the sight.

The hours pass. Suzie runs, jumps, and falls as she rolls in the surf. She notices her bruises from yesterday's beating as she looks down at her legs in the water. Suzie glances at her mom and Ray again and again. Mostly she loves her mom but hates Ray, but some of the time she hates them both.

Once home, Suzie grabs clean clothes and goes to take her bath. Her mom is there waiting to help her. Ray limps to the bathroom door.

"I'm hungry, baby," he says, stepping into the bathroom. Suzie pulls up her panties, which were mid-way down her thighs. Her mom, who is kneeling next to Suzie and trying

to undress her, keeps tugging Suzie's panties downward. "I'll be in there in a minute," her mom says. She tugs

Suzie's panties again. "Grab a banana to tide you over." Suzie has the top of her panties gripped firmly in her two hands, holding them so the fabric covers her. Suzie's mom stops, abruptly focusses her eyes on Suzie and says, "What the heck are you doing? Get undressed so you can get in the bathtub." Suzie stares at her mom and then glances up at Ray sheepishly.

"Oh, my gosh!" her mother says in a frustrated tone. "For god's sake, Ray, shut the door."

"Why?" Ray sarcastically spurts out. "She likes to show everybody in the trailer park her stuff anyway, huh, Suzie?"

Suzie stands there clutching her panties and looking at the floor. Suddenly she can't move.

"Oh, for goodness sake!" Her mother reaches out and slings the door closed in Ray's face. "You know, if it's that big of a deal, kid, we'll just shut the dang door. You can lock it too, ya know," she says while rolling her eyes. "Geez, come on, get undressed."

Ray yells, "I'm hungry!"

"You can have all the privacy you want, princess," her mother teases. She wiggles her hands in the air, acting as if Suzie's being ridiculous. Suzie slowly gets undressed and gets in the bath feeling a dense shame surrounding her— even more dense than the bathwater she is sitting in. Her mom stands up and says, "I've got to go get some dinner ready so I can get a few more minutes' sleep before work. Here, I'm locking the door. You silly thing, nobody cares about your naked body. You ain't got nothing to look at yet. You're too little." Her mother makes a face and smiles. Suzie sits up a bit and stares right at the door knob. It's locked. She likes the thought. She wonders what would happen if she locked her bedroom door.

Later that night, she feels Ray pinching her, "Wake up!" This time, he doesn't whisper. "Roll over," he demands.

Suzie is suddenly fully awake and terrified. Ray grabs at her clothes, putting his hand where she knows he shouldn't. He is reaching for something with his other arm down beside the bed in front of him. *That's his private place he is grabbing. What's he doing?* Fear has frozen Suzie and she doesn't dare move. She can't tell what's wrong, but he acts like it hurts him. She glances to the side at his face. He looks almost angry or sick. Something is very wrong, and she wants to run. She turns her head toward the window, the rest of her frozen with fear. He leans over and he puts his mouth on her, shoving his tongue hard into her ear. She leans as far away as she can stretch. *Help me, help me!* She hears herself calling those words in her mind, but she doesn't make a sound. Suzie feels saliva fill her mouth and a sick repulsion at the feeling of his nasty tongue on her. He lays his head on her chest and groans. Suzie feels she will vomit. She's trapped.

Moments later, without a word, he pulls his shorts up, and leaves.

Suzie doesn't cry. Slowly she sits up and leans against the wall. After several moments, her eyes focus in on Barbie's long blonde hair in the moonlight. Barbie is right next to her in the bed. Suzie picks her up. She looks at Barbie for a moment. She studies Barbie's face, her painted blue eyes and pointed nose, her perfectly arched eyebrows and beautiful cheekbones. Suddenly, she reaches up and grabs Barbie's head as hard as she can. Suzie pulls with all her might, bending Barbie's neck back, back and down, she pulls so hard. Barbie's head won't budge. Suzie sits straight up and grasps Barbie tightly in her right hand, and then slings Barbie across the room. Barbie hits the wall with a thud and falls to the floor.

She hears her mother's voice in her head. *No one cares about your naked body. You're too little.* Suzie looks at the floor where Barbie fell. She doesn't know why she hates Barbie so much. Tears now fill her eyes and fall down her face, settling and quickly disappearing on her pink cotton nightgown.

Night after night, Ray visits her room, and it goes on until it becomes a routine.

"Suzie." Tonight, he pinches her hard. "Wake up, stand up. Give me your hands."

Please, not again, she thinks. She can barely open her eyes. Fear has been replaced by exhaustion, repulsion, and anger. She wants to run. She wants to refuse, but she's afraid to disobey. She wants to tear herself right out of her body and let that inside part of her, the "real her," leave and go somewhere else.

Ray forces her to perform oral sex. She can't breathe. She coughs, chokes and gags, but this only makes him mad and he ridicules her. "Stop it, you baby." He glares at her. "If you love me, you'll do it," Ray chides. "This is what people who love each other do," he tells her.

I don't love you, she thinks. *I hate you.*

She wakes up in his bed. She's naked! "Hurry and go get in your room," Ray snaps. She quickly puts on her nighty and walks through the living room into the kitchen. She sees the big butcher knife in the dish drainer on the counter. She stops and looks up at it. Hatred is crouching right at her ear, leaning close to her as she imagines that she reaches and grabs the black handle in her hand. Very clearly in her mind, she turns back to his bedroom and walks up to the bed. Ray is asleep. Hatred is suddenly up in the air and swirls down around her face, circling her closely. Intoxicated with Hatred's pleasing presence filling her mind, she sees herself heaving the knife, gripping it with both hands, and plunging it down into his chest as deep as it will go. She does it again and again. She stabs his face too, over and over. She lifts the knife. It's so big, so sharp. She looks back toward his door and knows that if she even reaches for the knife to touch her finger to the handle, Ray will see her. But she wants to stab him. It feels so good just to stand there and let herself think about it. Suzie feels a warm, wonderful sensation in her stomach. She bites her lip, turns, and walks to her room.

Crawling in her bed, she whispers, "I wish I could kill him."

Shame is right there in her bed waiting for her. "You must be the most disgusting child on the earth for him to do this to you," he says.

Deceit swoops down and hisses. "This doesn't happen to any of your friends, only you."

"It's because you are sick and gross," Shame reminds her.

Even though it's daybreak, Suzie feels Fear. He's right there next to her.

"He can do it anytime he wants," Fear reminds her.

Suzie doesn't cry often, but today she does. She cries hard. She cries herself back to sleep.

Make it Personal

Can you see that one of the points in telling Travis's and Suzie's stories is to provoke readers into an awareness and understanding of the damage abuse does to a child thereby equipping them (readers) to strengthen their resolve to protect the children in their lives?

_____

_____

_____

Are you surprised that Travis didn't tell? Why? Why not? Are you surprised that there are no obvious signs of abuse in Travis's home life?

_____

_____

_____

Do you think you could tell if a child in your family was being molested? What signs would you look for?

_____

_____

_____

List as many things as you can think of that might help keep a child from being repeatedly molested?

_____

_____

_____

As you read theses excerpts from Travis's and Suzie's childhood stories, did the "millstone" verses come to mind? If Travis's and Suzie's parents and grandparents had known these Scriptures and how to teach them to their children, might the outcome have been different?

_____

_____

_____

Have the children in your life been taught the "millstone" Scriptures? If not, will you commit to teaching them what the Bible says?

_____

_____

_____

Have you ever wished someone would die? Do you still feel the same way? Explain.

_____

_____

_____

Notes

CHAPTER 9

Did Jesus Really Love Lazarus?

Therefore [even] when He heard that Lazarus was sick,
He still stayed two days longer in the same place where
He was.

John 11:6 (AMP)

A s I finished my day with Alison at the crisis pregnancy center, I felt something wonderful and dreadful. I felt confused yet keenly aware that the Holy Spirit was leading me.

Could all of this just be a coincidence? The devastation and hopelessness I encountered working with the Angelreach kids, the dream, Alison quoting the very verse I had read that morning about how Jesus wept?

As I drove through town toward Walmart, I was thinking about the events and dialogue in the Lazarus story. A thought stuck out to me about Mary, Martha, and Jesus that really surprised, convicted, and excited me. At that moment, I was turning left into Walmart and my hands came off the steering wheel as I raised them in the air letting my left knee hold it in place and exclaimed, "I get it! I get it!" You see, just like Martha and Mary, I was asking God, "Where were You?" or "Where are You?"

Please note that before my dream, I understood that in the Lazarus story Jesus says that He is the Resurrection and that He will raise us all (who believe in Him) like He raised Lazarus. But, as a result of that realization in the car, I set out to look much closer at every single verse in John 11, especially the dialogue between Mary, Martha, and Jesus, which I will share with you in a moment.

But first, let's examine why God wants this particular story about Lazarus included in the Bible. Consider God's audience for this miracle: the people who were present that day and those like us who would hear or read it later, right? In both of these groups, there are believers and non- believers. This miracle wasn't included so the people who were present that day would believe. They saw it with their own eyes…if it was just for Mary and Martha, then there wouldn't have been any point in including it in the written record. So why record it? A lot of Jesus's miracles did not get recorded. Check out the last verse in the book of John: "And there are also many other things that Jesus did. If they should be all recorded one by one [in detail] I suppose that even the world itself could not contain (have room for) the books that would be written" (John 21:25 AMP).

So, the story of Lazarus is certainly for us today as well. Jesus himself was raised from the dead, so for people who already believe, that would pretty much make the raising of Lazarus (just for a miracle's sake) look puny. Today's believers don't need this miracle to believe in the resurrection of the dead. The non-believers alive today would have had to have been present for Lazarus's resurrection to be convinced and believe based on this recorded miracle alone. This tells me that it's the dialogue that is important, not just the miracle. This miracle is a shadow, like so many other stories in the Bible. It's a type or picture of something much bigger.

I share this because I'm excited that God's Word has changed my life: so excited I can't keep it in. Furthermore, if my telling of it helps one person, it will have been worth the effort of sharing it. I started researching John 11. A week or so after the dream and talking to Alison, I came across a YouTube video titled, "This Illness is for the Glory of God" by John Piper. I'm going to talk about it for a moment and add my own observations.

Please realize no one including myself is right about everything, so when I quote someone (like John Piper) on one subject that doesn't mean I agree with them on every subject or that I recommend them as a teacher. Always check what people teach by comparing it to Scripture. John Piper would not agree with everything I teach either but we do agree on the Scripture from John 11. Here I found his perspective very helpful…so…Let's jump right in to John 11:

"Now, a certain man named Lazarus was ill. He was of Bethany, the village where Mary and her sister Martha lived. This Mary was the one who anointed the Lord with perfume and wiped His feet with her hair. It was her brother Lazarus who was [now] sick" (vs.1-2).

One of the first things John Piper points out is that the apostle John uses this reference to Mary, something that he doesn't explain until chapter 12, to highlight the close relationship between them. That is, Mary crying and washing (anointing) Jesus's feet with perfumed, very expensive oil before His death, burial, and resurrection. But since the apostle John is telling the story many years later, he refers to it, even though when Lazarus actually died, the event hadn't happened yet. This is the first of the three things that the apostle John says to point out the close communion, friendship, love, and the tender relationship that Jesus shares with these people with whom He fellowshipped.

"So (because Lazarus was sick) the sisters sent to Him, saying, Lord, he whom you love so well is sick." (v. 3)

This is the second time. Again, Apostle John points out that the Lord loved Lazarus. I think, being a woman too, that Mary might have phrased it this way to remind Jesus of the tender, loving relationship so that it would pull on His heartstrings and motivate Him to come quickly. "Lord, he whom you loved so well is sick." But I also believe that for all of us in the future, it is a reminder, especially to those who are seeking Him, that Jesus is capable and given to loving us extraordinarily like John Piper explains. For instance, if I sent for my father to tell him my sister Robin was sick, I wouldn't say, "Dad, the daughter you love is sick." That love would be assumed.

Jump with me for a second to verse 5. "Now, Jesus loved Martha and her sister and Lazarus."

That was the third time Apostle John tells us that Jesus loved and had a close communication with them. As John Piper points out, there is a really special thing going on here.

Not only is Apostle John saying it three ways, but the Scripture is inspired by God, so we can assume that this is the way it is supposed to be. I asked myself, why three times? Why did the cock crow three times? Why did Jesus ask Peter three times if He loved Him? Seriously, things happened in threes all over the Bible, especially when God is making a point. You have probably thought of some while reading that last sentence. Why would He (God) drive that point home? Yes, Apostle John wrote the book, but think of the big picture, the Holy-Spirit-inspired meaning.

Do you think that Jesus loves them (Laz, Mary, and Martha) more than He loves us who have called on His name, accepted Him as Savior, and are looking to and relying on Him daily? Do you think He loves us any less than he loves Mary, Martha, or Laz? No? Neither do I.

The first big point that I took away from the first few verses is that Jesus loves us. Do you remember how I said I was turning into Walmart and suddenly saw the Lazarus story lifted out of the Bible and across time in my mind? It's a picture, every little bit of the story is. He loves us! We are His family. Write it in the margin of this book: "Jesus loves me." He is shouting to His Church/Bride that He loves us dearly through this story. At least, that is what I see. Thank you again, John Piper, for helping me.

Back to verse 4: "When Jesus received the message, He said, this sickness is not to end in death; but [on the contrary] it is to honor God and promote His Glory, that the Son of God may be glorified through (by) it."

Jesus knew that the disciples would assume that Laz was in danger because that's what we all fear about sickness. Why else would they send for Him? That's why today we call on God and pray. We ask Him to heal our family members; we ask Him to intervene when we are in trouble and we can't help ourselves. We call on Him because we are scared. But viewing the situation from an eternal perspective, Jesus says that the sickness or suffering that we (right now) are calling on Him to heal or fix is not about death. On the contrary, the suffering is about God being glorified, and Jesus will be glorified as a result. John Piper's next question, mine and yours too, is:

how and why would God let someone suffer so that He could be glorified? A good, kind human would never do something like that, and Apostle John carefully pointed out three times that Jesus loved all three of them.

I can just imagine my dad telling me, "Oh, girl, you are fixin' to suufffffeeeer BIG TIME! But it's cool, seriously, no worries, cuz as a parent I'm going to be glorified so, just relax, calm down, and trust me."

Hmm. Let me tell you kinda like John Piper did. If my dad said that to me, there would be mutiny and high treason. I can hear me now, "Nope, no can do. I tell you what, Dad, find someone else to suffer. At least find someone else to suffer without complaining and pitching a wild, wall-eyed, crazy fit. I'm out of here. I will find a way to make this work. I will find happiness without you. What? Excuse me? You've got to be kidding me! You want me to trust you in my suffering? At that point, I'm sure I would just stare at him—my mouth gaping open and my hand on the door— completely confused.

I can remember taking a fall on my bike that removed all (and I mean all) the skin on my knee. My mom took me in the bathtub and proceeded to wash it. Are you kidding me? As I grabbed her hands and literally fought her, crying and squirming to make her stop, she reassured me that this was necessary for me to be healed. Honestly, looking back I'm surprised she didn't smack me silly the way I was acting. To her credit, she was very loving and patient with me. She calmly encouraged me and tried to convince me that this was best for me and that it would be okay. She assured me that it would only hurt for a little while, and it would be all better. However, at the time I was not buying it at all.

Looking down at my bleeding knee and feeling the burning, stinging, awful pain, that present misery was all I could focus on. What I could not understand at the time was, of course, that germs could cause a serious infection if untreated, and could kill me. The little present suffering was going to not only keep me from suffering more later, it could literally save my life. It was going to be, not only good for me, but best for me. Still, it was ridiculously hard for me to set my will and instinct down and trust my parents.

I realize that some of you reading this did not have a parent or parents who loved you in this way. For you, this is a foreign concept. For now, just recognize that this is how it should have been. The point here is that it is often the case that the wiser ones in our lives are going to teach us that suffering now is going to be in our best interest later. Am I implying that Jesus wants us to be molested for His glory or wants a child to suffer misery to the point of wanting to commit suicide so He can be glorified? No, absolutely not. God hates the way we treat each other. Please remember throughout this book (as we discuss this in detail) that free will, Adam and Eve style, is happening all over the timeline. People are making choices. We humans are hurting each other and ourselves. I for one have decided not to complain about God taking other people's free will away from them, unless I am willing to completely give mine up too.

John Piper suggests that we think of the word "sickness" in verse 5 of John 11 as "our present condition." So, with that in mind, I want you to think of a timeline (I heard this example years ago). Like a magic carpet, ruler, or piece of paper floating in the air in front of you, with time starting on one end of the timeline and ending on the other. Picture God standing outside of the timeline looking at it. God also exists outside of our timeline, which He created. Think about that for a moment. God actually *created* time. He lives everywhere including outside of time in an "is" kind of state. God just is.

As you look down at the floating carpet/timeline from an eternal perspective, remember, this "sickness" (Laz's condition), our present existence on the timeline, our personal pain and suffering, the stuff of life we are walking through every day, is not going to end in death (think eternally) but, on the contrary, it is to honor God and promote His glory, that the Son of God may be glorified through (by) it. I realize that you probably still feel empty, as the whole point is that God could stop the suffering. Don't get mad and judge God yet. Stick with me, because God can be trusted, and in this case, things are not what they seem.

Let's return to John 11, starting at verse 5-6: "Now Jesus loved Martha and her sister and Lazarus. Therefore, when He heard that Lazarus was sick He still stayed two days longer in the same place where he was."

John Piper explains that the word "Therefore" at the beginning of verse 6 means "because of this." Because of what? Because of verse 5. It may as well mean "on purpose" or to complete His intended statement in verse 5: "Now Jesus loved Martha and her sister Mary and Lazarus." So (on purpose because He loves them) when He heard Laz was sick, He stayed two days longer. So, Jesus waits on purpose? He does nothing. He didn't rush in and save the day for His dearly loved friends? He didn't stop the pain, and it's because He loves them. How do we wrap our minds around that in a big-picture perspective? First, He's saying that our suffering is to glorify God and Jesus Himself. Then He says that He is waiting because He loves them.

Jesus waiting is the second big point I want you to write in your margin or highlight. The big news is, He is waiting because He loves them, because He loves us. Write that down. Laz was sick and dying. They are suffering because of love. Is there a chance that He loves us so much He is willing to walk this suffering with us? That's right–with us! As the writer of the book of Hebrews reminds us in chapter 13, the end of verse 5, "He has said, 'I will never leave you nor forsake you.'" We are not alone when we suffer; the Holy Spirit is with us and in us. Now some of you are comforted by that, but others of you are thinking, "That's awful. How can He watch us and do nothing?" Stick with me. Remember my dream? Well, because of my pride, I judged God too quickly. Don't be like me.

Do you notice that John the apostle didn't use the word "therefore" (He waited) after the sentence about God being glorified but did use it after the sentence about Jesus loving Laz and the sisters? He didn't say Jesus was waiting so God would be glorified, he said Jesus was waiting because He loves them. This was not by accident. Yes, the sickness was so God would be glorified, but the waiting (Jesus not showing up and fixing the sickness) was because He loved them.

I have to walk this out and seriously contemplate how to reconcile who God says He is, and the fact that He claims in these verses that He is loving us, with how things look to me on the surface, all this suffering considered. I envy people who seem to handle whatever disaster life dishes out without a bit of disappointment in God or doubt of His love, but even knowing the truth, I struggle.

How might God be showing His love for Laz and the sisters by waiting? I think here we have to consider the possibility that God is showing His love for us by waiting and not fixing our life immediately or at all. John Piper asked his audience that question and so I forward it to you.

This is the deal: I really need to believe that the Creator (which logic tells me is there and my experience tells me is Jesus) is benevolent, good, and righteous. Yes, I admit I need it. I need to know He really cares about me. I need to look up to Him. I need to trust Him. I need Him to be my hero and I need to know He loves me. But when you are in the agony of pain that a serious personal loss causes, it is sometimes close to impossible to see God's hand or feel His close presence. Sometimes it's hard to even believe He is there at all or that He cares. But from the very beginning of this chapter through verses 5 and 6, Jesus is saying that His waiting is how He is loving us. To grasp this, we desperately need that eternal perspective.

Could God know something I don't know about the long- term (eternal) benefit of letting us walk through this "momentary mess" as John Piper calls it? After all, He is the God of creation. Can I trust Him? Maybe He didn't heal the cancer in your family or the heart defect. Maybe He didn't stop the fire from happening. Maybe He didn't keep your car from starting before that terrible accident. He let that baby die while you were begging Him to save that precious little one. The only way I can make sense of this is to jump my mind off of the timeline and look at it from an eternal perspective. That baby is not really dead. That baby's eternal soul only knows the reality of suddenly being in paradise, in the same dimension God is in, where there is no time and only the brilliance and splendor of a loving Creator. I need to see it through God's eternal eyes, even when it's difficult. He loves that baby even more than we do.

You know, to wait two days in full sight of the disciples

was really obvious. Why give everyone a reason to question you for the next two thousand years by waiting? Jesus wanted us to understand there was no hope at all for Laz, and that is just how we see our lives when we have been molested, have lost a loved one, or are suffering pain. We feel just like Mary did, like there is no hope for recovery, restoration, or healing. Often, we feel like all is lost.

The obvious reason for Jesus to wait is so no one would question that Laz was really dead. "Dead dead" you know, not "mostly dead" like in the scene from the movie *The Princess Bride* when Westley (The Dread Pirate Roberts) was declared "mostly dead" as opposed to "all dead" by Miracle Max who explained that "mostly dead" was really "slightly alive" and that the only thing that could be done when someone was "all dead" was to go through their pockets for loose change. But, seriously, if you let your heart absorb and focus on the deeper reason Jesus waited, you will gain great understanding here.

I know it would have looked a lot better for Jesus if He wouldn't have gotten the news at all and just showed up out of the blue, four days late, and saved the day. The fact that He waits two more days and makes no mistake of declaring it out loud to the disciples, begs the question: Why does He want us to know He waited? It was not just so He would be four days late. He could have done that easily. He wanted us to "know-know" He waited, and that points to the eternal picture. And then, in the very next sentence, Jesus tells us He waited because He loves us.

Because He loves us?

Have you seen the movie *Avatar*? I know there was some New Age weirdness, and some of the language was disappointing and offensive, but just think about the scene where Jake is with Norm and he gets his first look at his Na'vi body floating in the blue cylinder-shaped tank. Jake pushes his wheelchair around to the side where he can see it and carefully looks over his avatar. What if we could have seen our flesh suits before we got them and arrived here on earth? Do you remember the lecture his superior officer was giving the new arrivals to Pandora? He was warning them about this new world and the challenges they would face. I wonder if our lives and choices on earth would be different if we had received a briefing before arriving here. When we hear the Truth spoken to us today, do we even recognize it? Remember the scene where Jake gets into the bed that transfers his consciousness from his body with crippled legs to the blue Na'vi body with perfect working legs. Everyone in the audience gets sucked into the splendor when he simply wiggles his toes in the dirt and then runs full throttle through the grape vineyard, because we can all imagine how amazing it would feel to get to do that after being bound to a wheelchair for so long. We are just like that, spiritual beings transferred to this body. We are here on earth for a moment. Would Jake have appreciated the new Na'vi body as much as he did if he hadn't experienced being crippled in his other existence?

Knowing that this life on earth is temporary (we will one day get new eternal bodies) and not the main event compared to eternity, maybe we should ask, what is the real point of us being here? Remember, compared to eternity we are a vapor, a puff of smoke. In James chapter 4:14, he reminds us that our lives are a mist, here one minute and gone the next. Like when you are in the freezing cold climate and can see your breath when you exhale, but then it quickly vanishes before your eyes. We get way too attached to the earth suit that we and our children and parents come in. We, like Mary and Martha, are not looking at our lives from an eternal perspective. We forget that God loves the soul in these avatars more than we even love the actual bodies. We forget God's capacity to love that person with or without their body. We focus on our/their avatar instead of our/their soul to the point of being crazy angry with God if the avatar dies or doesn't look like or work like we think it should. We feel robbed if the avatar isn't beautiful or tall or maybe it is missing digits or is deficient in some way.

Do you know who Nick Vujicic is? If you would like to, go ahead and google: Nick Vujicic "God will not give up on you" or follow this link: **https://youtu.be/KJ1OEi2OhSU**. In this eight-minute-long video, Nick longs to know why God allowed an awful thing to happen to him. He asks God why He created him that way. He asks why God didn't give him arms and legs like everyone else has. Now, that's not the same as asking God why He allowed someone else's free will choice to devastate our life, but the answer is the same. You may also like "Nick Vujicic's Most touching speech" or follow the link https://youtu.be/nknzSWDcUgA . In this video, Nick asks three questions. 1) Who are you? 2) What is your purpose here? 3) What is your destiny when you're done here?

Nick says as Christians we are children of the Most High God, and that's exactly what the Bible tells us. "But when the proper time had fully come God sent His Son, born of a woman, born subject to [the regulations of] the Law, to purchase the freedom of [to ransom, to redeem, to atone for] those who were subject to the Law that we might be adopted and have sonship conferred upon us [and be recognized as God's sons]. And because you [really] are [His] sons, God has sent the [Holy] Spirit of His Son into our hearts, crying Abba (Father)! (Galatians 4:4-6 AMP). Wow, the Spirit of Jesus is sent into us, so when we cry Abba Father, it is just like when Jesus cries Abba Father. Nick also points out that it is not about us, it's about our Creator. He says we are here to glorify God. At first Nick demanded an answer from God, refusing to serve Him if He didn't explain why Nick was born without limbs. Just like me when I had the dream, Nick had an offended heart.

Nick says that when he was fifteen, he read John 9, a story about a man who was blind from birth. The disciples asked Jesus who had sinned to cause this "defect." They wanted to know whose fault it was, the man's or his parents'. Jesus replied, "Neither hath this man sinned nor his parents: but that the works of God should be made manifest in him." (John 9:3 KJV). The question Nick had was: WHY? Why did you make me this way? Nick says that in the story of the blind man, he found the answer to his question. It was God saying to him, "Do you trust Me?" You know being disabled from birth is not the same as being tortured by a pedophile your whole life, but the question from our hurting hearts is the same: WHY? Why didn't God stop the deformity in Nick's body when he was in his mother's womb? Why doesn't He stop a pedophile? The answer to that question is also the same: Do you trust Him? That changed Nick's attitude and then his life. And so Nick teaches, "If God doesn't give you a miracle...then be a miracle for someone else."

That's exactly what Nick did he followed the example that Jesus Christ set for us. Jesus prayed in the garden that God would take the cup (becoming our sin) from Him. In Matthew 26:39, Jesus pleaded for God to deliver him from suffering the cross. But, God did not do that, so Jesus became a miracle for us as He suffered through the Father's will. If we grasp ahold of this and trust God in our suffering and our loved one's suffering, then there is no suffering that we will go through that will be wasted or pointless. Nick says that when we ask Jesus why—why did this happen to me? that Jesus answers us with a question: Will you trust Me?

A friend just called me, very upset because a man pulled a gun on her in Houston traffic on her way home from getting an ultrasound for the little baby growing in her womb. Her reaction is understandable. Once she vented and told me the whole story, I let her settle down some and then suggested she take advantage of this opportunity and lift that young man (who pulled the gun) up to God in serious prayer. I reminded her that the young man is possibly headed for an eternity without ever knowing the love of Jesus Christ. This young man needs the conviction of the Holy Spirit, and he needs what only Jesus Christ can give him. She agreed, and we firmed a resolve to pray for this young man every time we think of him. Even in the small sufferings, we can make a difference and God can be glorified.

As far as our destiny when we leave here? The fact is we could die today in a car wreck or choking on a Jolly Rancher. That's just the way it is. There are no guarantees here on earth. Except for the one that Jesus Christ offers us freely. Jesus's first words spoken to us in the New Testament are: "Repent...for the kingdom of heaven is at hand" (Matt. 4:17 KJV). To repent means, to change one's mind about sin. Jesus was offered up for us to pay for our sin. It's a free gift with no strings attached, and it will surely change you into the new creature described in 1 Corinthians 5:17 (KJV): "Therefore if any man be in Christ, he is a new creature: old things are passed away; behold, all things are become new." Faith in Jesus Christ's death and resurrection is what changed Nick's life. If you watch a few more of his videos, such as the ones about bullying, you will get a very clear picture (at least through your tears) of a person living with an eternal perspective and with the potential to encourage and change the lives of those around him for the better.

Think about how we treat our flesh suits. If we saw ourselves and each other as eternal spirits or soul beings from an eternal perspective, and truly understood that it's just a wetsuit/avatar, would we adore or despise what we see in the mirror so much? Or might we be thinking about where we will spend eternity instead?

First Corinthians 15:34-58 (AMP) may greatly encourage you. I have included verses 34-35 and 42-44:

"Be sober-minded [be sensible, wake up from your spiritual stupor] as you ought, and stop sinning; for some [of you] have no knowledge of God [you are disgracefully ignorant of Him, and ignore His truths]. I say this to your shame. But someone will say, *"How are the dead raised? And with what kind of body will they come?"* So, it is with the resurrection of the dead. The [human] body that is sown is perishable and mortal, it is raised imperishable and immortal. It is sown in dishonor, it is raised in glory; it is sown in weakness, it is raised in strength; it is sown a natural body [mortal, suited to earth], it is raised a spiritual body [immortal, suited to heaven]. As surely as there is a physical body, there is also a spiritual body."

I hope this helps you to see our lives from an eternal perspective as soul-beings created by God. We will one day exist with Him in our new bodies, outside of time. These new bodies will have a physiological mass, meaning they will be God-created, scientific, for real, bodies. They will not be the bodies that suffered molestation, sickness, or ridicule. Thank goodness...right? We will live in the just "is" state with Jesus Christ just existing, with no tick tock of time stretched in front of us or regret and longing behind us. We will just be. How exciting is that?

Jesus loves Laz and his sisters, yet He purposely waits until all hope is gone. And He wants us to know it. He wants us to trust him. We understand that Jesus loves us the same as Mary, Martha, and Laz, yet He tarries, waiting as we are in our flesh suits, suffering and dying. He tells us point blank that the suffering will bring God glory, and He is waiting because He loves us. Please stop and pray. Prepare your hearts and ask God to help you to see and think eternally. Picture, as best you can in your mind, your spirit man that is alive yet stuck just for a short time in your flesh suit. Picture everyone's spirit man, those you know who are crippled, beautiful, ugly, mean, or involved in drugs or porn. Not just the ones looking at porn but the ones trapped, forced, used and exploited by the masses, all of those people are eternal souls. Your parents and your children are all spiritual beings living in flesh suits. Can you see their spirit beings? Now picture your new eternal, scientific, physiological body that awaits your spirit in eternity. You're going to need these pictures in your mind for the next chapter about Mary, Martha and Lazarus. For now, let's check in on Travis and Suzie.

Make It Personal

Do you think Mary and Martha felt like Jesus really loved them when their brother was sick and dying, but He did not come? Can you relate to them doubting God when they suffered?

_____

_____

_____

Do you think Travis and Suzie will ask God why He allowed them to be abused as they get older? What would you say to them if they asked you?

_____

_____

_____

Do you ever feel like you got ripped off in the flesh-suit department? Explain...

_____

_____

_____

Does thinking from an eternal perspective help you when you struggle while watching your or others' flesh suits fail? List the people in your life who have suffered in their flesh.

_____

_____

_____

Does it help you to realize that God is waiting precisely because He loves us and that growing in trust is why we are here? How? Remember Nick V. as you consider this question.

_____

_____

What is the worst thing you can imagine happening to you? Could you trust God even in that situation?

_____

_____

_____

Notes

CHAPTER 10

Travis and Suzie
Show-N-Tell and Soft Music

*"To this day, I can't stand the feeling of being forced,
coerced, or manipulated into doing something. No
matter what it is, even if it's good for me... it's
suffocating."*

— Travis

Ten-year-old Travis awakes in a panic. He hears a noise.
Oh, God, is it Kenny? He's coming. Travis can feel his
heart pounding in his throat. Frantically, Travis tries
to free his hand from under the tangled sheet. He reaches
up and shoves his eleven-year-old sister's shoulder. Theresa
doesn't respond.

"Please wake up!" he jabs her a second and third time.
Maybe if he can wake her up, Kenny will leave him alone. But
Theresa's out cold. She won't respond.

Kenny opens the door. Travis lays frozen, pretending he's
asleep. Kenny takes Travis's arm and pulls him to a sitting,
and then standing, position, ignoring Travis's sleepy posture.
Kenny's stocky, twenty-seven-year-old frame towers over
Travis. Kenny tugs and leads him out of the bedroom where
he and the other four kids were peacefully sleeping together
on the floor. Travis had thought that if he slept in the middle
of his nieces, nephew, and his sister, Kenny might leave him
alone. But nothing works.

Travis knows what's next. His heart sinks. He feels himself
shutting down.

As Travis is forced down the hall, he thinks about his

sister, Adrian, who recently moved in with Rebekah and Kenny to help babysit their little ones. She is now sleeping in the spare room. He hopes she will wake up and Kenny will have to stop, but then he fears she will tell everyone and that terrifies him. Travis knows that Rebekah has already gone to work at the hospital. He has no hope.

Once alone in Kenny's room, Travis again refuses to cooperate. "Open your mouth," Kenny demands. Travis refuses. Grabbing Travis's head forcefully with his free hand and pinching his face, Kenny brutally shoves himself against Travis, ramming himself repeatedly on Travis' nose, eyes, and cheeks.

Hot tears wet Travis's face, but Kenny doesn't stop. When Travis refuses to open his mouth, Kenny ejaculates all over Travis's face. Kenny then tenderly pets Travis's cheeks and forehead, whispering softly to him. "Dat's okaaaay. You're okay. All wittle boys like dis. Dey like it." Kenny wipes off Travis' tears. "Wittle boys all want dis."

The baby talk terrifies Travis. He feels something bizarre, sick, and evil.

Travis never gets used to the abuse. It is as if every time is the first and just as awful as the last, but there is no avoiding it.

Travis has show-and-tell at school. He can barely focus on what the third graders have brought in as he is busy counting how many seats before it is his turn. Travis thinks to himself as he watches the room mother passing out homemade peanut butter cookies. *What if my mother wouldn't have died? Would she have made those gingersnap cookies she used to make for my class?* Travis daydreams and happily pictures the other kids gathered around him, telling him how wonderful his mom's cookies are. The fantasy of his mother lovingly passing out cookies is broken by his teacher's voice and applause for his classmate, Lindsey, who brought her dog's old green collar to show- and-tell. Lindsey's golden retriever had recently died, but she kept Buster's collar. She had a picture of Buster, and she read a poem she had written about him.

Finally, Mrs. Guthrie calls his name. "Travis, come up here. It's your turn." Travis jumps out of his seat like it was on fire. He walks quickly up to the front of the class, carefully carrying a child-sized shoe box with about ten photos in it. His smile is mischievous and explosive. By the look on his face, you'd swear he had a baby alligator in the box. He sets the box down on the edge of the teacher's desk and slowly opens it. Carefully putting the lid next to it, he reaches in the small box.

"My father is a World War Two hero. His name is Travis Lavern Idom. He is my hero, too." Travis says this with a matter of fact, John Wayne kind of seriousness. "Here's a picture of him with a Japanese kamikaze soldier that jumped out of his plane and landed in the ocean. My dad's navy ship, the USS 852, rescued him out of the water. This is my dad holding the gun on him so he won't escape." Travis holds up the picture. The kids sit tall in their chairs and stretch their necks to see. "My dad said he thought the guy was happy to be a prisoner because he could have been eaten by sharks if they had left him in the water. My dad was in the navy for three years. After that, he was in the army for five years. He was a chief communications officer in the army. He was stationed in Japan on an army base."

Travis had rehearsed this every day for a week and was nervous but deliberate. "This was before my mom and dad got married." Travis now looks straight ahead of him, focusing on what he was going to say next. "My dad had a Japanese girlfriend who worked for him. She was being trained by my dad to help the Americans." He looked back down at the kids and he talked a little faster. "He trained thirty other women, too. They worked for him. Dad's first girlfriend's name was Emily Nock-ah-nee-shi and here's her picture."

Travis holds it up. Some of the kids stand up and lean forward to get a better look. Out of the corner of his eye, Travis sees that the teacher is laying down the papers she was grading and looking toward him, but he avoids making eye contact. He can't. Now is his chance and he has to say it fast.

"She was pregnant with my father's baby when the Korean War broke out and my dad was transferred to Korea, which means he had to move." Travis wanted to glance at his teacher as some of the kids were now looking at her, but he didn't dare. Instead, he started talking faster. "So he never saw her again, but I have a half-brother or sister that lives in Japan, and I hope I can meet them someday." Now every single child in the class is standing to see the picture. His teacher steps out from around her desk to look at it. "My half-brother or sister is probably about twenty-five years old now," Travis continues, as he looks up at his teacher. "My dad was forty-six when I was born, and all that happened before he met my mom," he finishes quick.

The teacher turns toward the class. "Class, sit back in your seats, please," she says sternly, yet coaxingly, as if wanting to hurry him along. "Travis, do you have other pictures?"

He shows pictures of his dad's ship and his dad's buddies. Travis feels amazing after he shares his dad's photos. At recess, the kids gather around him, wanting to see the pictures again.

"Your dad's a hero!"

"Wow!"

"Man, that's so cool!" The children treat him like a celebrity.

The bell rings and Travis heads in with the group of classmates still around him. Bobby sneakily slips up behind him and hits the box from underneath Travis's arm. Mrs. Guthrie rounds the corner just as Travis is yelling out and panicking that someone might step on his dad's pictures.

Mrs. Guthrie walks straight over to Travis. "Help him pick these up," she says to the other students as she squats to the ground and scoops up a picture. She gently lays it in the box and says, "Who did that, Travis?"

His face now red and flustered, he replies angrily, "Bobby."

"Don't worry, hun," she squeezes his shoulder tightly and presses her head down to his. Travis gets goosebumps all over his body. "It will be okay. I'll take care of him."

Travis so wants to let go of the box and reach around her and hug her tight. He wants to wrap his arms around her and bury his head in her side. He wants to be held, hugged, and petted for just a moment.

Mrs. Guthrie turns to go in the class. "Bobby," she says, "you come with me."

Bobby sneers at Travis as he walks by. Once back inside the class, the kids want to see the pictures some more and Travis quickly wipes the tears from his eyes. He forgets about Bobby's little stunt. Besides, Mary, who sits next to him on the back row, is smiling at him–a lot.

Like every other school day, Travis watches his family's small, one-story brick house coming closer as the school bus slows to a stop at the neighbor's house. Travis dreads getting off the school bus even more than he dreads the boys that bully him on the bus. Travis's home feels like a prison and his step-mom is a woman who is suffering and tormented with her own guilt and grief. She works hard. She cooks, and Travis loves the hot meals. She cleans, and Travis likes a clean house, but (because she doesn't know any better) she is demanding and unaffectionate.

Travis vacuumed the house this morning like he did every single morning before school, but he wonders now what new chores she will have for him today. It was nothing for Travis to come home and find every piece of clothing out of the drawers and thrown on the floor. "Refold them," she would say. "Do it again." Coming in and finding all of his clothes scattered everywhere after she had ripped them all from hangers in his closet because he had not hung them up straight or the way she had wanted was routine. Travis is still so excited about today's show-and-tell that even the boys on the bus couldn't ruin his happiness, and it may even have made the prospect of going home a little more tolerable.

"Okay, son, let's practice those times tables. What's five times six?" his father says before he even gets his books set down.

Travis counts by fives, using his fingers. Five, ten, fifteen, twenty, twenty-five, thirty. "Thirty," he answers.

"What's five times eight?"

Travis starts over, counting by fives. Five, ten, fifteen. The process is slow and thoughtful. Twenty, twenty-five, thirty. Using his fingers, he put down the last two fingers, looked up, and said, "forty." Without taking a breath, he adds, "Today I showed the kids in my class your war pictures."

"Oh yeah?" his dad replies. "Did you tell them that I found you floating on a log in the middle of the ocean?"

"No," Travis laughs.

Theresa interrupts, "No, he told them you had a baby in Japan with your old girlfriend!"

"You didn't?" his dad looks at him with big eyes and a half-grin, half-grimace.

"Yes, I did," Travis nods his head and smiles.

His dad laughs, shaking his head, "Oh, that should make the next PTA meeting a load of fun. Thanks, son."

"Jason says he wishes his dad was a war hero."

"Travis, I'm not a hero. I'm just a regular guy and, you know, a lot of good men died there. They are the heroes." His dad looked like someone had sucked all the air out of his lungs.

"I think you are too, Dad." Travis studies his dad's face. His dad looked out the window and just stared off into the distance.

"Dad, I need help with my math today. Can you help me with my paper?" Travis tries to change the subject."

"Oh, they are doing stuff I never even learned. Theresa can help you. She just had that last year."

Travis looks at Theresa and slumps his shoulders. "I'm not smart like you are. I wish I was. I'm dumb!"

"That's not true. You just need to try harder," Theresa says while scowling at him. "You are smart. Look how you rewired that radio last week, and we were going to throw it away."

"You're not dumb, son. I don't want to hear that again," his dad adds, then changing the subject, he asks, "How do you like your special counselor?"

"She's cool," Travis lightheartedly responds. Travis has had to go twice a week to counseling ever since he picked up his desk and threw it across the classroom when Bobby had given him a "wet willy."

"Theresa, why don't you make a song out of the times tables?" his dad suggests. "He never has any trouble memorizing songs for Sunday morning church."

Theresa smiles her big, beautiful smile at Travis and says, "Okay, then, we will make a song of his times tables!" Theresa could make just about anything fun. She got busy right away with the melody.

"I wash my hands all the time until they are so dry they bleed."
I never feel clean.

—Suzie

Suzie hears a car door slam and then the back door opens. "Hey, sweetie pie. You ready to get going for church?" Grams asks. "We gotta get you dressed." Suzie pushes her covers aside and crawls out of bed. She reaches up and hugs her Grams' neck. Soon Grandma says, "Hey, come on, let go, you're going to choke me." Suzie kisses her Grams on the cheek. "Good night, girl, you smell like cigarettes!"

Grams tilts her head and looks at Suzie. "You silly thing. Your nighty is on inside out and backward. Doesn't your mom help you get your nighty on after your bath?" Suzie thinks of the night before. "You look ridiculous," Grams teases. "Take that off." Grams tickles her, and the day starts. Church day is the best day of the week. It's for sure and Suzie can count on it. Her Grams' and Gramps' church is mostly black people and they love God, they love to cook, and have church socials. They are kind. Suzie notices, but doesn't care if they are almost the only white people there. After church, they go shopping for an Easter dress. Suzie chooses a purple one. Suzie looks at herself in the mirror. The dress is beautiful, a soft chiffon with white lace across the chest, waist, and trim. She smiles from ear to ear. She loves the dress. Grams ties the big full bow and pats her on the bottom. "Aren't you the prettiest thing ever in that Easter dress?" she asked.

Suzie grins again and takes a step closer to the mirror. The dress is perfect yet something isn't right. She can't see it, but she can feel it. She looks at her arms and legs. Her body is clean, yet something is wrong. Suzie twirls herself around and around, swirling the full purple ruffles. She stops and looks at her neck, chin, and face. All clean. Smiling, she glances up into her huge, panther-like eyes. As she fixes her gaze, she knows she has found it. There it is, she knew it was there. Shame and Deception are suddenly at her side, holding on to her tightly, one on each shoulder.

"You're a nasty, dirty little girl," they remind her. The finality of their proclamation seems irrevocable. It's true and she knows it. Her chest feels heavy. As she examines her eyes, the smile leaves her face. Suzie hates her own reflection.

"Suzie, do you like it?" Grams asks. "It looks so precious on you."

The purple Easter dress fools Grams, and Suzie is glad Grams can't see what Suzie sees. Oh, she loves the dress and really wants it, but it doesn't seem like it covers enough— as if it's a very pretty mask, only not a good one. Still, Suzie desperately wants to feel beautiful.

Suzie nods her head approvingly and smiles as she turns around for Grams to untie and unzip it so she can put her bright pink leggings and white Strawberry Shortcake T-shirt back on. Grams pays for the dress.

Suzie looks across the back seat and admires her new dress hanging to her left. She can't wait to wear it to church on Easter Sunday. All the girls will love it, she thinks. Her Grandpa stops the car at the little store two blocks from her grandparents' house to get nacho cheese Doritos and bean dip, Suzie's favorite. Suzie goes in with her Gramps so she can pick out her own drink. even though she always gets the same exact thing, Coke. When they get to the house, Grams cooks and Gramps will watch TV. Suzie helps with both. Suzie hates to see a Sunday end. She misses her mom but hates going home.

"Suzie, do you want to just leave the dress here so you'll have it for Easter?"

"Oh, no, Grams, please can I keep it at my house? I promise I won't wear it or mess it up. I just want to be able to look at it. Please, please?" Suzie begs.

"Okay, you don't have to whine. I know you'll take good care of it." Grams smiles at her as she gets out of the car and opens the door for Suzie. "Come on, kiddo, let's go show your momma that dress."

Suzie smiles from ear to ear and jumps out of the car. She hurries across the driveway and up the steps to the front door. But she stops abruptly, tilting her head. Ray is yelling. Then she hears her mother yell. "You're a liar and I am sick of it."

Ray snaps back, "What are you talking about, you crazy witch?"

"What's wrong, Suzie?" Grams says. She is standing at the bottom of the steps. Suzie looks back slowly, her eyes wide and full of knowing as she looks straight into her Grams's eyes. The smile that covered Suzie's face moments ago is now gone and a look of fear and an understanding that should never be on a child's face replaces it. Grams stops on the first step and looks into Suzie's huge, beautiful, fear- filled eyes. Suzie's face says it all, loud and clear. *Please don't leave me here.*

Grams can now hear the commotion, and softly, but with an irritated voice, says, "Scooch over, baby, let me get the door." Grams quickly climbs the steps and knocks on the door. "Hey, y'all in there?" she yells, irritated. Grams then leans down and rolls her eyes at Suzie. "The whole neighborhood knows they are in there." Grams rolls her eyes again. Suzie just stares at the corner of the door. They can hear some muffled but angry tones and some straightening going on, and then Suzie's mom opens the door.

"Hey there, sweetie," she says to Suzie as she steps out of the way to welcome them in. Her mother's mouth is smiling but her eyes are sad, and Suzie can tell her mom has been crying. As Suzie steps through the door, she feels a lifeless, empty surrender fill her body. Grams only stays about fifteen minutes, and as soon as she drives away, the angry words start again.

"What the hell were you even doing in her house is what I want to know?" Suzie's mom howls.

"I'll go wherever the hell I want to," Ray snaps. "I was just fixin' her plugged sink."

"Oh, sure you were! You can't even change a dang lightbulb around here! You ain't got no business in her house. You don't ever fix jack around here! The toilet's been running for six months!" Her mother's voice screeches.

"Get off my back," he yells.

"I'll get off your back, alright. I'm going to my mom's house. You're a cheating liar and I'm sick of your crap. Suzie's mom bursts through her bedroom door. "Come on, Suzie, we are packing." Her mother slams and locks the door behind her. Ray bangs on the door and Suzie hurries to the far side of the room. Ray breaks the door off its hinges and it falls to the ground, the bottom hinge giving way under his weight. Kicking and swinging, he falls right on top of it. Ray rolls to his side and staggers to his feet, grabbing the door up like it's a surfboard and hurling it toward the wall where Suzie is crouching. Suzie ducks down even more as the top end of the door slams into the wall just above her head. She lunges out from underneath it. Suzie's eyes are wild with fear as she runs to her mother.

"You go on, you piece of crap, and take that pain-in-the-butt kid with you!" Ray's face is full of hate. "You don't ever lock me out of any door in my house! You hear me, woman?"

Suzie is frozen with fear at her mother's side. Her mother yanks open her closet and grabs a handful of neatly hung clothes off the rod. "Hand me your pillow," she looks down at Suzie. "Now!"

Suzie immediately lunges to her bed, grabs her pillow, and runs back to her mom, grabbing her mother's thigh. Suzie's mother jerks the pillow out of the case and tosses the pillow on the floor. She then stuffs the handful of Suzie's clothes, hangers and all, into the pillow case. Suzie sees Ray coming and backs away from her mother till Suzie is back against the wall. She watches as Ray steps toward her mother and jerks the pillowcase out of her hand.

"You ain't going anywhere." His eyes are now evil slits, full of anger. "I will kill you first." His teeth are clenched. Suzie's mom grasps for the pillowcase as he holds it up out of her reach.

Her mom screams, "Give me the dang pillow case!" She turns and grabs another handful of Suzie's hangers off the rod in the closet. Ray drops the pillow case and reaches for the outfits, yanking the hangers out of her grasp as hard as he can. The edge of one of the hangers catches the side of her mother's mouth as he rips the hangers from her grasp. Blood pours from her mother's chin as she grabs her face and falls to her knees.

Ray chucks Suzie's clothes as hard as he can at the wall and yells at the top of his lungs, "This is all your fault, you stupid idiot! Look what you made me do. You're always accusing me of cheating, you friggin' psycho! Leave if ya want!" Ray turns and limps off, yelling and banging his fists against the walls in the hallway as he heads toward the living room.

Suzie's mom reaches out and pinches the bottom of the pillowcase, slinging the clothes out of it. Clutching it to her face, she lowers her head and groans in pain. She sounds just like a child crying until she speaks. "That sorry bas----."

Suzie is too scared to move and sinks to the floor, sliding down the wall till her bottom touches the dingy, cream-colored carpet. She curls up in a ball, still petrified with fear that Ray will come around the corner again. Suzie watches her mom sobbing. Her mother looks up at Suzie and, still holding her mouth, says, "Pack what you want to take to Grams's. We are leaving in five minutes. Hurry!" Her mom then lifts herself to a standing position and reaches out for the wall to steady herself.

The look of fear and determination in her mother's eyes lights a fire under Suzie and she jumps up quickly. Carefully hopping over the blood on the carpet, she grabs her laundry basket and starts piling her favorite toys in it as fast as she can. *Mom is finally sick of him and we are leaving!* Suzie grabs her Barbie and her Strawberry Shortcake doll, her coloring books, and a big box of crayons. She then yanks her drawers open and take out undies and pajamas. She looks toward the closet and remembers her Easter dress, but it isn't hanging there. It's on the floor. Suzie hurries over to it but stops before her hand reaches for it. She is afraid to pick it up. She can see drops of blood on the carpet. She is afraid there is going to be blood on the dress. She stands over it and stares.

Her mother's voice coming from the living room breaks her trance. "Look what you did to my lip, you dumb idiot!" Suzie lunges down upon the dress and jerks it up, flipping it over in one big swoop. There it was—blood on her brand-new Easter dress. Suzie drops the dress to the ground as fast as she had swooped it up. It's ruined. Suzie is suddenly aware of her body shaking. She doesn't care, she just wants to leave. She knows her Grams will be mad about the dress, but there's no time to worry now. They have to get out of here. *Hurry before he comes in. Hurry so he won't hurt us. Hurry, hurry.* Suzie drags the laundry basket to the closet and reaches up to yank her clothes off the hangers. The thought of moving to Grams was the best feeling she could imagine. Hope is pouring into her by the second, filling her spirit with energy.

Once she has her best outfits yanked down, she grabs her shoes and plops them on the top of the basket. *There, I'm ready.* One more quick trip over to the toy box just to make sure. Yep, she has everything she wants. She pulls the basket over to the bed and climbs up to wait for her mom. Suzie is terrified, but for the first time in a long time, she is full of hope. The tears won't stop, but she is thrilled. *Please, Mom, hurry.* When she gets to Grams, she can eat what she wants. There will be plenty of food and she won't always be in trouble. Best of all, Ray won't be there. *We need to leave now*, her mind screams. *Hurry, Momma.*

Suzie can see herself cuddled up on Gramps's lap. *Where's Mom? What's taking so long? She must be packing a lot.* Suzie spots the crickets in the peanut butter jar on her dresser. Her mom had poked holes in the lid so the they could breath. Suzie gets up and grabs the jar, carefully tucking it in between the side of the laundry basket and her shorts and t- shirts. Then she climbs back up on the bed.

Thump, thump, thump. She, hears Ray limping toward her

room. He rounds the corner and glances at Suzie. Immediately he turns his attention to the open dresser drawers hanging in disarray, then the open closet, mostly empty. Glancing back at Suzie, he looks straight in her eyes and quickly down, focusing on the basket in front of her. He tilts his head and wrinkles his brow. Slowly, he looks back up at her, his eyes glaring hatred.

"Huh," he laughs and sneers at the same time. Softly, and almost inaudibly, he says, "Got your hopes all up didn't ya, little girl? Huh?" he taunts. "Ya didn't hear me?" He jerks his head back and lifts his brows, "You ain't going anywhere. I'll kill her first," Ray mumbles as he turns from the doorway. "Stupid little tramp." *Thump, thump, thump.*

Fear gripped Susie's soul...*Hurry momma!*

Suzie doesn't move. She waits and waits for what seems like forever. Suzie then hears an odd sound. It's soft music coming from the stereo in the living room. She listens for a few moments and then slides off the bed and walks to her doorway opening. That sound is definitely not normal. Suzie stretches her neck to see down the hall, but realizes she will have to take a few more steps to figure out what is happening. Slowly, she creeps down the dark hall until she sees the smoky haze that lay across the living room like a huge, gray ghost hanging in mid-air.

Her mother is dancing slowly, Ray's arms wrapped tightly around her waist. Her mother's arms are around his neck as they sway to the music. Suzie can't believe her eyes. She stands there, astonished, as her cheeks fill with a hot rage. Her heart turns into a solid piece of lead and then sinks into the depths of a blackness too painful to describe. Her mother has betrayed her. Suzie can't breathe and the tears come. She backs up against the hallway wall, and using her hand and arms to guide her, feels her way back to her doorway, her eyes too full of tears for her to see.

Fear and Hopelessness lunge at her, swirling around her head. Taking turns, they torture her.

"Someday he's going to kill your mom and he'll kill you too," Fear hisses.

"You'll never get away from him." Hopelessness licks

his claws. "You are stuck and you'll always be miserable." Hopelessness laughs hideously. "She loves him more than she loves you. She doesn't even care if you're here. She's in there smoking and hugging him after what he just did. She'll never leave him no matter what he does."

"She's not even thinking about you." Fear and Hopelessness are speaking in unison now.

Without changing her clothes or getting tucked in, without brushing her teeth or saying her prayers, without eating dinner or having story time, Suzie crawls into bed and cries until exhaustion carries her to sleep.

Make it Personal

Do you think being abused is affecting Travis' behavior at school? In what ways?

_____

_____

_____

How do you think being molested affected Travis's and Suzie's relationships with the people closest to them? (for example, Suzie and her mom)

_____

_____

_____

How long do you think being abused will affect their lives?

_____

_____

_____

Do you think there should be a statute of limitations on pressing charges against child abusers? Why or why not?

_____

_____

_____

How do you feel about how Travis and Suzie are being treated? Vent here. Do you think God cares as much as you do? Why or why not?

_____

_____

_____

Children like Suzie often end up in foster care. Would you consider consistently praying for these children? Would you consider visiting a foster care center?

_____

_____

If you became aware of a possible situation involving a child and physical or sexual abuse, would you notify authorities or duck your head and mind your own business? What if the perpetrator was a dearly beloved relative—or even the family's bread winner?

_____

_____

_____

Notes

CHAPTER 11

Jesus is the Light of the World, But What Does That Mean?

Jesus answered, Are there not twelve hours in a day? If any man walks in the day, he stumbleth not, because he seeth the light of this world. But if a man walk in the night, he stumbleth, because there is no light in him.

(John 11:9-10 KJV)

Before the dream, I never thought much about free will. I wanted God to never let anything bad happen to me or my family, and I still feel that way. I wanted Him to protect us from hardship and disease. I'm sure you do too. And, just like Mary and Martha, who wanted Jesus to heal their brother, we get offended at Jesus when He doesn't protect us or come through for us. The thing is, God is way ahead of us and His plan is big! His plan is way bigger than Adam and Eve ever guessed in the garden and way bigger than Mary and Martha could have ever imagined. I'm picking up in Chapter 11 of John where we left off.

"Then after that saith Jesus to his disciples, let us go into Judaea again. His disciples say unto Him Master, the Jews of late sought to stone thee; *and you want to go back?*" (7,8) I paraphrased those last six words of Scripture in verse 8 because in my KJV it says "and goest thou thither again?" You almost have to say it in a Shakespearean era accent and, yes, I very much enjoy the thought of you doing that! Point is that the last time Jesus was in that area where Laz lived, they tried to kill him, and the disciples think He is crazy to go back.

"Jesus answered, 'Are there not twelve hours in a day? If any man walks in the day, he stumbleth not, because he seeth the light of this world. But if a man walk in the night, he stumbleth, because there is no light in him.'" (v.9,10)

Okay, so the disciples are worried because those in Judea had already tried to stone Jesus the last time He was there, but surely Jesus's reply doesn't just mean "Don't walk around at night," or "Let's go in the day, so we don't trip." Everyone knows that walking around in the daylight is much safer than walking at night when you can't see. So, the next obvious conclusion is that Jesus is speaking figuratively.

It's easy (for me) to read over this kind of stuff and figure Jesus is just being Jesus, and sometimes it's easy to assume (arrogance on my part) that I know what Jesus means from my perspective. But I wanted to be sure. So, I counted the word "light" in the book of John and it is used twenty-four times. All but twice it is referring to Jesus being the light of this world. The other two times it is clarifying that John the Baptist is not the light.

I like to use a method of studying my Bible that Kay Arthur teaches, so one of my two main study Bibles looks like Walt Disney's Tinkerbell skated across the pages of it with her magic wand. Numerous colored highlighters are patched in across each page marking key words. I formed the habit of adding my own words to color or highlight to Kay's list of suggested words, and in the book of John, "light" was one of the words I had added. Every reference with the word "light" is marked with a cute yellow lightbulb and is easy for me to find.

As I flipped through the pages of John's gospel, I wrote every single verse that had a light bulb, in order of occurrence, on a few 5x7 index cards, which is really weird because normally I would have just used a concordance. I'm sure I only did it this way because the house was like Grand Central Station that day and I couldn't concentrate as clearly as usual. So I took the slow, careful road. I'm so glad I instinctively wrote them down. When the house had cleared for a brief moment, I picked up my stack of cards to read it back to myself out loud. I was shocked. It appeared to me that these verses carried a theme, almost as if it were carefully woven throughout the book of John in a chronological fashion. These verses sing like a song or read like a perfectly written paragraph. Here are the verses, taken from both the King James and Amplified versions:

In Him (Jesus) was the life and the life was the light of men (1:4). The light shines in the darkness and the darkness has not overcome it (1:5). John came as a witness to bear witness of that light, that all might believe through him (1:7). John was not the light, but came to bear witness about that light (1:8). The true light, which gives light to everyone, was coming into the world (1:9). And this is the judgment: the light has come into the world, and people loved the darkness rather than the light because their works were evil (3:19). For everyone who does wicked things hates the light and does not come to the light lest his works should be exposed (3:20). But whoever does what is true comes to the light so that it might be clearly seen that his works have been carried out in God (3:21). He [John the Baptist] was a burning and shining lamp, and you were willing to rejoice for a while in his light (5:35). Again Jesus spoke to them saying, I am the light of the world. Whoever follows me will not walk in darkness, but will have the light of life (8:12). As long as I am in the world I am the light of the world (9:5). *Are there not twelve hours in a day? If anyone walks in the day, he does not stumble, because he sees the light of his world* (11:9). *But if anyone walks in the night he stumbles because the light is not in him* (11:10). The light is among you for a little while longer. Walk while you have the light, lest darkness overtake you. The one who walks in the darkness does not know where he is going. (12:35). While you have the light believe in the light, that you may become sons of light (12:36). I have come into the world as light, so that whoever believes in me may not remain in the darkness (12:46).

Are you kidding me? All sixteen verses, with the word light in them, found throughout the twenty-one chapters in the book of John, written in order, shout the message "Jesus is the Light of the World!" It's amazing that there are whole chapters in between some of these verses, and when written in order, they are amazingly fluid and intense. Just for fun,

I looked at the verses in Matthew, Mark, and Luke to see if I could find the same type of theme concerning the word "light." I did not. I found verses using the word "light' as in "a candle" or "my burden is light."

You know, God just makes me laugh. He makes so much sense when we look for Him. I set out to prove Jesus was speaking figuratively in John 11:9-10 and found a treasure chest. I suspect He has watched many other seekers discover this before me, but I am so happy that He let me find this little treasure on my own.

If we reject Jesus Christ as the Light of the World, we will stumble, as we have no light in us. We have no salvation in us. We can't save ourselves. Jesus is telling Thomas that there is a method to what Thomas sees as madness. Verses 9 and 10 are a major point, and for so long, I just read right over it. I think Jesus is giving the disciples, and us, a hint, a clue, ahead of time about the mystery of what He is fixing to teach them and us. God is so fascinating!

"He said these things and then added, our friend Lazarus is at rest and sleeping: but I am going there that I may awaken him out of his sleep. The disciples answered, Lord if he is sleeping, he will recover. However, Jesus had spoken of his death, but they thought He referred to falling into a refreshing and natural sleep. So then Jesus told them plainly, Lazarus is dead. And for your sake I am glad that I was not there; it will help you to believe (to trust and rely on Me). However, let us go to him." (John 11:11-15 KJV)

Here I believe Jesus wants us to know that He sees our deaths here on earth differently than we do. Verse 11 is a billboard on the side of the road of life and it says, "TAKE THE NEXT EXIT! Come see death from my perspective. It's not the end, it's only temporary." Jesus then says He is going to go wake Lazarus up from his death/sleep. It's not hard for us to walk into another room and wake someone up from a nap, is it? Jesus is showing us just how He sees it. It's just that easy for Jesus to call us forth from death. From His perspective, it's just like we might go and wake someone up from a nap. That's amazing right there, and I never want to take those words for granted again.

So, what does He tell them next? That He's glad He wasn't there when Lazarus died. Well, that is pushing the point home, if I've ever seen it done. They (the family) are suffering, Laz is dead, and Jesus is glad He was not there *for their sakes*, because they are going to grow to rely upon and trust Him. I don't know about you … but to me, it feels like a rug was just jerked out from underneath my feet again. The problem is, I didn't land on the ground. It's more like I'm flailing through the air and trying desperately to grasp some understanding that sets me on a firm, reliable foundation.

We are suffering now. People are dying. Is Jesus glad He isn't coming to help us in our current situation as we suffer in this free will, death-and-disease-filled world, just as He was in this situation with Mary and Martha? And is it so we will learn to trust Him? Sure, His Word says that the Holy Spirit comforts us, but right now I'm pondering God not fixing the awful, horrible, sometimes just unbearable circumstances of our lives because that's what we really want from Him.

What is it about a relationship that makes it worth having? Trust. If you can't trust the person you are in a business deal with or in a marriage covenant with, where does that leave you in the relationship? Jesus didn't make a cameo appearance and just show up one day by beaming Himself down on someone's coffee table and saying, "Here's the deal. I'm the physical manifestation of God's character in the flesh and you can trust me! 'Nuff said, now go tell the world." God is love. He did what love would do. He gave us free will to show us what is in our hearts. Then He came as a child, grew up here, walked in our shoes, and suffered. He submitted His will (flesh) to the Father (soul) and gave us an example to follow.

Do you ever talk to yourself? I do, and I realize that my mind may want one thing but my body often wants something very different. For instance, I struggle with turning to food for comfort. I have conversations with myself in my mind all the time. My flesh-will exerts itself, "This is what I want to do." My mind disagrees or warns me, logically knowing what should be done, yet taking into consideration the desires of my flesh, and the battle is on for me (my soul, heart and spirit) to concede to my flesh.

My husband asked me that question (do you ever talk to yourself?) once when I was trying to wrap my head around the concept of Jesus praying to God the Father in the Garden of Gethsemane before His death on the cross. I couldn't understand how Jesus could be God (His mighty right arm) in the flesh, which would basically mean He was praying to Himself. My husband pointed out that it wasn't any different for Jesus to pray to the Father than it is for us to have a good talk with ourselves, our will and our flesh conversing. This helps me understand how Jesus struggled in His mind, His will, and His flesh.

"In the days of His flesh [Jesus] offered up definite, special petitions [for that which He not only wanted but needed] and supplications with strong crying and tears to Him Who was [always] able to save Him [out] from death, and He was heard because of His reverence toward God [His godly fear, His piety, in that He shrank from the horrors of separation from the bright presence of the Father]" (Hebrews 5:7 AMP).

This was Jesus (God's mighty right arm or His flesh) growing a relationship with us by suffering. He understands our weaknesses. Here He (His flesh) modeled obedience to God the Father's (God's Soul and Spirit) will by not giving into sin when His flesh had to want to. When was the last time we experienced strong crying and tears because we shrank from the possibility of separation (sin) from God's (Soul and Spirit) presence? I can honestly say that before I cry about my desired sin, I will easily give into it. Did Jesus know before He took our sin on the cross (became our sin) that He, at that moment, would be separated from the Father? When was the last time we as Christians wanted to avoid sin so badly, not after we sinned but before we sinned, that we cried out and wept because we could not bear the thought of separation from God? It is interesting to me that Jesus (as flesh) sometimes sees Himself/flesh separate from the Father, evidenced by the way that He calls Him "My God" repeatedly in the New Testament. However, God uses terms in the Old and New Testament when referring to Jesus, as if they are One. Similarly, we (as individual persons) feel more independent and separate from our parents but when we have children we see them as the most precious part of ourselves walking around in different (their own) bodies. God is so cool.

Once when recalling one of my children suffering in pain, I literally said "How did my heart get outside of my body?" I felt as if my own self was in another flesh. Look at this amazing picture Father God has given us.

Everything Jesus did here on earth was to build trust with us. He victoriously fought temptations to sin. He then submitted to God, becoming our sin for us. He showed us how to trust our heavenly Father, even when we feel as He did—deserted. Remember Jesus's words as He died on the cross:

"And about the ninth hour (three o'clock) Jesus cried with a loud voice, 'Eli, Eli, lama Sabachthani?'—That is, My God, My God, why have You abandoned Me (leaving Me helpless, forsaking and failing Me in my need?" (Matt. 27:46 AMP). Jesus (God's character in flesh) knows the pain of feeling forsaken.

You know, sometimes I think about how I desire my earthly father to be proud of me. I don't want him to see me as ugly, worthless, dirty, or with any other undesirable quality. My father's disapproval, even for a split-second, bothers me. Jesus knew that He was becoming our sin. The very evil, ugly, revolting thing that God cannot look upon. Think about actually becoming the very thing that your dad finds disgusting or repulsive. It would just kill me to become something my dad despised, but then to feel his wrath poured out on me on top of it would be unbearable. For my earthly father to furiously punish me and turn from me because I had become the very thing he detested would hurt so bad. It hurts to think about what Jesus (God's character in the flesh) allowed Himself to go through, and that doesn't even cover the physical torture.

Remember the timeline we talked about earlier? We pictured a carpet or a ruler. Jesus came and walked on our timeline. He walked down that road with the disciples to face the mourners, and He met Martha and Mary on that road. He did it to teach us something huge. If we recognize that He is the Light of the World and our redeemer, and we repent, changing our minds about our sin, we step into relationship with Him. That's where trust is built.

The thing is, we have to humble ourselves before God and realize that it is not all about us and our happy, organized, perfect, lives. In three of the gospels, Jesus is calling us to deny ourselves and follow Him.

(See Matthew 16:24, Mark 8:34 and Luke 9:23.) Jesus was there in Bethany that day trying to show us what is important here. He is offering us a completely new perspective, an eternal one.

"Then Thomas, who was called the Twin, said to his fellow disciples, Let us go too, that we may die (literally, be killed) along with Him." (16)

No one knows for sure what Thomas meant here. The following is just my observation after studying the text, looking at the Amplified version, looking up a few words in my concordance, and considering Thomas's overall personality. This is not a thorough study and there are volumes of excellent resources by seasoned professionals who have differing opinions. But, because I think my reasoning is basically helpful to me, I'm going to share it in hopes that it will help you.

In my opinion, there is a chance that the disciples (at least Thomas), had no real clear understanding of Jesus being the "Light" of the world. Many people think Thomas was just stating that he was willing to die along with Jesus. But if that were the case, then why did Thomas flee with the other disciples when Christ was crucified and died for our sins? Also, Thomas refused to believe when told Jesus was risen and alive. My point is Thomas never even expected what was going to happen.

I could be wrong, but I don't think Thomas had much faith in Jesus's decision to go back to Bethany. I don't think Thomas had a clue. Does it sound like Thomas understands that he can trust the "Light of the World, God-made-flesh, Creator, and Mighty King" who is standing right there next to him? Noooo! If I'm correct, then the statement that Thomas made pretty much sums up half of my Christian walk, at least up until now.

You see, in the past I experienced a lot of just shaking my head and going forward with my life, even though I felt like it was all a big mistake. Funny thing is, what I believed in my heart (just like Thomas) came out of my mouth (just like Thomas). I knew that disaster was probably right around the corner because I was walking through disasters every day.

Where I worked had to be a mistake, who I was married to (a struggling drug addict) was definitely (in my opinion) a huge mistake, that mold-filled house I lived in was a big mistake. I didn't understand a lot of what had happened in my life or why I was where I was. I couldn't make sense out of why I was headed in a certain direction or why so many things had gone wrong. Even now, I feel like I don't have control over some of my life. So often, I find myself just going along with it, hopping from situation to situation and trying my best to put out the fires.

In the past (every once in a while) I'd say something facetious, like I think Thomas said, and without much faith I might add. "Well, tomorrow's another day and it can't get any worse" or Murphy's law, "Whatever can go wrong will go wrong." Or my personal favorite, Isaiah 22:13, "Let us eat and drink for tomorrow we die." The truth is that a lot of us have this "stuff happens and then you die" mentality. How many of us have seen that famous bumper sticker and said those very words?

It's because we are just like Thomas and we don't see the big picture. We don't see the Light. We don't recognize the power of Christ at work in our lives. We only see our circumstances. We don't trust Him. If we did, we wouldn't be saying such negative things. The worst part is we desperately need a revelation of the Light, and Jesus knows it. We are literally lost in the darkness without Him.

If I had been there and been speaking that day instead of Thomas, I might have facetiously said, "Well, we all may as well go and get stoned too." The definition of the word "stoned" here is not a reference to smoking pot or other pharma-remedies we use to escape our daily problems, but rather, a very shocking reference to a horrid practice where angry mobs viciously throw rather large rocks at someone's head until they die. I wonder how the Holy Spirit feels when I chronically complain about my difficult circumstances or outright suffering. If I'm wrong about Thomas, I hope he will forgive me. I know I'm right about myself, and that definitely needs to change.

"So, when Jesus arrived, He found that he had already been in the tomb four days." (v. 17)

Everyone present that day at Lazarus's funeral understood that anyone would have died after three days shut up in a tomb with no water or food. However, in their culture they believed that the soul of a dead person hung around the body and the grieving, sad relatives for three days. And it was possible to raise them at, say, two or two-and-a-half days. But the belief was that the soul leaves the body after three days. I read that on the Internet some time back, I don't know where. So, basically, at four days, to raise him from the dead would be to call his soul back from Paradise. That would have been considered a major miracle to the Jews. I think the eternal perspective point is that all was lost. There was no hope for healing or restoration. We can relate to that now because we feel that "all is lost" feeling at the loss of a husband, child, a parent or other loved one, a relationship, or the loss of a dream. Disappointment and heartbreak can surround us like a sudden storm, without warning or mercy.

"Bethany was near Jerusalem, only about two miles away." (v. 18)

Looking from an eternal perspective, verse 18 tells me that Jesus is right around the corner (two miles away), figuratively speaking, and perfectly capable of coming to my rescue. This understanding sits at the bottom of my soul like a five-hundred-pound anchor that I can't move. It tethers me so I have to deal with it. Sometimes, I want to cut that chain worse than I can describe. It makes it so much harder to understand our pain, yet God wants us to know He is right there, close by, just like He was for Mary, Martha, and Laz. And He is watching, very aware of our dilemmas, yet He is still waiting. What is He waiting for? For us to trust Him.

It is sometimes easier to keep or create a safe distance from God when we think about the fact that He is so close yet allowing us to suffer. Maybe we are thinking that if we don't pursue a close relationship, we will stay off His radar and suffer less. If we ignore Him, maybe He won't use us or allow us to suffer for His glory. Pretty clever, aren't we? After all, like Suzie asked me during her interviews... if God allowed what happened in the past, what else will He allow? The truth is that Suzie's family was ignorant and neglectful, and her abuser had free will. The truth is that Jesus warned us, just as He spoke to His disciples right before He was crucified in John 16:32-33 (AMP):

"But take notice, the hour is coming, and it has arrived, when you will all be dispersed and scattered, every man to his own home, leaving Me alone. *Yet, I will not be alone*, because the Father is with Me. (Italics mine) I have told you these things, so that in me you may have [perfect] peace and confidence. **In the world you will have tribulations and trials and distress and frustration; but be of good cheer [take courage; be confident, certain, undaunted]! For I have overcome the world. [I have deprived it of power to harm you (eternally) and have conquered it for you."**

Just like Jesus knew His Father was with Him as He went toward the cross, Jesus tells us in John 16:33 that we will have trouble and trials and frustrations and distress, yet to be of good cheer...be confident and undaunted! He has overcome the world! He has conquered it for us! Why is life so sad and difficult? Because we don't really believe Jesus's words.

"And a considerable number of Jews had gone out to see Martha and Mary to console them concerning their brother. When Martha heard that Jesus was coming, she went to meet him, while Mary remained seated in the house." (v. 19, 20)

Warning: this next bit is pure speculation. I know some of you just busted out laughing, possibly spitting your soda on this book, maybe you're thinking that most of my comments are pure speculation. Hey, I'm just reminding you.

I wonder if Mary knew that Jesus was coming and purposely chose not to get up to meet him, possibly because she wanted Him to "know" she was upset with Him. Or, perhaps she was hurt enough to not want to look Him in the face. I can't be sure, but what I do know is that the closer you feel you are to someone, the worse it hurts when they (seemingly) let you down. The more you have opened yourself up to loving and admiring someone, the more devastating it is when they refuse to help you or when they are not there for you. Here, it occurs to me that because of the difference in the way the sisters related to Jesus, Martha usually doing and Mary usually adoring, that the two of them might, because of the way they saw their relationship with Jesus, respond differently to the fact that He didn't show up and help them.

For me personally, the more I praise and worship God, and the closer I get to knowing Him, the harder it is for me to comprehend when He lets me get a toothache or a kidney infection. In fact, it hurts awfully. Not just the pain I'm going through, but I feel betrayed and abandoned at some level, even knowing what I believe. You should hear me crying out to God. I sound like this: "Lord, how is it okay with you for me to have a kidney infection and be going through so much physical pain right now? It's me, your daughter, you know, the one who sat in the closet last week while everyone else spent the morning together enjoying breakfast, and I worshiped you because I love you so much. You know me? I'm your little girl, the one that sings to you. I love to worship you and adore you. I acknowledge you every chance I get. I fast sometimes, too, and you know how much I like food. I want to read your Word, Lord. My kidney hurts, please help me, please, I can't take this pain. Think of all the other times you have helped me." (Sometimes I list them.)

"Why won't you help me now?" Yes, I beg.

As I cry out to Him, sometimes my problems get fixed right away. He works a miracle and the dentist, (after I already told the dentist to pull my rotting tooth), out of the blue, offers to do a root canal and temporary crown for $200. If any of you have had any dental work done lately, you'd know for sure that that is a bona fide miracle! You know what's funny? When the receptionist at the dentist office told me how much a root canal and a crown were going to cost, I told her that a casket and burial would probably be cheaper. She looked at me with this "I can't believe you said that" kind of stare, which I returned, as I still wasn't over the sticker shock on a root canal! It really was a miracle.

The next time I'm suffering and pray, it's totally different.

I struggle for two years and need six surgeries as the result of a boating accident. It is hard for us to handle personal suffering no matter what our relationship with God. Mary and Martha were very close to Jesus, and because of their relationships, both had high hopes as far as how they expected to be treated. Watch for Martha's faith in the next scenes. I have noticed that a lot of my Martha-type friends have extraordinary faith.

Martha is on her way to see Jesus, and Mary is still sitting in the house, disappointed, and slightly miffed, I think. I believe that's exactly where I would have been, right there next to Mary, confused and staring at the fireplace. I might even have slammed a cupboard, pushed my food away, and scolded the dog. Heartbroken that my precious Jesus didn't come immediately and rescue me. He let my loved one die. The way I might have seen it, He obviously doesn't care like I thought he did.

"Martha said to Jesus, Master if you had been here my brother would not have died." (v.21)

WOW! How many of us have a question or two for Jesus? A question like, where were you when my sister died of cancer?

Martha didn't ask Jesus a question, you say? You're right. She was much more direct. Her words were more like an accusation. She was saying, "This is your fault. My brother died because you didn't come." Why do I think that? Let's say hypothetically that my sweet daughter-in-law, Brandi, wanted to go to a garage sale and she couldn't take her sick children along. So she called me and explained that there was a baby bed on sale for $20 that was normally $150. She then asked me to come and watch the kids so she could go buy it. If I delay a day or two when it is in my power to come, and she misses the sale, what would I think she was saying when I walked in her house later and heard the words, "If you would have been here, my child would have a bed." I would hear, "It's your fault my child doesn't have a bed." Of course, that is what Martha is saying. She is disappointed. Can we assume she blames Jesus? Oh, I think so. Just like we blame Him when we ask questions like, God, where were you? Where are you now? I thought you loved me. Why does my brother have a brain tumor? Why did my father abandon me? Why was I sexually molested?

In Crystal McVey's YouTube video **https://youtu.be/ Bwp6PZbCU**, "Nine minutes in Heaven- (Heaven-Testimony): we see an example of someone who has questions for God. I know that you may be a skeptic, and a lot of people out there *are* liars, and so we have to be careful who we believe. But I also know by comparing personal testimonies to Scripture which testimonies sound like a bunch of nonsense and which sound completely truthful, compared to Scripture. Decide for yourself if it lines up with Scripture and if you believe her. If she is correct and telling the truth, then you may not have as many questions as you think you might when you finally see Jesus.

In Crystal's testimony, did you notice how as soon as she sees the Light (Jesus) her question changes, even as it is coming out of her mouth? She starts to say, "Why did you let me be molested? Why don't you love me?" Instead, she falls prostrate on her face before a love that made her feel she would explode, and she blurts out, "Why didn't I do more for You?"

Martha, like Crystal, knew that Jesus could have stopped the suffering and, just like God heard me the morning of my dream, Jesus has heard all of our pain throughout the ages. Can you imagine? Every single one of us looks toward Him (the Light of the World) and wonders why certain things were allowed to happen. He has heard our pain and our accusations. Just exactly as He heard Martha and Mary that day. As I look back on that morning, knowing what I'm learning now, I am amazed at His mercy and His long suffering.

The Light of the World invites us to have an eternal relationship with Him. He wants us to be His eternal Bride. But we don't care about *Him.* We just want Him to fix and explain why He hasn't saved us from the distress, frustration, trouble, and suffering in our lives?

We all have had a "tomb experience." Mary and Martha's suffering was caused by the death of their brother—lying lifeless and decaying in a tomb while the solution seemed so close, but yet so far away.

After reading chapter 13 of this book, I hope you will be compelled and elated to lift your head and see why He walked down that road to Bethany. I hope a new perspective will change your attitude and life forever.

Make it Personal

List the things in your tomb. What loss are you focused on?

_____

_____

_____

Do you think children like Travis and Suzie might be hurt, angry, or confused about God's love for them? Do you know people who may be hurting and need to view life from an eternal perspective? List them.

_____

_____

_____

Do you distance yourself from God so you won't be noticed? Do you think that will keep you from suffering? Or do you have another reason? What is it?

_____

_____

_____

In what areas do you need to totally trust God?

_____

_____

_____

Do you ever (like Jesus) fight sin off until you cry bitter tears? Before you sin...not after? List the sin(s) you would like to have victory over.

_____

_____

_____

Do you ever say facetious things like Thomas did? Why do you think you say those things? Will the new perspective presented in this chapter change that habit?

_____

_____

_____

As you examine your heart, have you completely denied yourself to follow Him...Or is it more important that He "fix" your life and give you what you want?

_____

_____

_____

Notes

CHAPTER 12

Travis and Suzie
A Boy's Best Friend
and Sleep Overs

Looking back, I wish I would have told on him or fought him off. I was so scared and ashamed of what people would think of me if they found out. I desperately wanted to hide what he was doing, even if it meant silently suffering while family who could have saved me were in the next room.

— Travis

T he phone rings and soon after, Travis's step-mom says, "Y'all need to get your work done. Rebekah is coming to get you to go for pizza and you can spend the night." Rebekah was always calling and asking if the kids wanted to go on a fun outing like the zoo or maybe the movies or skating. She was truly a wonderful big sister.

Of course, Travis loved doing fun things with his sisters and he wanted to join in, even if they were just going over to Rebekah's so the girls could do an exercise tape together or make cookies. But it was a constant battle. He knew if he went, he might be molested. But missing the zoo or the movies was an awful choice too. Besides, what reason would he give his step-mom for why he didn't want to go? She would force him to say, and then the kids at school would find out.

Travis can't let that happen. Travis's step-mom is always angry at him and he knows it would be really bad for her to find out. She might blame him. The thought of people knowing is the worst thing he could imagine. Travis would rather suffer the abuse than have anyone find out this disgusting thing was happening to him.

God, make him stop!

Kenny selfishly makes demands. Aggressively, and without compassion for Travis's sobbing, he keeps insisting and Travis reluctantly complies.

Finally, Travis gags, almost throwing up, and he knows it's over.

"Twavis, did you ever do dis for Micky?" Kenny asks, using that repulsive baby talk voice.

Travis is still crying and spitting. The look in Kenny's eyes is curious and evil. Travis doesn't respond out loud, but as he spits again, he knows what he wants to say: *I'm not doing this for you. You're making me do it. My brother Micky would never ask me to do this.*

Travis hates Kenny for asking him such awful questions about the girls at school and their privates. Kenny's sickening grin makes Travis want to vomit.

"All little boys want that from girls, Twavis. You'll tewl me, won't you? You'll tewl me all about it, right?"

Travis looks away and ignores him, but his heart is bursting with hate. Travis knows that the assault on his body has ended for now, at least until the next time. He has learned to cope by denying himself the luxury of dwelling on it for very long if he can help it. At least, until he's at home and all alone.

"Travis!" yells Theresa, "Where are you?" He ignores her as he has been walking thru the woods long enough to be attacked by the voices that routinely torment him. Rarely was Travis all by himself, even if it was just the TV that kept him company. But when he got alone for a few minutes, the evil ones always found him. As he took a walk through the woods, his dog Poochie leading the way, they traveled tethered together alongside him and whispered.

"You're disgusting and you know it, don't you?" Shame taunted.

Travis sits down on a huge oak stump and rests his head on his knees. He wraps his arms around his head, covering it.

Deceit leans in close. "God hates you. He always has. He has hated you from the time you were born, don't you know that? You're so stupid. You're an idiot to think He might love you. Why even pray to Him? He doesn't care about you at all. No one loves you." Deceit is relentless.

Shame leans in close. "You must be the worst child in the world for God to let this happen to you. What is wrong with you?"

Deceit interrupts as a threat gurgles its way out of his deformed, twisted mouth. "If you tell, everybody will hate you and they will all blame you. You will never ever have any friends."

The lies and fear pour down Travis's shoulder and across his chest like vomit, and then soak into his flesh, disappearing as if soaking into a rag. The fear-filled poison spills into Travis's heart and soul until he gags and chokes. Travis cries until his face is hot and soaked with tears. He lifts his head to wipe his running nose on his sleeve and then shoves Poochie with both hands, giving him a hard push away. He then bows his head again and places his brow on his crossed arms.

Poochie has been trying to lure Travis out of his deep despair. Poochie tries again to nuzzle Travis by nudging his moist nose up under Travis's armpit. Travis turns his face away from Poochie's muzzle and cries. Poochie presses his body close to Travis's side and rests his neck and head across Travis's upper back. Travis lets his heart crack open for a moment, and the groans flow out of his mouth as the pain oozes through the break like lava down a black rock mountain. Poochie doesn't give up, but soon he lies down on Travis's feet, lifting his head every half-minute or so to look up at his charge.

"God," Travis asks softly, "do you hate me? Why do you hate me? Why won't you make him stop? Why don't you let him die? You could send an angel with a sword to cut his head off. Please, God. Please!" Travis's sobs are hard enough to choke him as he coughs and spits on the ground.

Deceit is right there. His gray, wet lips whisper right next to Travis's ear. "God doesn't care, or He'd do something to help you."

Again, Shame whispers to him in a teasing manner, "If they knew, they would laugh at you. You'd be the laughing stock of the whole town and they would all hate you even more. You are worthless, that's why Kenny does it."

Poochie stands and pushes his nose in between Travis's arm and forehead, but Travis again turns his face and shifts his body the other way. "Stop," Travis demands. Poochie has watched this long enough. Crouching down, he shoves his muzzle under Travis's arms and in between his legs, pressing his nose up hard into Travis's face, and quick as lightning starts licking Travis's tears.

Travis is almost shoved off the stump. He reaches out with both hands to keep himself from falling and wraps his arms around Poochie. As Travis pulls him close, Poochie's tail wags furiously. He has won.

"He hurts me, Poochie," Travis cries softly into Poochie's neck fur. "I can't make him stop."

Poochie straightens his head, pulling it back a bit and tilting it. Poochie looks deep into Travis's sad, tear-filled eyes, then licks his face again.

"I can't tell no one. I just can't. I hate him."

Poochie sits down in front of Travis, again looking intently into Travis's eyes, tilting his head, and whining a soft, long groan.

"I wish I could just die. I just want to die."

Poochie paws at Travis's lap and licks his tear-streaked cheek some more. Travis knows that Poochie is saying he cares, that he understands. Travis throws his arms around Poochie's neck and squeezes tighter. Poochie pushes his head and then his upper body into the side of Travis's head and neck until Travis loses his balance and flops to the ground. Poochie quickly jumps over him, licking his face excitedly, his tail furiously wagging. Travis tries to cover his head with his arms, but Poochie has the advantage now. Travis can no longer resist and his spirit starts to soften, allowing a slight curl of a half-smile to alter his sad, pain- filled face. He sniffles and grabs the top of his T-shirt and wipes his face. Rolling to his side, he sits up and turns his head away from Poochie's frantic affections.

"Travis," Theresa yells again, "come on, come on! Let's ride bikes!"

Travis hears her, but just barely. He knows she has probably circled the block looking for him, but Travis can't come out of the woods now, even though he halfway wants to. He waits for her to ride off again.

Poochie walks around and sits directly in front of Travis, looking at Travis and then turning his head toward the direction of Theresa's last call, fully expecting him to respond to his sister's voice.

"You are the only one who understands what I'm going through," Travis whispers as he reaches for Poochie and nestles his face in Poochie's reddish-brown fur. Poochie sits patiently, still and tall, letting Travis lean his head on his shoulder. Travis rubs his head back and forth on Poochie's strong neck. It's as if Poochie knows that Travis needs his strength and companionship.

Poochie, of course, never says a word. His existence is enough. Poochie's faithful presence and huge, brown, concern-filled eyes are the best gifts a dog could give a young, hurting, ten-year-old boy, especially because Poochie will never tell Travis's painful secret.

Travis finally wipes his eyes. "Come on, Poochie. Let's go find Theresa."

Poochie follows Travis out of the woods and across their yard, his tail wagging. Travis bumps the silver kickstand with his foot and, hopping on his bike, heads down the trail. Poochie takes the lead and life goes on.

*"I often prayed, 'Hide me, please God,
so he doesn't come and get me.
Please, God, don't let him come tonight.'"*

—Suzie

As the next year passes, Suzie is molested several times a week, sometimes nightly. Ray makes Suzie special drinks with Coke and hard liquor. He makes her drink it. Suzie gets very dizzy. Sometimes it hurts. Her privates burn, but mostly she's just sleepy. The special drink nights are not good nights, but they are better than some of the other nights.

Sometimes he pinches her awake. "Suzie, you see these girls in the pictures?"

Suzie is so tired. There are magazines spread across half of the bed.

"You are going to be sexy just like she is." He points at another girl. Suzie looks at the pictures he points at. She feels a terrifying presence in the room. She feels something evil. She wonders if it is inside her. There's something mesmerizing about these girls in the pictures. She wants to look more. Something inside her knows it's bad, but she can't look away.

Suzie's jaw aches so badly, causing tears to trickle down her face. *Do what he says so it will stop. Make it stop.* Suzie is now very used to the ritual pinching and constant coaxing and anxious demands. She complies without complaint, like a little robot. Like a slave, she does whatever he tells her. She hates it, and she is so so tired. Suzie wants to take a bath by herself. Having to bathe with him makes her madder than any of the rest of it. It's almost as bad as when he shoves his nasty tongue in her ear, which makes her sick to the point of gagging. He is ugly, every inch of him, and she despises him with all her heart.

Suzie dries his back because he says she has to. He has a scar all the way down his back from top to bottom. He is covered with tattoos, and she hates every single one of them.

"Suzie, this is what you do when you love someone. Do you love me?" he asks in a whisper.

Suzie doesn't respond. She suddenly feels like she can't breathe. She is rotting from the inside out.

Suzie wakes up the next morning to the front door slamming. Her mom is home from her night shift at the restaurant and is singing a made-up song, "It's your last week of third grade, wake up, little girl, get up, get dressed, get dressed, you're gonna be late." Suzie is immediately excited, remembering that today is the day that her school will be on the news. All the kids in her school will be spelling out the word "TEXAS" (with their bodies) on the soccer field, and Suzie is the center of the X. She will stand there while the helicopter flies over her and takes their picture. Suzie jumps out of bed and, just as she swings her covers off, she realizes that her panties are on the floor. She hurries off the bed and frantically puts them on while looking at the light blue sheet that hangs over her doorway, giving her some supposed privacy now that her door is gone.

Her mom peeks around the curtain just as she drops her nighty and says, "Come on, small fry, let's get a move on it. The bus will be here soon."

Suzie doesn't have to be told twice. Today will be a great day. This week will be a great week. The end-of-school parties are this week. Suzie pictures the cupcakes and punch they will have at the parties. She smiles as she gets dressed, picking a soft pink sundress with rose buds on it that Grams just got her. Suzie eats her Lucky Charms and watches her mother do the dishes from the night before. Her mother keeps a very clean house, and Suzie likes that their house always looks nice. Some of the houses in the park are gross, really gross, but not hers.

Suzie slides off her chair and carries her bowl to the sink. Her mother reaches up and flicks some water at Suzie's face and giggles. "Stop, Momma," Suzie laughingly protests.

"Oh, don't be such a stinkweed, Suzie. A little water won't hurt you," her momma says as she dries her hands. Suzie knows her mom is teasing her and she pretends to be mad with a huge pout displayed across her face, but busts into a smile as her momma reaches over and tickles her. Suzie laughs when her mother pats her backside and says, "Go get your shoes on."

Suzie runs down the hall and looks for her shoes. *Where did I put them?* She stops in her doorway and thinks for a moment. *I know I put them by my bed last night. I wanted to hurry this morning.* She walks toward her bed. *They should be right here beside my bed.* Just then, Suzie remembered Ray tossing something in her toy box when he was pinching her awake last night. He cussed as he tossed it in. She steps over to the new toy box Grams got her and, sure enough, there they were. She hated the reminder.

"You deserve what he does to you," Shame hisses as she bends over to reach into the toy box.

Suzie sits on the floor to put her shoes on. Suddenly, her room feels like it has been picked up and moved a million miles away from anyone who loves her. She feels so alone.

"You are filthy. Yes, you deserve it," the whisper softened. "All of it." Shame had her full attention. It was like she was instantly drugged. "He only does it because he knows you're dirty, just like those girls in the magazines. You are a nasty little girl and all the boys at school know it as soon as they look at you." The whisper was so soft, her heartbeat was suddenly drowning it out.

Suzie finishes buckling her sandals and she is now sitting on her floor, legs stretched out straight in front of her. She is staring at the hem of her dress, counting her heartbeats. Suzie closes her eyes and takes a slow deep breath, concentrating with great determination, ...twenty-seven, twenty- eight... twenty-nine...

"Come on, Suzie, let's go!" her mother yells from the front door. Suzie snaps out of her trance and looks around the room for her backpack. She jumps up, stopping to look at her bed. In her mind's eye, she sees Ray kneeling by her bed the night before. She examines her thrown back rumpled covers and pillow. Suzie grabs her covers and chucks them off the end of her bed. She quickly picks several toys and tosses them up on her bed. A baby doll named Ella and a Strawberry Shortcake doll, a stuffed dolphin, and a Barbie. *There that's better.* She turns her head from the scene, grabs her backpack, and hurries under the sheet that masquerades as a door, putting her nightmare behind her.

Once summer vacation begins, Suzie begs her mom every single day for weeks to have her friend Hope over for a sleepover. Finally, Suzie's and Hope's moms decide on a Wednesday so Suzie's mom will be home to make sure they have a good time.

As Suzie awakes, she thinks, *Hope is coming tonight! Mom's making cookies! I'll show her my toys. We will color in my new Strawberry Shortcake color book I saved just for tonight. I'll let her pick any picture she wants to color, even if it's my favorite. I have pink glittery nail polish for tonight and we'll play Barbie dolls. Maybe Mom will fix our hair.*

Suzie hops out of bed and starts making it right away. She folds her Scooby Doo blanket and neatly lays it across the bottom of her bed. She opens her dresser drawer and makes sure her new, dark pink pajamas are folded and ready to put on later that night. As soon as her room is clean, she sneaks out of the trailer as quickly and silently as she can. The morning is muggy and quiet. None of the other kids are up yet, so Suzie heads for the creek. She takes off her shoes and gently slips her feet into the muddy creek bottom. Suzie is very still. Catching crawdads takes patience, but she has it down to a science.

Later that night, Hope spends the night with Suzie, just as planned. It was everything that Suzie had longed for: cookies, painted nails, coloring, dolls, and giggles. Everything is perfect until late in the evening when the phone rings. Suzie's mom slips her head around the curtain to let the girls know she has to leave for work. Suzie can't let that happen. She stands up and begs her mom to stay.

"I've got to go, Suzie. He'll fire me if I don't."

Suzie wants to burst into tears, but not in front of Hope. Suzie sucks the pain deep into her chest and sits back down, forcing a half-smile across her face.

"They need me," her mom lifts her eyebrows, "and you will be in bed soon. You won't even know I'm gone."

Suzie's heart sinks, but as suddenly as her heart hits

bottom, she has a thought, a terrifyingly wonderful idea. Suzie looks up from the Monkey's game that she and Hope are playing and lets her mind go. *Maybe Ray will take Hope to his room tonight instead of me.* The thought brings a crazed, confused new feeling to her. Suzie shrinks at the thought for a second. *How can I wish that? But I do. I want him to take her this time.*

In her mind, Suzie knows she has betrayed her new friend, but she was sure she would rather Ray take Hope to his bed instead of her, no matter how wrong that was. And she wouldn't change her mind. Suzie looks at Hope's long blonde hair and thinks how pretty it is, much prettier than her frizzy brown curls. She looks up at Hope's face and feels sad, but still certain that she would rather it happen to her friend and not her. Hope's eyes are beautiful. Suzie feels excited and dreadful. *I couldn't have picked a prettier friend out of all the girls at school. He will want her, he has to. Just like he wants me and the girls in the magazines.*

As Suzie's mom tucks them in, Suzie lays her head on the pillow next to Hope's. She encourages herself. *It is perfect. Everything is just right. Hope is on the outside of the bed and I am safe, on the inside.* Comfort fills Suzie's heart and she feels safe and secure. *Ray will take my new friend to his room tonight instead of me.*

Make It Personal

Did you realize just how awful molestation might be for a child before you read Travis' and Suzie's stories? Are their stories opening your eyes?

_____

_____

_____

Do you think that adults who were molested as children should be pressured or persuaded to keep the sickening details to themselves? Why or why not?

_____

_____

_____

Do you wonder if, in some way, the abused person's silence protects the perpetrator?

_____

_____

_____

Who benefits the most by keeping these deeds in the dark?

_____

_____

_____

Do you believe there is a hell? Do you believe God is just to send the sinful there?

_____

_____

_____

How do you think God will judge a person who ignores a child who is being abused? Should a family member who ignores and doesn't report abuse be subject to jail time?

_____

_____

_____

If you can relate to Travis or Suzie's story: Have you forgiven all of the people responsible for what you suffered? If not, list the ones who you need to release to God. Please read the "Must-Read Conclusion" at the end of this book titled "What Forgiveness is Not."

_____

_____

_____

Notes

CHAPTER 13

The Offended Heart

*But some of them said, Could not he who opened
the eyes of the blind man have kept this man from
dying?*

(John 11:37 NIV)

I wonder if anyone present in the days before Lazarus'
funeral had said to Mary or Martha, "Where is your
messiah? Where is your precious, trusted Jesus now
when you need Him?" Guess what? They didn't have to say
it. We all feel it. When something awful happens, don't we
feel forsaken? Not only are we in pain caused by our awful
situation, but then we worry and are sometimes tormented at
the thought that others who see us suffering will judge us. We
hate that they may assume we are just not important enough to
God for Him to bother with helping, protecting, or saving us.
We cringe at the thought of others deciding that we are being
punished or that God is distant, angry, or indifferent toward
us. Our fear is that others will see our wretched situation and
think we mean nothing to Him. Can we bear the shame of it
without being offended at God's Holy Spirit?

The young people at Angel Reach feel exactly like
Travis and Suzie did: abandoned, unloved, unimportant,
and worthless. A person who feels abandoned might have
thoughts that sound like this: "My father died when I was a
baby, I guess God must not even care about me." Or, "God let
me be raped because I'm trash and I don't matter to Him." Or,
"My parents gave me away like people give away dogs. I'll
never matter to anyone." Of course, these circumstances may

be true, but the way we feel about them is not.

The fact that things are going wrong does not mean you've been abandoned by God, just like Abel, Mary, Martha, Laz, Travis, Suzie, and the youth at Angel Reach were never out of God's attention or affection either. Feeling abandoned is something that everyone deals with at some point. King David cried out in Psalm 22, "My God, My God, Why have you forsaken me? Why are you so far from helping me, and from the words of my groaning?" David had not been forsaken, yet he felt that way. King David's words were a prophetic foreknowledge of what Jesus Christ would suffer for us. Read Psalms 22 as if Jesus was saying it as He hung from the cross.

Jesus himself was a man of sorrow and acquainted with grief. Jesus was not abandoned by God, yet He suffered dearly. "He was despised and rejected by men, A man of sorrows and pain and acquainted with grief; And like one from whom men hide their faces. He was despised, and we did not appreciate His worth or esteem Him." (Isaiah 53:1 KJV) Remember, this is in the Old Testament, written approximately 450 years before Jesus is born.

Jesus knows how we feel. He Himself cried out from the cross, "My God, my God, why have you abandoned Me [leaving Me helpless, forsaking and failing Me in My need]?" (Matthew 27:46 AMP)

Luke records that after making that last statement, Jesus cries out with a loud voice, "Father, unto thine hands I commit My spirit! (Luke 23:46 AMP).

It is astonishing that Jesus feels and expresses being abandoned by crying out a question, yet He commits His spirit to God, trusting His Father, and even says, "It is finished." As recorded in John 19:30, this statement acknowledges that Jesus was willingly completing God's understood purpose for His earthly life, even after He felt abandoned. Jesus is not offended at God's will or offended that He had to suffer to accomplish it. He isn't even angry at the people who put Him on that cross. "Forgive them, Father, for they know not what they do." (Luke 23:34 AMP)

It is an unfortunate state to be offended at God, even when you are, like me, saying all the right things, not even realizing your heart is holding offense toward Him. I didn't completely trust the integrity of God's heart, and I truly didn't realize it. According to Scripture, an offended heart can block miracles and possibly prayers from being answered or heard.

"And on the Sabbath He began to teach in the synagogue; and many who listened to Him were utterly astonished saying, Where did this man acquire all this? What is the wisdom [the broad and full intelligence that has been] given to him? What mighty words and exhibitions of powers are wrought by His hands! Is not this the carpenter, the son of Mary and the brother of James and Joses and Judas and Simon? And are not His sisters here among us? And they took offense at Him and were hurt [that is they disapproved of Him, and it hindered them from acknowledging His authority] and they were caused to stumble and fall." (Mark 6:2-3 AMP)

"*And He was not able to do even one work of power there* except that He laid His hands on a few sickly people and cured them." (v.5)

I would venture a guess that the people He healed were the ones who remained unoffended. Even people with strong faith in God can be shaken off their foundations when they suffer or see their loved ones suffer. Martha sees Jesus in the flesh in front of her, so she has an advantage over my young friends at Angel Reach. Yet, Martha struggles. Notice what she confesses she believes, even in her confusion:

"And even now I know that whatever you ask from God, He will grant it to you." John 11:22 (AMP) (Martha speaking).

Is Martha hoping that Jesus might bring her brother back? Is she suggesting in a slightly manipulative way that Jesus can have anything from the Father and He might prove it right now? Her words "even now" make me wonder. "Jesus said to her, your brother shall rise again." (v. 23) "Martha replied, I know that he will rise in the resurrection at the last day." (v. 24)

This statement in verse 24, that she knows her brother will rise in the last day, seems to contradict her earlier statement in verse 22 that Jesus could get any prayer or request He wanted from the Father. Was she afraid to ask and be told no when she knew He could do it? I consider here the possibility that Martha was the only one there that day who suspected a miracle, even as she doubted. One day, I'm going to ask Martha if that was the case. I think she exhibits a great faith here. The problem is that at the same time, she was offended. Do we love Jesus for who He is or for what we "know" He can do for us? Many of us do not doubt for one minute that God can help us. In fact, that's the biggest part of the problem: we know He can help us! On the flip side of the coin, who would tolerate being wanted only for what they can do for someone else? Do you see the danger there? I don't want to be loved or wanted solely because I clean and cook. There is more to me than that. I don't want to be treated constantly like a party favor either. My husband doesn't want to be wanted solely for his paycheck, and who can blame him? God is no different.

I can hear myself now. "Oh, Jesus, this is a great opportunity for You to prove that You are the Father's Son and that He will do anything you ask. You could bring my brother back to life and people will believe You are Christ, just like I do." Or I might sound like this: "God, if You give me a baby, I will believe and so will everyone who is praying for me to have a child. Jesus, if you'd heal this cancer, everyone who knows us will believe in You and they will be saved."

I have not only done it, but I've also seen others beg—asking for a child, spouse, or miracle. And we are cunning when we are pursuing our miracle (our will). The whole time Jesus must be thinking, "You don't love or want Me. You're not even close to satisfied in My salvation gift or eternal marriage proposal. You just want Me to know that I should have fixed the whole problem, disease, or deficit." I wonder how Jesus feels.

You may say, "Well, it's not wrong to love your brother or want healing or to want a baby. These are all good things." Well, most everything we want from God is good, but do we want it more than we want God? Do we want our miracle more than we want God to be glorified? I'm guilty. I tried to beat down the doors of Heaven so I could have a godly marriage. What could be a more righteous thing to pray for or expect from God? Wanting a godly marriage is a wonderful thing to want, and I had hundreds of good reasons for God to give it to me, but did I want it more than I was in pursuit of God on a personal level? Oh, yeah! My (godly) marriage was an idol and more important to me than my relationship with God. I know that because it was the main reason I went to God. I begged God to change my ex- husband's free will. I pleaded with God to just make my husband change and do what's right. Yes, I wanted God to get ahold of his heart for his sake, but mostly because his actions were making me miserable. Dear reader, please understand this: you can pray for your wayward relative, but God will not force them to change. They have a free will.

Furthermore, when you hear a woman testifying on the local radio station that God has answered her prayer and that her husband has accepted Christ, understand that even though she is giving God glory for her loved one's salvation, God doesn't ever force someone to pursue, obey, or choose Him. God does not love that woman more than you because her loved one chose to follow Christ.

Please consider this carefully: If you yourself were choosing a wife or husband to spend eternity with, would you choose someone you knew would always put their parents, their children, and their sisters and brothers or loved ones before loving you? No, because a marriage is the closest intimacy we can have, and God has a right to expect His eternal bride to love Him more than anything else including our families.

Luke 14:26 says, "If anyone comes to me and does not hate their father and mother, wife and children, brothers and sisters yes, even their own life such a person cannot be my disciple." Ouch! Now, do I hate my family? No, of course not. But do I hold God responsible for their health, their safety, and their spiritual condition? Yes, I admit it. I have!

I will ask you the same question I have asked myself. If my son rejects God and he ends up in hell, will I be offended at God and hold God responsible for that? Or can I look at my son with tears in my eyes and say, "It is not God who is sending you to hell. You chose hell by rejecting God." After all, whose side am I on? If my father or spouse rejects God's love and curses his way through life, am I going to be angry at God for not doing more to convince or persuade them?

Whom do I really love?

"Jesus said to her, I am (myself) the Resurrection and the Life. Whoever believes in (adheres to, trusts in, and relies on) Me, although he may die, yet he shall live." (v 25)

This is how my heart translates Jesus's words. "Look at Me, Martha. I am the Resurrection. Look at Me." The whole time she is pointing to Laz, her dead brother. "Martha, I am the Resurrection, Your eternal sustainer, for you and Lazarus. Your Groom, your Father. Just focus on Me for now, and I will take care of everything. Look at Me, build a relationship with Me, desire Me, pursue Me, trust Me, know Me, rely on Me, want Me."

But Martha wants her brother back. Jesus continues....

"'And whoever continues to live and believes in (has faith in, cleaves to, and relies on) Me shall never [actually] die at all. Do you believe this?' She saith to Him, 'Yea Lord: I believe that thou art the Christ, the Son of God, which should come into the world.'" (v. 26, 27)

Martha's statement of faith reminds me so much of so many Martha personalities I know. I admire this about them. Here, Martha exhibits amazing faith; Martha believes He is the Messiah. But, as you can see, she doesn't grasp it any better than I did the morning of my dream. She knows He's from God but doesn't understand that Jesus (the Light of the World) is not her personal Johnny-on-the-spot, life-fixer-upper. He is pursuing her trust, her love and her devotion, her heart. He is after an eternal relationship with her. He pursues us in the same way now, even right now. Right this moment He's pursuing you.

Did you notice in verse 26 that Jesus says, "whoever continues to live and believe"? Those words "whoever continues" remind me that it is not just an awareness of Him that Jesus wants us to have but an ongoing relationship, even when things go wrong. Especially when things go wrong, and Jesus waiting until Martha's brother was in a tomb is proof.

Have you ever considered the word "believe"? It is an action word like "run," "sing," or "live." You can stop any of these four activities; the word "believe" by itself implies an ongoing action of its own.

"And when she had so said, she went her way, and called Mary her sister secretly, saying, 'The Master is come, and calleth for thee.' As soon as she heard that, she (Mary) arose quickly, and came unto Him. Now Jesus was not yet come into the town, but was in the place where Martha met Him. The Jews then which were with her in the house, and comforted her, when they saw Mary, that she rose up hastily and went out, followed her, saying, she goeth unto the grave to weep there. Then when Mary was come to where Jesus was, and saw Him, she fell down at His feet, saying unto Him, 'Lord, if thou hadst been here, my brother wouldn't have died.'" (vs. 28-32)

Poor Mary, I really feel for her. I am just like her sometimes. I enjoy sitting at Jesus's feet and worshipping and appreciating Him, which makes me, like Mary, most vulnerable to disappointment. I know God's plan is perfect, yet I still struggle with why He doesn't help me when I know He could step in and save me. Please understand that I am not criticizing people who are Martha personality types or saying that they do not feel the pain as deeply. The pain is going to hurt the same, but they may not handle it the same. They may not be as confused or let down as the Mary types who are more prone to sitting intimately at His feet. I am envious of the Martha types and their ability to just believe and have faith, along with their ninja-like mastery of servanthood. I have many Martha types for friends and I am well acquainted with their fierce love for God and their unwavering devotion to family. I have noticed that the doers are dependable, energetic, enthusiastic, often ambitious, willing, tenacious, thoughtful, courageous, and encouraging. They will give until it hurts. They are also disciplined about spending time with the Lord.

I have also noticed that we all have some mixture of Mary and Martha in us. No one is just a Mary or a Martha 100 percent. I also think we have Mary and Martha seasons. As a primarily Mary type, I notice that Marys have to be careful to not be lazy or hermits, hiding their light under a bushel. I have to decide, and then convince, coax, and sometimes force myself to get involved or follow through, and that's something I continually work on.

When I put myself in Mary's sandals, I think she may be

respectfully saying, "Where were You? Why didn't You come? This wouldn't have happened if You would have shown up when I needed you." She is on the ground in front of Him and is showing by her tears and by her respectful body language that she was deeply wounded and had counted on Him.

I'm saying "respectful" because she's not throwing the kitchen utensils at him and screaming ugly insults. I see many angry people doing this with their words today. I was recently listening to an atheist who hates a God she claims doesn't exist. I know this because when she was asked, "What if you are wrong and there is a God you will answer to?" she shrugged her shoulders and said, "Then I'll go to hell." She then followed with "but I wouldn't want to worship a God who allowed this suffering anyway or who forced you to choose Him or else go to hell." You see this atheist is really mad (offended) at the idea of God's authority, and just like this atheist, many more of us are angry because of what's in our tomb. Mary was heartbroken over her brother's death. She, like this atheist, knew that any God worth worshiping could have saved the day.

Notice that Jesus doesn't respond to her like He did Martha. There's no dialog recorded between them. I'm curious about that. Is it possible that Jesus expected more out of Mary than he did Martha because of the nature of their relationship? It's just speculation, but I remain curious.

It is also very intriguing to me that Jesus made Mary get up and come to Him. He knew that she knew He was coming and had been spotted on the road. He made her get up and come to Him just like Martha did. He stayed there and waited for Mary. I wonder about that. I mean, in the grand scheme of what was occurring that day, it wasn't absolutely necessary. So why did He wait there for her? What was going through His mind? Did He want them to have some privacy? Did He want to see if she would come? Did He want to see just how offended she was? I don't know, but He must have had a reason. He cared.

When Jesus therefore saw her weeping, and the Jews also weeping which came with her, He groaned in the spirit and was troubled (v. 33)

I think we might be able to assume He was hoping for a different response from Mary. Wow! He groaned in His Spirit! What exactly is His Spirit? You know my mom has a very quiet peaceful spirit, she has a calming influence on everyone around her. She has taught me what the Spirit of God is because it motivates her every action. The Spirit of God is the driving force in every decision she makes. If you are wondering about the spirit someone has, check what motivates and animates them. What do they care and talk about? Your spirit is your driving force. Your director and your cause. It causes you to react the way you do and to make the choices you make. I have attended churches where the body was all about outreach to the community and those churches had a spirit driving every decision focused on the mission of service and love towards their fellow man, and I have attended churches where the overwhelming driving force was order, programs for the body, discipline, growing numbers, and money. It doesn't take long to get the feel for someone's spirit. Have you ever been around someone who is always complaining? Well, that is a direct reflection of the (driver) spirit within them. Have you ever been around someone who is ambitious? Ambition to succeed is a driving spirit. Jesus's spirit is driven by glorifying God and love, and that driving force within Him was groaning.

This word "groaned" (*embrimaomai*) in the Greek has a surprising definition. It means primarily to "snort with anger." It means to fret or be painfully moved. To express "indignation" against and to "rebuke sternly," groan or murmur against. The word troubled (*tarasso*) in the Greek, is to stir or agitate in a physical sense, referring to his spirit. I was familiar with both of these definitions from the Strong's Exhaustive Concordance before I had the dream, but I had heard preachers much smarter than myself say that Jesus was angry because of their lack of faith or He was angry at Death itself. Or that He cried as a result of His compassion. I no longer believe they are correct.

The word compassion is used twelve times in the four gospels referring to Jesus having compassion on the multitudes or a person, and it is the Greek word *splagchnizomai*. It has to do with the bowels and a yearning deep inside of pity or sympathy. That is not the word used here.

In the afternoon on the day of my dream, it occurred to me, once I settled down and stopped having my pity party, that when God answered me, as I cried out to Him and opened my Bible that morning to John 11, that Martha, Mary, and I were all doing the same exact thing. We were all questioning/ accusing Him of not caring while asking why He doesn't show up. We were all offended at Him. Me flying above the houses shooting the perpetrators at will and Mary and Martha grieving and offended over their brother. I think Jesus was hurt and weeping for just that reason; after all, He was God in flesh. It also occurs to me that because God is Love, the very worst thing we can do to Him is accuse Him of not caring.

And (Jesus) said, 'Where have ye laid him? They said unto him, Lord, come and see. Jesus wept.'" (vs. 34,35)

This breaks my heart. I think Jesus feels falsely accused and judged by the very loved ones He desires to reveal God's glory to. Jesus must have felt like He was casting pearls before swine, as they were not concerned about seeing God's glory but only about their brother. Jesus wasn't crying for Laz, as He knew He would be raising Him from the dead. Jesus also knew that Lazarus's eternity was not at stake. Now you might think that He was crying because He felt sympathy for Mary, but not Martha? I mean, He had seen Martha first. He cares enough about her to have a dialogue with her. She was undoubtedly upset. Here's another thought: He didn't cry in chapter 12 of John when Mary was crying a bucket of tears and wiping His feet with her hair. Jesus (God with us) is groaning in His Spirit here, and I want to understand why.

When we attend a funeral we always assume that the one closest to the dearly departed is hurting the most. They are the ones we feel for. Why do we not consider that Jesus loves these dying, hurting or suffering people "more" than we do? Why do we assume that our love for them is stronger or deeper than His? Do Martha and Mary assume that they love Lazarus more than Jesus does? Of course, they do. Why is that? If God has the capacity to love so much deeper than we do (after all, He is love) then it only stands to reason that He, being the closest to the sufferers as He created them, will be even more upset than we are about what has happened to them.

Just because His deliverance or justice doesn't happen on my timetable doesn't mean He doesn't care. Yet in my dream, I assume I care more because I'd stop the abuse or pain right then and there if I could. Is there a possibility that God hurts even more than we do when his children (our loved ones) are sexually molested, commit suicide, or suffer? They are His children first. He created them. How utterly ridiculous and truly infinitesimal is my love for these hurting and abused compared to God's love for them. Even if they are my family, I shrink in disgust when I consider the Almighty Creator and compare my puny concern for them with His.

"Then said the Jews, 'Behold how He loved him!' And some of them said, 'Could this man, which opened the eyes of the blind, have caused that even this man should not have died?'" (vs 36, 37)

Do you see the two things that are occurring in those last two verses? Some of the Jews are noting that Jesus loves Laz and some of them are offended because He didn't step up sooner and stop the pain. The question these people had is, if Jesus could create new, working eyeballs in a stranger's head, couldn't He have stopped this from happening in the first place for His good friends?

"Jesus therefore again groaning in himself cometh to the grave. It was a cave, and a stone lay upon it." (v 38)

There's that word "therefore" again, referring to the verse before. My translation is "Therefore or because the guests questioned Jesus not helping, He groaned in Himself." Also, the word "groaned" is the same Greek word *brimaomia* meaning "snort with anger" or "stern rebuke" we saw earlier. This should make it very clear that Jesus groaned because of their accusation that He could have helped but didn't. Which is exactly what we do every time we ask Why? ...or...Where are You?

I wonder how it felt to be there on Lazarus's resurrection day and have not one of the people who truly loved Him looking at Him with delight and anticipation. Not one person just wanted Him for His presence or for who He is.

Think of the centuries of people who question, blame, and

turn up their nose, judging God even to the point of mocking Him, falsely representing Him, or deciding to believe He doesn't exist because of all the suffering caused by sin and free will. Now think of the hordes of people wanting something from Him. Think of the judgments God has received from us since we have grasped the knowledge of good and evil.

In the garden, the Serpent tricked us into taking the 'Knowledge of Good and evil'. Now that the weapon is in our possession; the accuser helps us load the magazine... bullet by bullet. *"God is not really good... if He were good, He wouldn't have allowed your wife or mother to die of cancer...If He cared, He wouldn't have let you be molested, or your brother get crushed in a car wreck...He could've stopped that drunk before he got in the car... He could have healed that disease and your child or loved one would still be here...if God loved you, your mother/father wouldn't have abandoned you!"* Sound familiar? The magazine/clip firmly slams tight into the receiver.

The enemy of God helps us aim it at our Creator. *"God doesn't even care. God is right here watching all of us and He doesn't lift a finger. He let that man molest/rape you and never helped you"* Satan deceives us, lying to us, coaxing us into measuring God's goodness against our knowledge.

The god of this world supports our arms (figuratively) to help us place the sight perfectly on our loving Savior. We place our finger on the trigger as God's judge and jury. *"God wouldn't send someone to hell just because they rejected Him... what about people who have never heard about Him? ...and what kind of God would kill His only Son?...I'd rather not serve or know a God like that."* As we pull the trigger, the weapon explodes in our face...we walk away from God and the enemy laughs. First he tricked us into taking the Knowledge; now he helps us use what we see as good or evil to separate us from God eternally.

Aren't we the good ones after all?

I recently watched the latest remake of the Ten Commandments and got so miffed at the way the producer depicted God as a child who was not necessarily precocious as much as He was capriciously cruel, tantrum-filled, and just flat random. This child/god was spouting a kind of belligerent temperamental-ness not even typical for the worst behaved of brats. It made my stomach churn. I wondered aloud how amazing God is to take all of the abuse the human race (including myself) dishes out about Him, yet He tarries and waits for us, intending to do good for as many as will choose Him. His mercy is astonishing. We are just like Mary and Martha, so many of us looking toward His coming so He can explain His absence. Again, we are offended.

It doesn't matter how we judge God or how we depict God. It doesn't matter what these morning talk show hosts say about God. He is who He is and our accusations don't change Him. But that doesn't necessarily mean it doesn't anger and hurt Him. After all, we are made in His image, and it hurts and angers *us* when we are falsely accused or depicted in an untrue way. I'm sure He is not pleased when we distort His character or motives. Amazing that God tolerates our insults and doesn't shoot us like the rabid dogs we act like. (See Romans 2:5.)

For those of you who, like me, have been taught that Jesus was angry at their lack of faith, let me point out that there are other places in the Bible where Jesus addresses his disciples' lack of faith, but we don't see this word *brimaomia*, and He doesn't weep. He shows frustration with statements like, "How long will I have to contend" and "Oh ye of little faith." Thank goodness, He's not like Darth Vader who evokes his terrifying powers from the Dark Side as he chokes off the windpipe of his naysayer. And I quote, "I find your lack of faith disturbing" as his general falls to the floor and starts kicking from lack of oxygen.

All light heartedness and jokes aside, I suspect Jesus felt very lonely that day when He said, "'Take ye away the stone.' Martha, the sister of him who was dead, saith unto Him, 'Lord by this time He stinketh: for he hath been dead four days'" (v. 39). Even His closest friends had lost hope in Him. Martha is calling it just like she sees it: "It's too late."

I want to ask you a question. Where in your heart is there a situation that you have said, "It's too late. All hope is lost. This can never be redeemed or fixed, and because of this my life is ruined and God has failed me." Martha says to Jesus, "Don't bother, it's not fixable." She's describing just how awful she sees it. She thinks she knows something God doesn't know. We all think we have it all figured out.

Could it be (maybe this is just a wild shot) that Jesus wanted them and all of us to see that it was in the hopelessness of the "all is lost" situations that He can still be trusted? Beyond hopeless, beyond reason, beyond understanding. You might be thinking, "Well, four days in a tomb is totally different than your mom dying when you're five, and going your whole miserable life without her protection, love, and affection." Yes, but if you trust, really trust, that your life is a vapor and your Deliverer is coming, it will make all the difference. Jesus answers Martha's warning.

"Jesus saith unto her, 'Said I not unto thee, that, if thou wouldst believe, thou shouldest see the glory of God" (v 40) What is glory? I looked the word "glory" up in my

Strong's Expanded Exhaustive Concordance. The word "glory" carries with it the understanding of glory becoming apparent or going public in whatever way God reveals Himself. Words like "exhibited," "manifestation," "shown forth," and "exaltation" are used to describe what is happening with His glory. In Exodus 33, Moses had pressed God to see His glory even after God's Spirit routinely came to his tent in a pillar of smoke and spoke with him. God's responded by telling Moses He would let His "goodness" pass by while Moses hid his face in the cleft of the rocks. Think about that. God reveals His glory by letting His "goodness" pass by. God's glory is directly related to His goodness.

In Lazarus's death, God's glory was exhibited for Martha, Mary, and for His Bride to see publicly. Think of it— Jesus chooses to give us a peek and reveal God's glory (His goodness) to us by taking something dead and rotting (a hopeless situation) and speaking the dead thing to life. This is a foreshadowing of the resurrection of His Bride. Jesus wants us to be really focused on the tomb because we are about to see the glory of God. I'm sure it occurs to Martha and Mary that if He can do it once, He can do it again and again. The sisters realize at that moment that they won't really die. No wonder in the next chapter of John, Mary is at Jesus's feet pouring out expensive oil and crying while wiping his feet with her hair. Right here is where Mary gets her eyes opened. She is His Bride and one day will be resurrected by Him. Mary will be His forever! Jesus is her Eternity. Jesus is her Eternal Life and Lazarus's too. Can you imagine what our lives would be like if we could get our eyes off of our flesh suits and our family's flesh suits and think eternally? "Then they took away the stone from the place that the dead was laid. And Jesus lifted up His eyes and said, "Father, I thank thee that thou hast heard me." (v. 41)

It's noteworthy that the first thing Jesus does when He is praying is thank the Father for hearing Him. I think thanking or worshiping God at the beginning of every prayer is the only way to start a prayer.

"'And I knew that thou hearest Me always: but because of the people standing by I said it, that they may believe that You have sent me.' And when He thus had spoken, He cried with a loud voice, 'Lazarus, come forth.' And He that was dead came forth, bound hand and foot with grave clothes: and his face was bound about with a napkin. Jesus said unto them, 'Loose him, and let him go.'" (vs. 42-44)

Can you imagine how it might have made Jesus feel if things had been different when He came walking down that road toward the sisters' home? What if Mary or Martha had run up to Him and been so comforted to see Him coming that they jumped into His arms, buried their head in His chest, and loved that He was with them? What if they had cried, "I'm so glad You came!" What if they had welcomed His embrace and greatly appreciated Him for being there. Not for the miracle (what He could have done if He had been there) but for who He is? Just for His presence or the comfort that His Spirit brings. What if Mary or Martha had exhibited a heart that was not offended at Him? What if one of them had been expecting a miracle or just completely trusting Him no matter what, even to the point of joy? I can't imagine how that might have touched Him.

Do you remember the two criminals who were hung on the crosses on either side of Jesus? (See Luke 23:32-43.) There we have another example of the two heart-attitudes toward

God. One man is offended and yells out that Jesus isn't the Christ, because if He were, He would have saved Himself and them as well. This man is angry and accusing and blaming. He knows that any real God or Savior could easily stop the painful situation. The other man confronts the first one, asking him if he even feared God. I find that interesting.

He pointed out that Jesus was innocent, but the two of them were guilty. In other words, he confesses his sin. He then humbly asks Jesus to remember him. Can you imagine the physical pain Jesus must have been in at that moment? Yet, in his pain He assures the second criminal that he will be with Him in paradise.

What will it look like the day you or I see Jesus face to face? Picture Jesus walking down the road toward you like He did toward Mary and Martha on His way to (your tomb experience) Lazarus's tomb. We will see Him face to face when we die or He returns. Will we be excited and totally enthralled, jumping up to run and meet Him just for who He is, or will we see a malfunctioning miracle machine that owes us an explanation about His absence? That's exactly what Mary, Martha, and the offended criminal on the cross saw.

I ask myself if I will be troubled, focused on my parents health or my kids success or careers or ministries or my loss or the past or physical pain or what was fair and who did me wrong and why God didn't give me this or that? I don't want to be struggling to make sense of it. It also occurs to me that just like the two criminals on the cross, one of the two sisters (Mary) was possibly expected (in a hopeful kind of way) by Jesus to respond differently than she did...maybe that's why Jesus cried? Did Jesus expect or earnestly hope that Mary, who sat at His feet, would trust Him at a different level, setting an example for us? Remember, God gives us free will.

I want to be completely free of the cares of this world and consumed with Him only, just Jesus. I want to be on that road like Mary and Martha, only when I see Jesus coming, I don't want to be crying. I don't want to be a desperate, broken mess with a backpack stuffed full of questions about my life or speculating why He didn't do something. He is showing us that death is not the end! I want to be rejoicing and saying,

"Jesus, I knew You'd come! I'm so excited! I kept my eyes on You only. I trusted You. And better yet, I'm ready to be your Bride. I want You first. There's not another thing on this earth that is more important to me than You. I don't need an explanation. I don't need to see the 'front side' of the tapestry, just You. Before I want a spouse or children or success or a good reputation, or my family's lives or my health, or my friend's approval, I want You."

When we see a person who is dying of cancer or disease, yet lifts their hands toward Heaven and praises their Creator, we see someone who is packaging their 'Knowledge of Good and Evil' back into a box and is handing it straight back to God, relinquishing back to Him what Adam and Eve took in the garden.

When we see a person who was born with no arms or legs or was abandoned, abused or neglected… thanking, worshiping and serving God, we see a human who has rejected their knowledge of good and evil and presented it back to our Creator, trusting 100% in His Glory and Goodness. Which places us right back to where we were in the garden…trusting God completely.

I want to have 100% relinquished back to Christ the 'Knowledge of Good and Evil' that Satan tricked us into taking and instead fully trust in Gods goodness and glory no matter what I see here on earth.

I pray He will have no cause to look at me (like He did with Mary and Martha) and say, "Linda, if you'd have just believed," or "Linda, didn't I tell you?"

Make it Personal

Can you see how an understanding of free will, the millstone scriptures, and an understanding of Mary, Martha, and Lazarus's story could greatly benefit someone who was abused as a child or is suffering? Do you know someone you could pass this book along to?

_____

_____

_____

_____

Do you see why thinking eternally can be life changing for people like Travis and Suzie? How will thinking eternally help you? What three steps can you take to keep thinking eternally at the forefront of your mind?

_____

_____

_____

_____

Did you realize that an offended heart toward God can block God answering your prayers?

_____

_____

_____

_____

Do you think Jesus was weeping at Lazarus' tomb because He was hurt or angry that they were accusing Him of not caring? Have you ever accused God in your heart of not caring? If you decide to completely trust God, even in the suffering, and completely clear your heart of offense toward Him, do you think that could change your prayer life?

_____

_____

_____

What does the statement "I am the Resurrection" mean to you personally?

_____

_____

_____

Have you ever begged God for something? What was it? Did you want it more than you wanted a relationship with God?

_____

_____

_____

_____

Will you be angry at God if one of your loved ones rejects God? If you need help or support as you ponder these questions please contact us through idomministries. com.

_____

_____

_____

CHAPTER 14

Travis and Suzie Hunting Dogs and Love Tunnels

"I think it's the things we refuse to talk about that suck the life out of our relationships."

—*Travis*

I t's Saturday. Rebekah invited Travis and his sisters for a fun afternoon at the park together, pizza, and then overnight in her and Kenny's trailer. After Rebekah leaves for work and the other kids fall asleep, Kenny seeks out Travis.

Travis, now twelve, hears the door knob turning and thinks about scurrying under the bed to hide. But there is no way out. The desperate longing to run is squelched by the fear of the other kids finding out what Kenny is doing to him. As Kenny pulls Travis by the hand down the hall again,

he sees Rebekah's bedroom doorway coming and he knows what is going to happen on the other side. For four years, Kenny has abused Travis without mercy.

Kenny pushes him on the bed and takes Travis's clothes off, even though it is obvious that Travis is upset. Kenny looks at him approvingly and pets him. Travis feels fearful, ashamed, and unprotected—like at any moment Kenny may do something awful, something worse than he has done before. Kenny has never raped him, but he treats Travis like a male would treat a female in every other sense. Kenny often grabs Travis to kiss him, and Travis instinctively turns his face away, unable to control his revulsion. Kenny touches and mouths on Travis's twelve-year-old chest like a man would a woman's. Travis is confused and repulsed, feeling nothing sexual or pleasant, only the slobber on his chest. When Kenny mounts Travis to rub himself on Travis body, Travis doesn't know what to think. Disgust floods his spirit.

Kenny routinely puts his mouth on Travis's privates to try to incite a sexual response. Travis's body didn't respond the first several years, but the older Travis gets, the more difficult it is to stop the automatic physical reaction to stimulation. Travis resists with all his might, thinking of things to distract his mind during the assaults. The cactus in the desert, fishing, the kids at school picking on him, his dog, or fire ants biting him. The uglier, smellier, and more frightening he could pretend it was, the better. Travis concentrates as hard as he can so his body won't give in. Kenny sometimes gives up, but other times, because Travis refuses to let his body go, Kenny keeps trying for what seems like forever. Travis holds on so long that his raw skin swells and burns. The swelling lasts for days at a time and hurts so badly he can barely pee. The first time this happened, Travis thought it was going to stay huge, like a purple plum, forever. Or that it would rot off. Travis was petrified that someone at school or his family would see what it looked like. It hurt so bad in class he could barely wait to get home so he could ease into the lukewarm bath water for the only relief he could find. It hurt terribly to get wet, but always felt better afterward.

Travis pretends he would strangle Kenny, choking him to death. *Just let it be over with* is Travis's constant prayer. Kenny was Travis's enemy number one, but Travis's body was becoming enemy number two.

Travis has become a master at controlling his response, yet it doesn't always work. Travis dreads Kenny's advances. Travis wants out of his body. The fact that Travis has to take his used, disrespected, defiled and abused body down the hall and get back into his bed wounds Travis deep inside. And that's when the voices start. Treacherous accusations that scorch his soul blister their way across Travis's tender heart.

Each time Kenny molests him, Kenny gives Travis a five-dollar bill or a silver piece. Kenny would often beg Travis to perform oral sex. "Please, Travis, please? Come on, I'll give you ten dollars," Kenny whines. Travis knows from experience that Kenny will tire of begging and, in frustration, force him anyway. Travis reluctantly and resentfully, and sometimes eagerly, takes the money. After all, he should get something, shouldn't he? Sometimes Kenny promises him money and doesn't give it to him. It doesn't matter. Travis knows he has to do it anyway, and Travis hates Kenny just the same, with or without the money.

As the school bus rounds the corner, Travis sees his dad mowing the lawn. That means Travis will probably have yard work today. He waves at his dad and heads straight for the pen in the back yard where Poochie stays while he is at school. Poochie greets him with tail wagging, standing front feet up on the side of the pen. As soon as the pen door opens, Poochie shoots out like a rocket and flies past Travis. Travis tries to grab him. He's thinking about the week before when Poochie jumped several feet up the side of a leaning tree and grabbed a squirrel. Travis yells angrily at Poochie to come as he didn't want to have to bury another squirrel. Trying to keep Poochie from digging them up wasn't fun either. "Come on, Travis, let's go," his dad calls.

Travis hops up on the riding mower motor and turns himself forward with his legs Indian-style. Once he is seated on the engine, his dad lifts his foot from the brake and off they go to make their regular trip around the neighborhood. Travis loves to ride on the hood of the mower while his dad shouts and waves to any neighbors who just happen to be out and about.

As soon as Travis's chores are finished, he heads for Randy's house. Randy is the new kid in the neighborhood, and even though they had a wrestling match that turned into an all-out fist fight the first day they met, they have become good friends.

Travis remembers how they went straight at each other and were soon on the grass, first one on top and then the other. Randy is a year-and-a-half older and a good bit bigger than Travis, but Travis is strong for his size, quicker, and more determined. Travis didn't want to fight, but Randy had something to prove to the other boys in the small wooded subdivision. Travis remembers going home mad and confused at Randy's behavior that first day, but during the following months they have become practically inseparable. This was all due to Randy's persistence. Travis pedals his bike toward his new friend's house and wonders what Randy would say if he knew about what Kenny does to him.

Travis knows he will never tell him.

"As an adult, I crave God's love. It's the only love that's true. If someone has a heartbeat, he or she will betray you."

—Suzie

Suzie is awake the second the curtain moves. Ray tip-toes around the toys that she and her sleepover guest, Hope, had left on the floor. She peeks, barely opening her eyes, as he approaches the bed. Ray kneels and gently lifts the covers off Suzie from the back side, reaching across Hope.

Suzie opens her eyes and looks straight at him. She wants to tell him, to make a suggestion, even to beg him, "Take Hope instead. Take her!" It's all she can do, as he picks her up, to keep herself from blurting out, "Look at her hair. She's pretty. Why not her?"

Ray lays Suzie on his bed just like normal, but this time he turns and walks out of the room. Suzie is sure he is going to get Hope and bring her in there too.

A minute later, Ray returns, but without Hope. Instead, he's carrying a bottle, a glass, and a pink silk hanger with a black lace cami hanging from it. Suzie recognizes it as one of her mom's pretty nighties. He stands Suzie up by the bed and strips off her new Strawberry Shortcake pajamas she had saved for her sleepover. Naked, Suzie stares down at them lying crumpled on the floor, as if they were nothing special. He dresses her in the black nightie. He snaps it between her knees as it hangs down way too long. On her small body, it fits awkwardly as if it were still on the hanger. She reaches repeatedly to grab the loose straps as they slide over her tiny shoulders.

Ray pours brown liquid out of the bottle into a small cup and gives it to Suzie. "Drink it."

She obeys and lifts it to her mouth. It smells strong, like the stuff Mom cleans the toilets with, but Suzie takes a big swallow so she won't get yelled at. It burns all the way down into her stomach. She coughs and chokes violently.

"Here," Ray says. He is irritated as he opens a bottle of Coke that was sitting on his headboard and adds it to the vile brown liquid. She is used to the yucky drink and the magazines that are spread across the bed, but the lingerie is something new.

The next morning, Suzie wakes to Ray frantically shoving her across the bed and grabbing her PJ's from the floor where he had dropped them the night before. She can barely focus her eyes, but she immediately senses that he is scared. Now she hears her mom's keys jingling and the front door opening.

"Hurry, Suzie, get dressed," he hisses. "Give me your leg." He shoves her in her pajamas and lifts her in the bed, covering her as if she belonged there. Then he grabs the lingerie, bottle, glass, and magazines and shoves them under the bed. He slides himself into the bed and put his hand up to his mouth, his index finger to his nose. "Shh." He squints his eyes at her, daring her to say a word.

Suzie understands from those hate-filled eyes that he would hurt her mom if she dared to give him away.

Suzie's mom rounds the corner with a shocked, concerned look on her face. "There you are, sweetie. Why aren't you in bed with Hope?"

Ray quickly answers for her. "Aww, she was crowded and said that her little friend was taking all her covers." Ray patted Suzie's head, ruffling her curls. "It's okay now, Suzie. Go get your little friend out of bed so y'all can play."

Looking up at Ray, Suzie sees his bright smile as he yawns and stretches. *What a liar he is.*

"Come here, baby," Ray stretches his arms out toward Suzie's mom. "I missed you. Did you have a good night? Come cuddle with me." He pats the bed next to him.

Suzie glances at her mom as she gets out of the bed. She notices a funny, suspicious-type look on her mom's face. Suzie turns her head away as fast as she can and scurries out the door without looking back or hugging her mom.

"She's just in a hurry to go see her friend," Suzie hears Ray say as she walks across the living room into the kitchen. Suzie hopes her mom doesn't ask her about being in the bed with Ray. She would have to lie, because Suzie knows Ray would kill her mom if she told.

Suzie stands motionless in the doorway of her room. Hope sleeps peacefully in the bed, the hint of a smile on her face, as if having a pleasant dream.

Shame limps up behind Suzie. "This never happens to other girls, only you. It's because you're gross and disgusting," he taunts. Suzie creeps across the room until she is directly in front of Hope, then she quietly sits on the floor. Suzie likes Hope, but right that minute, she hates her too.

As she studies her face, anger wells up inside Suzie's chest. "She was awake last night," he says, "and she knows what happened. She just isn't going to say. She will tell all the girls at school and they will all hate and tease you," Fear suggests as he appears at her side.

Terrified but needing to know, Suzie whispers, "Hope, are you awake?"

Hope does not answer. She is fast asleep. Relieved, Suzie crawls in over her guest and pulls the covers over her shoulder. *Why can't I be like everyone else?*

"You are different. You're nasty." Shame answers. Suzie knew it was true.

The next evening, Suzie sits on her bed and colors in her Rainbow Bright coloring book, one leg folded under her and the other hanging loosely off the bed. Her mom had cooked fried chicken and mashed potatoes for dinner with corn on the cob. It was Suzie's favorite meal and she was full. Ray was smoking his drugs in the living room again, but tonight it smelled different. Suzie sees a heavy layer of smoke drifting down the hall. She notices that the smoke is a different color. Susie can hear her mom and Ray in the living room, and they are much louder than normal. She is concerned but knows she will get in trouble if she goes out to see what's happening.

As Suzie tries to color, she has trouble focusing on the page. The lines are fuzzy. Her head feels weird and when she looks up, the rooms spins. She senses someone looking at her from her curtained doorway. She knows that it's Ray, but she feels oddly indifferent about it. She can feel him looking at her even though she is staring at her color book. Again, a wave of dizziness comes over her. Almost like when she drinks the brown liquid for Ray. She closes her eyes and lets her head spin. It feels kind of good. She waits for it to go away.

Her mom doesn't work tonight, so she reminds herself that she is safe.

A dark, half-figure appears in her peripheral vision. She can barely make it out, so she turns and looks up to be sure. Suzie screams out in terror as a hideous creature lurks at her door. It looks like Ray, but his eyes are a glowing, yellow fire with red crust around them. His hand is deformed as he holds back the curtain, his knuckles are swollen and his fingernails long and sharp like grey daggers. Suzie jumps from her bed and runs to her closet, slamming shut the flimsy sliding glass door. Susie holds the door closed with all her strength. Screaming, she cries out in terror for her mom. Suzie can feel the monster right outside her closet door. She can hear him growling and coaxing her out. He wants to hurt her again. Out of sheer horror, Suzie pees herself. She's wet and too terrified to move. Trembling with fear, she presses her hands and feet against the back of the door and weeps.

On Sunday, Suzie attends church with Grams and Pops, just like always. This night is different though. After the evening service, they gather near the altar for prayer. The pastor encourages the grown-ups in the congregation to line up on either side of the center aisle and form a bridge with their hands clasped together, forming an archway. Then, from the youngest to the oldest, the kids are instructed to go to the back of the church and walk down the center aisle under the clasped hands of the adults. He called out their ages and the children smile huge smiles as they walk slowly into the tunnel of love. The children in the tunnel are prayed for and blessed by all the members on either side.

When the pastor calls for eight- and nine-year-olds, Suzie steps up. As she looks down the tunnel at the loving faces, she feels she might cry before she even enters the tunnel. Looking up at the mostly black congregation, she is overwhelmed by the love in their eyes.

"Come on, sweetie. Step up here. The Lord God Almighty is going to bless you."

Suzie puts her finger up to her lip and chews on the side of her nail as a huge lump forms in her throat. She walks cautiously into the tunnel.

"God bless you, my daughter," an old man says.

"Lord's gonna use you some day, beautiful child." A woman nods her head. The love in their hearts apparent as they speak.

"He has plans for you, don't you forget that, young lady!" "God will protect you and keep you safe."

Tears well up in Suzie's eyes as the lump in her throat swells.

"God will protect you. He will always keep you safe.

Don't doubt it," another man proclaims.

"God bless your coming and your going, child," the next grown up says.

Suzie blinks and the tears tumble down her face onto her dress.

"God, use this beautiful child for your glory," says the next. "Don't let her be harmed, Lord Jesus, protect her."

Another says, "Keep her from the enemy."

"Awe…you sweet thing, He loves you. He loves you so much."

Suzie wants God. She can feel His presence.

"Don't you cry, sweet baby girl. God is your ever-present help in times of trouble," the next lady proclaims with a determined and certain authority.

If she could have pushed a button and been able to walk up to God right that minute, Suzie would have, even if it meant never coming back. Suzie walks as slowly as she can, enjoying every second of this. She longingly soaks up every smidgen of the life-giving love that rains down as they speak.

"You are the head and not the tail. You are blessed and highly favored."

"Amen, amen. God gonna give you joy, little girl. You git ridda them tears."

As she steps through the last bridge of hands clasped above her head, a woman declares, "You're a good girl, and God loves you." She desperately wants to go back through the tunnel. She looks longingly down the aisle behind her as the other children follow.

The other children play and run around the church afterward, but not Suzie. She takes a seat on the altar and watches as the others go through the tunnel of love. She looks at their faces and listens to their blessings.

Make it Personal

Did you realize how much of a sexually abused child's sufferings happen inside his or their mind?

_____

_____

_____

Would you like to help a child like Travis or Suzie? Please stop now and pray about that.

_____

_____

_____

Will you pray for the minds of the wounded children in your life or sphere of influence?

_____

_____

_____

Do you think all pedophiles should remain on probation for life? What other earthly penalties or punishment do you think child abusers should receive? List below.

_____

_____

_____

Do you think God can be trusted to know a pedophile's heart and to judge him or her justly? Look up 2 Timothy 4:1 and meditate on it over the next few days. Memorize it and share it with others who need to trust that God will judge.

_____

_____

_____

Can you trust God enough to take Travis's and Suzie's abusers off your hook (that means letting go of all bitterness and vengeance, but it does not mean you shouldn't speak up or press charges and get them off the streets and protect others) and put them on God's hook, completely relying on God to deal with their heart?

_____

_____

_____

Do you need to forgive someone who hurt you too? Who was it? What did they do? Make a list; be thorough. Write in code if you need to...God knows.

_____

_____

_____

Notes

CHAPTER 15

The Perpetrators ...Walking it Out

My son, do not despise the Lord's discipline and do
not resent His rebuke, because the Lord disciplines
those He loves, as a Father the son He delights in.

(Proverbs 3:11-12 NIV)

Kelsey walked into the Angel Reach office where I sat filling out daily reports and asked if I had a minute. As I looked up I noticed her puffy cheeks and red nose. "What's wrong?" I asked, knowing in my heart it had to be about Eric, a young man and client of Angel Reach whom she was mentoring.

She sat down in the chair next to my desk and asked me if I could possibly have a talk with Eric. He had tried to commit suicide again, the third attempt in as many years. Kelsey and her husband had mentored Eric for five years, and when I say that she loved him, I can honestly tell you that she loved him like her own.

My heart ached with sadness as I tried to explain to Kelsey that I wasn't qualified to counsel Eric about suicide. I wasn't a certified counselor or a psychologist and lacked even the most basic training in that area. I reminded her that I could say something hoping to be helpful, but instead trigger some unexpected weakness or memory, only making things worse. I assured her that she should speak to the psychologist Eric had been seeing for years.

Kelsey was desperate. The doctors he had been seeing didn't seem to be helping him. She said she had listened in on some of the Life Skills classes I taught on Monday evenings, and felt that because I was good with the kids, I could possibly help him. Tears slid down her cheeks as she begged for my help.

I don't know if there is anything in this world more persuasive than a crying mom trying to get help for a child. Finally, after many attempts to dissuade her, and against my better judgement, I agreed to have a talk with Eric.

As I sat alone in the small, cozy office, I peered out the huge window facing the street and watched her approach Eric, who was sitting in the passenger seat of her car. Through the huge wrought-iron fence, I could see her stylish skirt blowing around her slim figure in the warm breeze. In her forties, Kelsey was attractive, cheerful, and energetic. Eric was really lucky to have such a warm, committed mentor.

Eric was also a kind, friendly sort. He was rarely an issue for the Angel Reach staff and very soft spoken. I had taken him to work and picked him up every week for several months, so he and I had talked about everything under the sun. Even with all the time we had spent together, we had never spoken of his suicide attempts. I watched as she gestured to him to get out, and he opened the car door and stepped out onto the grass. I felt dread at the thought of saying something that could make things worse.

I prayed as he headed up the walkway toward the front of the house. "God please help me to help him and not hurt him in any way. God give me the right words ..."

Eric opened the gate and headed up the stairs. I recalled a conversation from a year before when he had told me he had been molested as a six-year-old by a family member and how he had ended up in foster care. His family life was full of violence, drugs, and a relative who should have loved and protected him. Instead, that man stole his innocence.

Knowing that I was talking to someone who had been sexually molested caused me to consider that maybe the pain from that experience was what was eating him alive. As Eric came in and hugged me, I determined to tell him my dream and see if he needed to forgive his perpetrator and let go of the bitterness from his heartbreaking past. Eric sat down next to the small round table in the middle of the room and leaned over, resting his blond curly head on his palm.

"Hi", I said. "I'm glad to see you up and about after that stint in the hospital last week. A whole bottle of Tylenol?" I raised my eyebrow and bit my lip as I tilted my head. "You're lucky you are still alive and have a functioning liver. You know you need that, right?"

I tried to joke as we were both used to each other's personalities. Eric knew I cared about him. "Tell me what's wrong," I said.

Eric mumbled a laundry list of problems with his ex-girlfriend, his job, again the ex-girlfriend, his friends, the ex-girlfriend, his boss, and finally the ex-girlfriend.

"All boys have girl trouble," I told him. I mused that normally young men didn't attempt suicide because some girl cheated on them. He shrugged his shoulders and distractedly brushed some (invisible to me) lint off his jeans. "I want to tell you about a dream I had, okay?"

"That doesn't sound too bad," he replied, looking up at me and grinning a bit. He leaned back and got comfortable, crossing his arms in front of his chest.

I told Eric of the beautiful peaceful sky that I screamed into for help that quiet morning last April. I recalled for him the hate-filled, rancid feelings I had while flying over the houses and shooting the perpetrators. Eric listened intently as I described the man in the shower with the small child. As I was telling him about the accusations I made at God, asking Him why He didn't help us, Eric's face changed. He started fidgeting in his seat and looked past me out the window. I knew I was on the right track. Eric was hurting.

Deciding that he needed to forgive his perpetrator was easy after seeing his reaction to my anger and disgust as I drifted toward the man in the shower who was molesting the small child. I told the story to him exactly as I told it in the first chapter of this book. When I got to the part of the story after the dream when I was with Alison and had shown her the video of the Angel Reach kids, which included him, I shared how upset I got when Alison told me her brother was raping her almost every single day. I told him how lost in sorrow I was. I repeated what Alison had said about her brother being God's child too. As I told him how Alison believed that God's heart was breaking for the choices her brother made to rape her, and that God loved her brother very much, Eric looked down at the floor.

A tear slid down his face onto his white-and-green collared shirt. Sensing that Eric was ready to possibly forgive the man who had stolen his innocence by sexually abusing him, I rolled my office chair closer to him and put my hand on his arm. "Eric, can you forgive that man who hurt you when you were six years old?" I asked. "It is not for him; it is for you."

He didn't respond, so I told him about Cain and Abel and how I would love my son, even if he murdered his brother. I knew Eric had a younger brother whom he constantly talked about. "Think about it," I continued. "If it were *your* younger brother, who you send money and gifts to all the time, who had done what your perpetrator did, could you hate your younger brother? Would or could you just stop loving him?" The tears rolled off his face, but he shook his head. "I'm going to hell anyways, so I may as well just get it over with…the sooner the better!" He leaned back in his chair and abruptly turned his head to the side.

I sat back and searched my heart for a reason why the conversation took that radical turn. "What do you think you have done that would cause you to sentence yourself to hell? Is it something that Jesus's sacrifice on the cross can't save you from?"

I never suspected what Eric then eked out through his choking sobs.

"I hurt …I molested … a little girl who lived in my foster home when I was twelve years old. And God will never forgive me!"

Stunned, a huge lump filled my throat. Eric was obviously overcome with pain and self-loathing, but not as a result of being molested by his family member. I never would have shared my dream or any story where I was trying to brutally exterminate the perpetrators if I'd suspected for one second that sweet, gentle Eric might have done that after he himself had been molested.

I can be so naive.

I could feel heat rising in my face. There I was—sitting not only with a wounded young man, who had been molested (by a loved and trusted member of his family) as a child, but with someone who was broken-hearted over his admittedly grievous choices. Eric obviously knew even at twelve that what he did was wrong. And somewhere out there was a teenage girl still dealing with the trauma of being molested by him at six years old, as Eric had been.

The groanings of Eric's excruciating sobs were breaking my heart and jolted me back into the moment. "Eric, I understand now. You need to forgive your perpetrator, but just as importantly, you need to forgive yourself."

Eric's immediate response was, "I can't. I'm disgusting. God will never forgive me. How can He? I'll pay for what I did. I'll rot in hell!"

I explained that that is exactly why Jesus died on the cross for us, and that if he believes Jesus dying on the cross wasn't a good enough sacrifice for his sin, he was calling God's plan and Jesus's blood not good enough. I assured Eric that he was loved, and that the fact that he was brokenhearted over his sin was good. I reminded him that even though God punished Cain for murdering his brother, He still showed him love and grace. I told him about David and how he took a man's wife and had her husband murdered, but God restored David to Himself when David repented. Then we talked about trying to locate the girl he had molested so he could ask for forgiveness and offer restitution. Finally, we called Kelsey in and shared what Eric had confessed with her. In all those years, he had never told anyone, not even his doctors or counselors, what he had done.

Within a few weeks of that conversation, I moved to Arizona to help my mom for a while. About a year later, while visiting Texas I went out to lunch with Kelsey to catch up with her and tell her that I was thinking about writing this book, and that I hoped to include Eric's story. She shared that there had been no more suicide attempts after our talk that day in the office, and that shortly after I left, Eric had asked to speak at one of the Monday night Life-skills classes. He gave a testimony to the twenty-three aged-out foster youths, then clients of Angel Reach. He shared his story of being sexually abused and how he had hated his perpetrator. He heartbrokenly told them that even after he knew how bad it hurt to be molested, he did the same thing and sexually abused a little girl when he was twelve. He cried as he shared his story and the realization of how Jesus died on the cross for him and that he needed to forgive himself and his perpetrator, because he wanted God to forgive him. He shared how he had wanted to make restitution for what he had done.

Kelsey said that after he was done speaking, nineteen of the twenty-three kids came up and asked for prayer. Not because they had been molested, although they all had been. They came for prayer because they also had molested younger kids in the foster system, and they were dying inside because of their guilt. Kelsey said it was the most freeing, heart-breaking night they had ever had.

I was astonished.

Please understand that these foster youth have no one to hug them and teach them about good touch. Most of them grow up with a state employee telling them to turn the music down and stay in their room. Their mother and father is a TV, and they are looking for love and affection any way they can get it. It is a breeding ground for abuse. Do you want to help? Please foster a child and give them a safe place to sleep. Teach them the Scriptures in Matthew 18 and help them to make good choices. Please remember that if you have children of your own, you need to protect them first and that will take some extra diligence on your part.

In the years that followed my dream, I have been shocked at how often I thought the dream would help a victim to forgive the perpetrator, only to realize that God had other plans. To my astonishment, the perpetrator was often where God was aiming.

In Psalms 51:17 (AMP) David says, "My [only] sacrifice [acceptable] to God is a broken spirit; A broken and contrite heart [broken with sorrow for sin, thoroughly penitent], such, O God, You will not despise."

It is true. He knows our hearts. No matter what we have

done, He loves us. I ask myself if my son were a Nazi war criminal, would I hate him? I can honestly say I *would* hate that my child had grown up to become a deceived, pride- filled mass murderer. But my heart would ache for him and what he could have been. I would admit he deserved to die and be in hell separated from God for eternity, and I'm not certain I could even bear to look at his face, but my soul would cry for him. It would hurt. I recall Corrie ten Boom's book *The Hiding Place* where she learns from her sister, Betsy, how to love and pray for her tormentors, offering to love and care for them after the war. This is the kind of love God calls us to as we become like Him. He wants us to know what it feels like to be like Him as we truly discover how to love our enemies.

Just for the record Eric was twelve (a minor) when he offended, and the statute of limitations (not that it applies) was up. The best we could do was offer him support as he decided how to make restoration and pursue repentance. I believe telling his story and confessing his offence unlocked the door to healing.

It was about 8:15 in the evening, and just minutes after I had finished typing the chapter about the dream, when a friend called and told me that her estranged husband had just called her and told her a story about a dream I had. Excuse me? My dream? Yes, the very dream I had just spent the whole day writing about. What? I was completely caught off guard that the story of my dream had reached her ears.

My friend explained that her husband had been deeply moved when hearing about it. He was emotionally broken over the thought that God's heart is breaking for the perpetrator, and he had called her crying. I stopped breathing momentarily as she continued to tell me that her mother had told her husband about my dream. Now, I was even more shocked. At this point, I had probably told fewer than ten people about the dream, and one of them was my friend's dear mother, an eighty-nine-year-old woman suffering from dementia. I visited her regularly in the assisted living facility.

My friend and her husband were separated over some serious marital issues. Because of some of the things he had done (I won't be specific), I knew he struggled with sexual sin and had been in that dark place for years. My friend left him in order to have male members of the church hold a mirror to his face and help him address his sin. What he did didn't involve any children and wasn't an issue for authorities, but was definitely perverted sexual sin in God's eyes. His wife was careful not to spread details, but some things had to be discussed, and I helped her when she left the house and moved to a safe place. What made this so shocking was that he was very often the one counseling others to get their Christian act together. He was what I would have called a "man of God," appearing rigidly disciplined and upright to the outside world.

When my friend told me a few vague, but blunt facts that led to her leaving her husband, I have to say, I was flabbergasted. I never saw it coming. Not them—the "have it all together" family. But what she confided in me earned him a special spot in my "sexual pervert" box. Yes, that's correct. You see, I have these boxes I put people in (not recommended). I have lots of boxes (God and I are working on this).

About a month after I helped her move and seperate from her husband, my very upset friend called again to tell me her husband was against our friendship. He believed I was in rebellion against God because I had divorced my first husband. What? Seriously? Can you hear the wheels screeching and burning rubber (on my spirit tires) as I emotionally hit the brakes?

That hurt so badly. He had no clue as to what I had endured, and how hard I tried to save my marriage from the horrors of drug addiction. In my mind, I pictured myself pinching the skin on his neck as if he were a kitten, lifting him out of the sexual pervert box, and moving him several boxes over to the "stupid, sexual pervert" box, where I had left him all those months.

Back to the evening my friend called—the day I had typed

up the dream chapter. As she continued telling me about her husband's remorse, I was thinking, "Ugh, I haven't thought about him for months. And I've never thought of praying for him. That's right, not once. Even after all I had learned about God's love toward all his children. You want to know why? Because I don't like him. He passed harsh judgement on me, and I didn't deserve it.

I suffered horribly losing my husband to drugs. Picture me watching helplessly as my hopes for a Christian marriage and family glugged down the toilet right before my tear-filled eyes. My three sons and my step-daughter's lives and hearts being torn to pieces … tiny pieces! Watching my husband waste away on drugs was the worst pain I have ever suffered, and I have mascara stains all over every set of sheets I own to prove it. In the end, my husband abandoned me for the drugs and the affections of numerous other women who didn't mind the drugs, and so we divorced.

As I was thinking these self-condoning and self-condemning bitter thoughts and trying to mask the fact (by putting my hand tightly over the mouthpiece of the phone) that I was ugly crying, I realized that my friend was asking if we could get together and have coffee and do some catching up so I could tell her all about the dream and my book. Oh, coals of fire!

I hung up the phone and let the truth sink into my pores. I took deep slow breaths and tried to control my anguish, but the tears still flowed. It was dead quiet, and the house was so still. There was a presence in the room with me and I could feel Him. The Holy Spirit just sat there with me (no, I could not see Him) in a spiritual way as I got a good look at myself. I, for the first time, earnestly prayed for my friend's husband. And right then my angry heart opened to the love of God for him. I thought of Adam and Eve's two sons and how I love my boys. Could I pray for her husband like I might pray for my own child gone astray? I was alone with this sudden realization that God had given me insight into His love for the "bad guy," this perpetrator, and how much God loves those children, His children, like I love mine. Yet, I had plopped my friend's husband with all of his faults and his judgment of me right square in the middle of the "You're a waste of human flesh" also known as the "stupid pervert box." The thing is, I thought I was doing so well. Really, I did. I was praying for people I heard about on the news like I'd never done before, every time I heard a bad report. Well, not every time, but the majority of the time.

I had changed and often when I heard a horrible newsflash, immediately after praying for the victims, I started praying for the person who had offended as well. There was a young nineteen-year-old in my town who was driving drunk and killed several people in a family. I asked myself, "How would I feel if that were my son who drove drunk and killed precious people?" Then I prayed for the loss of the people left devastated by his bad judgment. But this time, I also prayed earnestly for him (the offender) and his family. I still prayed for the children at Angel Reach, but now I prayed for their offenders. I prayed for the grandfather who pimped out his eight-year-old granddaughter in the backseat of a car in a Walmart parking lot, knowing that he will face the judgment of God if he doesn't fully comprehend and reject wholeheartedly his sin. My heart cries out, "Can that grandfather ever understand the damage he has done?" I truly don't know. But still I prayed for him.

Can God make the damage done to that girl go completely away, or be completely healed? I believe He will. I believe that when Jesus said to Mary, "Didn't I tell you if you only believe you will see the glory of God" (John 11:40). And the miracle of Lazarus coming to life is the picture of our healing. He will give us new bodies that don't have a trace of the memory of the abuse we have suffered. All we have to do is trust Him until that day.

It's hard to pray for these people who abuse their children, steal, rape, murder, cheat, and lie, but I do. At the same time, I realize that there is often this huge, huge hole in my love bucket. There was my friend's husband, God's child, fully deceived and given over to a demented sexual spirit, and there was me with only disdain, condemnation, and judgment to offer him. Ugh.

Isn't it just like God to wait until the very day I spend eight hours writing about this dream, and three years since I had the dream, to have a friend call whose husband heard about the dream from a woman who is suffering from dementia, whom I would have bet couldn't even comprehend my words. I was immediately convicted and aware of God moving in this circumstance to reveal to me that my heart was still in need of repair. I always need repair. How could I look right past my friend's husband who desperately needs the knowledge of God's great love for him when that's the very lesson I'm writing about? I'll tell you how. It's because it is much easier to pray for those who hurt strangers, even though that's not easy. I did and can do that very freely now. But, let them hurt us, let them touch that sacred or severe place of pain in our heart or mind, and it's a different story. I repented that night. I pray that He will help us to love like He loves.

I want to be crystal clear here and point out that you can both offer forgiveness and love to anyone, even a seemingly hardened perpetrator, and still 100 percent hold them accountable for their actions. It is not wrong to expect them to face consequences for their offences. In fact, it is the best thing for everyone involved, especially the children. I personally don't think any adult who molests a child should ever be released out into the general population again, regardless of their spiritual growth. Our children are too precious and we owe them stricter laws for offenders. We should hope and pray that the perpetrators come to a full knowledge and understanding of their offense, with brokenhearted repentance, and still keep them off of the streets. It's not just about "saying you are sorry." Remember…only God knows their hearts, and He is never fooled.

Make it Personal

Do you earnestly pray (as if they were your own children) for those who hurt and offend you? List three reasons why you think God wants us to do this. Also list three reasons you feel hesitant to earnestly pray for a person who offends or hurts others.

_____

_____

_____

Were you surprised that Eric, like so many other foster kids, molested a younger child, even after he had been molested and knew how bad it hurt?

_____

_____

Were you surprised that Eric was so repulsed by his behavior that he tried numerous times to kill himself? List other actions that you think might make someone feel unforgivable.

_____

_____

_____

Do you have anything in your past or your present that makes you feel unforgiveable? List below.

_____

_____

_____

List three reasons you think the Bible tells us to confess our sins one to another? What happened when Eric shared his mistakes? Are you willing to share your faults and mistakes to help others? Why? Why not?

_____

_____

_____

What happens if we all just leave things the way they are? List anything you fear might happen if you were to share your past mistakes openly.

_____

_____   ᵃ

_____

Why do you think it was so easy for me to stuff my friend's husband in a box, slap a title on it and leave him there without even a thought of a prayer? What did I lack? How might I have responded if that were my son?

_____

_____

_____

Notes

CHAPTER 16

Travis and Suzie
Monopoly and Mayhem

*"Do people really care what you have been through?
Do they really want to understand you? Or, do
they just want you to keep quiet?"*

— *Travis*

Travis hears a car pull into the driveway. It's his sister, Adrian. Although she has lived on her own for years, she often comes to visit and spend the night. They often set up the Monopoly game, and this night is no exception.

Within thirty minutes, Adrian owns all the railroads, utilities, and hotels on the board. Travis is the first one to go broke, so Theresa offers to let him play with her as a team. Cindy gives them her dwindling dollars to help them beat their older sister.

"It's not fair for y'all to gang up on me like this," Adrian protests.

"Geez, Adrian. You're twenty-one. You could give us a break, you know," Theresa teases.

Soon, Theresa and Travis are out of money and all four of them are picking up the pieces and putting the game away. Adrian asks where she should sleep.

"We can't sleep with her snoring," both Theresa and Cindy chime in.

"I'll sleep on the couch," Adrian offers.

"No, you can have Travis's bed and he can sleep on his floor," their step-mom says in her firm manner. "I don't want anyone sleeping on the couches. It'll mess them up."

Travis makes a place to sleep on his bedroom floor, giving Adrian the bed like his step mom had instructed. As Adrian pulls back the covers and gets into Travis' bed, he recalls something he hadn't thought about in years. Although it had stopped when they moved in with their new mom, the thought crosses his mind, *Is Adrian going to hold me and put my hand on her breast like before?*

Travis feels a familiar presence in the room, like something or someone else is in there with them. Adrian is older now. She's twenty-one. Surely. she won't do it. But Travis can't stop thinking about the cuddling when Adrian used to hold him when he was five and six. He gets confused and tells himself to go to sleep and forget about it. Finally, he dozes off.

A couple hours later, he wakes up when Adrian gets out of bed to go to the bathroom. When she returns, instead of getting back into her bed, she lays next to Travis on the floor. She lifted his covers and gets underneath them. And she's naked!

The presence is there again. The same feeling he gets when Kenny molests him. Adrian scoots up close to him. This is an all-too-familiar experience to Travis, who is used to being awakened in the middle of the night and used like a rag against his will.

Adrian reaches around him and touches his privates until he responds. He has a small frame for his age and very skinny, so Adrian easily picks him up and puts him face down on top of her.

Travis knows this is wrong, but he is used to being mistreated and used. He doesn't really know anything about girls other than what boys at school say. He hasn't seen any R-rated movies, bad magazines, or even held a girl's hand. He has no idea what to do.

Adrian places his hips where she could move him around and tries to put him where she wants him. But quickly gives up and pushes him off, dropping him next to her. Then without a word she gets up, grabs her robe, and goes to the restroom.

What happened to the cuddling? Travis suddenly feels the sharp, stabbing pain of rejection. His mind races. *Did I do something wrong? Why do I feel awful? Is that it? Why doesn't she speak to me? Why didn't she hold me like before? Is that love?*

His confusion skyrockets. Kenny tries to kiss, pet, and love on him in spite of how much Travis protests, cries, and hates him. Adrian doesn't even want to hold him. Travis feels a heart-breaking, disappointing and bewildering turmoil inside. He wants Adrian to come back. He wants to cuddle and be held. *Maybe she'll decide to come and hold me and talk to me.* He hopes she will.

It doesn't take long for his confused feelings about the whole encounter to turn to disgust and hate. The shame and perceived rejection of being sexually attracted to his sister and wanting her attention and cuddling, but then her pushing him aside, is more than his young mind can bear. It feels like dangled affection, and he is starving for it. He knows Kenny doesn't care, because Kenny knows he hates it. Kenny forces him, even though he cries. Now, after his first, brief encounter with a female, to realize he wants it desperately and she doesn't care either... she is just like Kenny. Using him. *I'm just a piece of meat!*

Travis' sexual response to Adrian's molesting burns his soul like a hot branding iron. Just as if it had stamped the words, "sick, disgusting, dirty little pervert" in his flesh. Now Shame and Guilt have more ammunition to pummel him with, and it reinforces the tormenting thought that he is not worth loving.

Travis is, of course, at the age where most boys start thinking and fantasizing about the opposite sex. This encounter pours gasoline on that smoldering fire. He hates the feelings he has when he thinks about girls at school, because they always lead to his only feminine sexual memory, the night of rejection with Adrian. What should be normal physical attractions to the opposite sex are fretful times of self-loathing. His sexual desire literally disgusts him. He hates himself for wanting so badly the very thing that Kenny had coached him, drilled him, and teased him about for years. He doesn't want to want it. It is always so nasty the way Kenny grins when he asks about girls. Adding to that is the shame of his twelve-year-old body's unprovoked response to his sister, which makes him feel more disturbingly filthy and dirty every day. Travis can't think about the opposite sex without Adrian and Kenny popping up in his head. He wants to think about girls and not have those images bursting in and taking over his mind. Travis feels robbed and cheated. Travis is angry.

It doesn't take long after the incident with Adrian for the tormenting spirits to come, but now there is a new one. The new arrival is much more treacherous than the others, but it couldn't have come unless the others had prepared a way for its presence. Immediately upon experiencing any sexual desire, Shame dives in upon Travis like a vulture on a carcass.

"You know you would do it again. You know you want it. You are so sick. What's wrong with you?" Shame is now so much a part of Travis that when Shame appears, he resembles dead, branching limbs extending out of Travis' sides and wrapping around his torso. Shame's distorted head tilts to one side as he presses his gruesome, gray, lifeless lips against the side of Travis's head. "She's your sister. You're worse than Kenny. You're evil and no one knows it. But you do, don't you?" Shame whispers.

Travis is sitting on the edge of his bed when Guilt joins Shame and creeps across his bed, leaning in close to him. Guilt's hoarse, dry voice scratches out the words, "God will never forgive you. You have done the worst thing there is to do. You're going to hell."

Hopelessness slinks across the floor closer to Travis and, looking up into his tear-stained face, reminds him again like he has done before, "You can't stop. You can't stop wanting it, you're addicted, you need it, and you can't stop Kenny either. You're ruined. You will never be normal. No one will ever want you. Kenny will never stop."

Deceit pushes his way past Hopelessness and Guilt, shoving his face into Travis' and snarls, "You're going to be exactly like him. You are going to hurt people just like Kenny hurts you. Kenny told you, didn't he? He said you would love it and he was right. He knows you. You are just like him."

Travis's hands are now clasped tightly to both sides of his head. He is trying to squeeze the thoughts out of his brain. "I have to make this stop!" Travis sobs. Travis hits his forehead with the palm of his hand over and over as hard as he can, as if he could knock the awful thoughts right out of his head. "I can't take this anymore. I can't, I can't!" he cries out into the empty house. "I can't take it!"

Warning...if you have a friend or loved one who committed suicide, you might want to skip to the last paragraph of Travis' story or move on to Suzie's part of this chapter.

Slowly, a gray fog pours into the room from every crack and crevice. The other tormentors clear the way, retreating to the edges of the room and remaining silent as they watch Suicide fill every molecule of space around Travis like a ghostly cloud.

"You poor boy," whispers the soft, soothing voice of Suicide. His beautiful, smooth face appears out of the smoky, silver mist when he speaks and then vanishes again into the dark gray softness as it folds and rolls around, circling Travis' body head to toe. "Get the knife, Travis," he coaxes with an air of confidence. "You can make this stop," he whispers.

Travis is exhausted. In a complete daze of traumatic shock, Travis leans over and picks up the box from his headboard where he keeps the big knife he got for Christmas. Wiping the tears from his face, he squeezes his eyes tight, forcing the tears to turn loose and fall so he can see. He takes the blue-pearl-covered knife out of the box and opens it, exposing the blade. He runs his thumb over the shiny, sharp metal.

"Cut yourself, Travis, just cut it off," Suicide softly whispers, lulling him like a drug promising a sweet release. "It'll be all over soon. You'll bleed and then you'll go to sleep." Suicide quickly swirls around Travis to the other side of his head. Interrupting Travis' dazed exhaustion, Suicide demands in a shrieking whisper, "Cut it off, Travis. It's all they want. If it were gone, they would leave you alone. Cut it off!"

Travis pulls his pants off and places the sharp blade of the knife under his penis, close to his body. He grabs the object of all of his suffering. Travis inhales Suicide's sweet aroma deep into his soul.

"Just cut it off. Hurry! Do it now," Suicide urges.

The others come closer and join in, reciting the lies they've been spewing for years. It sounds like a symphony. The crescendo a sublime, anxious, seducing lullaby of death.

"Just cut it off. Just cut it off. Just pull up on the blade fast and this will all be over. No more pain. Kenny and Adrian will leave you alone."

Will I die? God, I want to die! Will I go to hell? I just want to die and go to heaven with Mom. Travis' frantic thoughts added to the confusion swirling around him.

Deception torments him. "You're just a piece of meat and no one loves you or cares for you except for that. Cut it! Cut it! God doesn't even love you. If He did, He would have helped you. You asked Him over and over. He never hears you. You begged him. Hurry. Cut it. Now. Do it and you'll be free. No one will hurt you again."

Travis is certain that Suicide's beautiful promises are the most truth-filled words he has ever heard. Travis's hands tremble and he takes very slow, deep breaths.

"You can have control. You'll show them all. No one can force you again."

Travis looks straight into Suicide's compassionate eyes, and he wants it—he wants control. He rests his weary head in Suicide's embrace. Travis pulls up on the blade and feels the knife on his flesh. Tears fall and he begs, "God, please… please forgive me …"

"My heart was like a stone, but somewhere deep inside of me, I desperately wanted him to love and protect me. I can't even believe I'm saying this. It's so confusing."

—Suzie

Suzie climbs the tree at the end of the dirt drive where their trailer house sits. She lets the sizzling summer breeze blow through her curls as she gets comfortable in the branches and thinks about the new apartment they will be moving to next week. *I'll miss Hope, but I'll have a new room with a door and there will be lots of kids there. Maybe I can get a bike or some roller skates to play on in the parking lot. They have a small playground and a pool. There's a McDonald's right next door.*

She will miss Kitty and the creek and crawfishing and Mrs. Evans, the old lady who often lets her come in for lunch and...."SUZIE!"

Suzie startles at the sound of Ray calling her name. She thinks about hiding in the branches, but it's too late. He has already spotted her.

Darn it! He sees me. I'm such an idiot! Suzie scolds herself as she turns to climb down the tree. She takes her time as her short legs make it difficult. And she's in no hurry. If he is calling her into the house in the middle of the day, that means her mom has already left for work. Suzie is thankful that her ears are still sore from when she got them pierced, so she has a good excuse for Ray not to kiss them.

Ray has her mom's favorite salsa and chips sitting on a tray on the bed with two Cokes. Ray never let Suzie snack, so she knows he is up to something. He is so stingy with the food that she always feels like she's stealing when she takes something out of the refrigerator.

The TV in the bedroom is on. The look in Ray's eyes is sick and depraved and, of course, there are brand new magazines on the bed. Suzie thinks about the big beautiful tree and hates herself for getting caught. Just once, she'd love to have a day of peace.

Later that afternoon, Suzie is sitting at the creek edge. She sees something move and turns her head to focus on it. She spots a cricket. Normally she would hop up and catch it right away, but her mood is different today. She just watches it for a bit. It jumps, landing right in front of her. Suzie slams her hand over it and clutches it in her grip. She can feel it struggling between her ring finger and her palm. She lifts her hand close to her face and looks at its tiny legs sticking out. Suzie doesn't smile or talk to it like she usually does. She doesn't try to put it in a container to show her mom. She just watches it struggle. Suzie watches it for the longest time. Then without much thought or reason, Suzie reaches up with her other hand and carefully pulls one of its legs off. She immediately looks around for a stick. Suzie finds a sharp rock and tries to poke it into the abdomen of the insect.

Suzie loosens her grip and now has the cricket just pinned by its head. Suzie feels so angry inside, and watching the cricket squirm makes her want to smash it into mush. Suddenly, Suzie slings it away from her overhanded as hard as she can. "See what you made me do?" she yells as tears run down her face. Suzie looks around again, but this time she wants to kill something bigger, like a worm or a caterpillar.

She finds a lot of bugs that day and she sticks them all. She stabs caterpillars with a rusty nail she found. She watches them writhe and twist. She doesn't know why, but it makes her feel strong, like she is the boss. It makes her feel better.

It wasn't until later that night as she lay in bed that the sting of guilt assaults her heart. She remembers what Ray had done that day and she desperately hates the fact that for the first time it had felt good to her. She hates Ray and wishes he would die, just like those bugs. She hates herself too. Suzie then remembers the worms and how they squirmed; she recalls how the crickets had struggled to get away. She wants Ray to feel that pain. But, Suzie hates that she had hurt the bugs and she sobs. At the very same time she desperately wishes she had something else she could destroy. Suzie grabs Barbie and bends her arms as hard as she can as she grits her teeth and groans. Her hands are shaking, Suzie is furious.

That night she cries hard, but no one hears her.

When Grams pulls her car into the parking lot of the new apartment to drop Suzie off that next Sunday evening, it is immediately obvious that something is going on. Suzie's mom sits outside on the tailgate of their truck, flicking her cigarette onto the pavement. Hopping down, she presses her sandal onto the butt and mashes it. Before Suzie knows what is happening, she's in the front seat of the truck between her mom and Jeanie, one of her mom's friends. They were going to find Ray.

"He better not be at her house. I've done everything for him. I know he's sleeping with her. I know he is! How can he be doing this to me?"

Suzie looks up at her mom and sees her wipe tears off her stressed but still beautiful face. They head down a dirt road. Her mom is driving very slow.

"Can you see his car?" her mother asked Jeanie.

"Yep, there it is." Jeanie points to the side of a small A-frame house. It was almost dark, and you could just make out Ray's small, beat-up Buick parked under the trees.

"I can't believe this!"

"You can't go in there! He'll kill you," Jeanie warned.

"What am I going to do? That sorry witch is trying to steal my man!" her mom wails, her sweet young face distorted with anguish.

Suzie realizes what Ray is probably doing with this other woman in the strange house—the same thing he does with her when her mom is at work.

Suzie's thoughts run wild. *What if Mom finds out that Ray does that stuff to me? Will she hate me just like she hates that woman in the house?* Suzie looks at the steps and the porch leading to the painted red front door. *I want to see her. What does she look like? Maybe she is like the girls in the magazines. Why doesn't he love my mom? Mom is as pretty as the girls in the magazines. Why does he do this to me and that lady? I never want Mom to know. I can't make my mom cry.* A lump forms in Suzie's throat, and she knows she will never tell her. Tears start to well in Suzie's eyes as she realizes that she is the hated and despised...she is the "other woman."

Once settled in the new apartment, Suzie realizes that she can't get away as easily or as often as she could in the trailer where her bedroom was close to the back door. At the apartment, she has to cross in front of Ray to get to the door, which is right next to the TV and the only way out of the apartment. Ray is always in the living room.

Suzie is hungry, but there isn't much to eat in the new place, either. No fruit, Ding-Dongs, or bags of chips for snacking like at Grams and Pops'. Suzie searches the shelves of the refrigerator and grabs a piece of bologna out of the package, hiding it under her shirt till she gets to her room. Suzie's room is like it has always been. No decorations or pretty matching curtains. Just plain, except for her old, worn-out Strawberry Shortcake comforter and her Scooby Doo fleece blanket, which are two of Suzie's favorite things. It is summertime, and although the days are usually long, for Suzie, the nights are often longer.

His bed or her bed, Suzie can't remember which they were in, but she remembers the day. It started in the living room as she asked to go out and play.

"Come here," Ray says as he put his cigarette out in the ashtray and lifts her small, nine-year-old body onto his while he stretches out on the couch.

Ray gropes her crotch even though they are both fully clothed. He shoves his tongue deep into Suzie's ear as Suzie fights back the nausea. Vomit wants to choke her throat. Within minutes, he is grabbing the magazines off the top shelf of the bathroom and handing Suzie her mother's lingerie. Suzie knows the drill and sits down on the bed in her mom's nighty to look at the naked woman in the magazine. Soon she is on top of him, naked and nauseous, but he is in control. Before he gets what he wants, a loud knock is heard at the front door. They both hear Grams very distinctive southern drawl.

"Hey y'all, open up."

Ray's expression immediately flips to furious anger and he glares at Suzie as if she is the devil herself. This is almost as disconcerting as her Grams' impatient yelling. "Hellooowa! I know you're in there. Come on already."

Ray is tossing Suzie's clothes at her and grabbing his jeans. "Coming, just a minute," he barks as he pulls his pants up and slicks his hair in place with one hand while he scoops up the magazines and shoves them under the bed with the other.

Suzie is just as fast and tosses her mom's lingerie into the open closet, pulling the door closed. Ray is on his knees in front of Suzie, grabbing her shirt and pulling it over her head as she steps into her white shorts. Suzie looks at Ray's panicked face. It is priceless. How she wishes she could freeze it that way. He now looks like he wants to throw up when minutes ago it was her who wanted to puke.

Once dressed, Suzie runs out into the living room and waits, glancing back toward Ray, who is only ten or so steps behind her. She looks at him for the signal to open the door and, in perfect form, Ray puts his first finger to his mouth and warns her with a look as he squints his eyes and reaches for the door knob.

Later that very afternoon, Suzie is playing at Grams in the spare room where Grams keeps all her toys and where she sleeps when she stays over at Grams' house. Every few minutes, Suzie returns to her grandmother's side as Grams watches "Little House on the Prairie." Suzie perches on the side of Grams' recliner, one leg up and one leg down as she brushes her Barbie's stiff, shiny hair. The music coming from the TV is frightening. There's a little girl with brown wavy hair walking through the woods.

"Who is that girl, Grams?" Suzie nervously asks.

"It's Sylvia, honey," Grams looks at Suzie. "You should go play, honey," Grams coaxes as she glances toward the bedroom.

Suzie sees the birds on the TV screen suddenly fly in every direction, spooked by something that is following the little girl in the woods. A man's hand cups over the little girl's mouth when she tries to scream, and the little girl's flowers fall out of her hand to the ground. Suzie's heart is suddenly pounding, and her eyes are glued to the TV.

"I know what is happening to that girl," Suzie blurts out as if it were happening to her right that second. Suzie's cheeks flush and get hot as she realizes that Grams heard her. She didn't mean to say it aloud, but the words flew out of her mouth like a trapped bird darting from a cage. Suzie instantly knows by the look on Gram's face that she may have to lie to explain her sudden outburst. Suzie has to think fast.

"You do?" Grams looks at Suzie with a quizzical look, raising both eyebrows and then holding her breath as their eyes stay locked tight on each other. "Do you think that has happened to you?" Grams suddenly straightens up and turns her body toward Suzie. The look on Grams face turning to deep, authentic concern.

Suzie has never once thought out what she might say if an adult besides her mom asks her about what was happening. She certainly never entertained the thought that someone might be understanding or sympathetic. Suzie immediately thinks of her mother's anger in the truck, when she was looking for Ray and the other woman a few weeks back.

"Your mom is going to hate you forever," Deceit yells at the top of his lungs. His huge, gaping mouth is right next to Suzie's head.

"You're a liar. They know you lie sometimes, so your mother won't believe anything you say," Shame whispers with a relaxed confidence that causes Deceit to turn frantically and growl like a mad dog.

Suzie turns her head slowly and looks into her Grams' eyes. *Even if Mom hates me, Grams will still love me.*

Suzie realizes at that very moment that she can tell. She can tell it all to Grams. She can tell that Ray hurts her. She can tell that Ray won't let her take a bath by herself, and that he won't leave her alone at night. Suzie remembers Ray's face when he panicked earlier that day.

"Suzie, is Ray touching you on your private places?" Gram's words are firm, but she tenderly reaches up and wraps her arm around Suzie's waist. As if Suzie had prepared her whole life for this moment, Suzie takes a deep, slow breath and, with her eyes locked on her Grams, cautiously nods her head yes.

She has to look away from her grandmother's inquisitive stare. A huge lump forms in Suzie's throat as a flood of relief instantly fills her heart. A huge black storm cloud has suddenly parted and sunshine is hitting her face for the very first time in years. The floodgates of her heart's dam burst open and she starts to cry, letting in a torrent of cool, healing water. It pours into her desert place as her grandmother holds her close.

The lump in Suzie's throat tightens and tears trickle down her rosy cheeks. Suzie's huge, beautiful green-blue eyes look back at Grams as her grandmother grimaces and cups her hand up over her mouth. She looks back at Suzie, tears also streaming down her face. Grams sits straight as a board and forces out the words with delicate determination. "Is that what he was doing today when I came to get you?" Grams leans her head forward and bends down, looking straight into Suzie's eyes.

Suzie takes another slow, shaky breath and breathes it out even slower, gritting her teeth as she remembers what he was doing. Hot tears fall from her sweetly freckled face. Suzie nods her head up and down repeatedly.

Grams loudly exclaims in a half cry as if she just realized the answer to a million-dollar question. "That's why it took so long to answer the door today?"

Suzie looks deep into her Gram's tear-filled eyes and whispers a soft, broken-hearted, "Yes."

Make it Personal

Travis feels the sexual abuse by his sister when he was twelve caused just as much or worse mental torment as Kenny's. List as many reasons as you can to explain why this could be true. How do you think it made Travis feel?

_____

_____

_____

Do you think that Adrian, at age twenty-one, had any idea that she was seriously harming her brother or causing him such guilt-filled hatred of himself?

_____

_____

_____

How do you think parents can raise up kids to understand the harm done when we touch others inappropriately? Do you think these talks should be introduced at an early age? If you need help, visit www. idomministries.com We are planning an age-appropriate curriculum for children through age eighteen based on the Scriptures found in Matthew 18.

_____

_____

_____

Do you think Suzie might have told about Ray's molesting her sooner if she had been asked sooner?

_____

_____

_____

How do you think that the abuse Travis and Suzie suffered as children will affect them as adults?

_____

_____

_____

Do you have a clearer understanding of the loss experienced by people who have been sexually molested than you did before you read about Travis' and Suzie's lives?

_____

_____

_____

What do you think Grams will do now that Suzie has told her? What would you do?

_____

_____

_____

Notes

A MUST-READ
CONCLUSION

What Forgiveness Is Not

Would you ever consider telling an elderly veteran who was crying over a battle where comrades were literally blown into pieces that "he just needs to forgive" the enemy? Of course not. You would understand that his pain and tears were over the unimaginable loss of close companions.

So why do we so often assume persons wounded by sexual molestation are crying out of hatred or unforgiveness toward their abusers? The truth is, many of these sexually abused were hurt by people they looked up to and still love and care for. Why is it that when they talk about their trauma we immediately assume they hold a grudge against the abuser, and therefore need to forgive him or her in order to move forward. And why do we imply that the moment they forgive, they will no longer hurt over the abuse? This is nonsense and so very damaging to victims.

In the past (before I married Travis) if the awkward subject of "someone being molested" came up, my instinct was to try to say something constructive and move on in a "let's get life back to normal as quickly as we can" kind of way. That "something constructive" usually centered around forgiveness. After all, I was trying to help the victim's pain go away. I found out the hard way that my instinctive reaction was not helpful. Although I do believe forgiving is of prime importance, there are some confusing border lines here.

Remember, the victims we are counseling (or just trying to love and support) are usually adults, but in order to forgive, they must take that little girl or boy in their heart back to the horrible place (in their memories) and face the anguish. It's worse than fighting a three-headed dragon. You see, the child was the one wounded, not the grown-up. That child whose spirit was crushed, is still in there, usually paralyzed by the trauma. I know that for certain. Please show mercy when reminding a victim of sexual molestation (or any other child abuse) that they need to forgive. They hear it a lot. Everyone knows we are supposed to forgive.

Also please try to understand that just because they are crying or hurting or talking about it does not necessarily mean that they haven't forgiven. Sometimes they just need to express their pain and loss or be protected from the source of the pain. They need to know that what happened to them wasn't okay or their fault and that people do believe them and care. They mostly need to know that something is actively being done about it. Forgiveness doesn't and should never mean you're not allowed to talk or cry about it again. One reason wonderful, caring people will tell a sexual molestation victim who talks or cries about their abuse to forgive is because they can't comprehend the anguish of the victim's loss. As a result, they assume the person has bitterness in their heart toward the perpetrator. However, a person who has been molested as a child has lost more than we can ever appreciate having, and at such a tender age. One of these losses is their dignity. Oh yes, children feel that tremendous loss, as being molested devalues them to their core. Their ability to trust man and God is also ripped away. Their ability to receive love also crushed. Can you imagine never being able to feel truly loved? Always doubting that you are good enough? Can you imagine struggling to believe anyone could possibly love you? What would it feel like to be incapable of experiencing any value in yourself? That is a reality for many abused people. Their innocence smashed. The loving, tender experiences they were robbed of, that should have happened within the safe boundaries of a caring godly relationship, are gone. Yanked away. For those abused by loved ones—used like a tool instead of a precious, valuable member of the family—the wound is deep and devastating. Their value as a person has been annihilated and needs to be healed and restored. They become completely filled with shame. Think about that for a moment. It's as if they become shame.

Time makes us more able to talk without tears, but tears are not always an indication (as some believe) of anger, bitterness, or unforgiveness. You would never accuse a person who cried over the death of a loved one fifty years later or a young mother recalling a stillborn birth five years later of being bitter or unforgiving, even if someone else had caused it. You would simply assume that they were hurting over a tremendous loss. Well guess what? These sexually abused ones have lost also. They've lost their innocence, lost their youth, lost their virginity, lost their happiness, lost their ability to trust, lost their security, and lost their self-worth. Often, they've lost their family unit. They have faced loved ones not believing them, calling them liars, public humiliation... on and on. They have faced fear you will never experience. Sometimes they can't even mentally identify what they have lost, yet they feel the pain.

I think the healthiest thing we can do is just let them cry or talk and put our arms around them and say, "I'm here. I'm with you. I care. I'm on your side." Don't say things like... "You really need to stop focusing on this... after all that is in the past" or "I sense some bitterness when you're talking about it and you really need to work on forgiving." That's just like saying "Your pain is just too much to bother with; you're too sensitive or you need to get over it." Or saying, "You're really taking all that stuff that happened in your past way too seriously and you're being way too dramatic." That's no way to help someone heal.

Many people don't express their pain verbally and bottle it up inside because they don't want people to wrongly believe that they can't forgive. There are also people who have truly forgiven and then doubt the fact that they forgave because they've been convinced that they should never hurt again. They mistakenly think that if it still hurts (in the slightest), they have failed and can't forgive. The guilt of (supposedly) not forgiving plagues and torments them. They live in fear of hell every time they experience pain over their loss, on top of everything else. This is a horrific burden on top of their severe pain.

Guess what? It's okay if it hurts sometimes! That's right. Victims of sexual abuse have lost some precious and important things that they will never get back, and it hurts and it's okay to say it! Try saying that to the next person who shares their secret pain with you. If they have opened up to you, they obviously are hoping you will hear their heart. Try saying "I know it hurt horribly and it is okay for you to say it hurts. I'm sorry you suffered through that. I'm here for you."

You know what else really helps? Imagine that you had walked in during the abuse. Tell the victim exactly what you think you would have done if you had caught the offender, red handed. It may sound something like this: "I would have taken a baseball bat and beaten them till I was too exhausted to swing, if I had been there and caught them!" I know it sounds crazy, but this is often very comforting for a person who felt unprotected, bullied, and vulnerable. Just knowing someone would have jumped in and stopped the abuse, if they had known, is so reassuring. Remember though that some of these wounded ones were molested by people they love dearly, and this gets tricky. It is soul crushing and horrifically painful. They may feel guilt for casting a negative light on their loved one even after they were brutally abused. Proceed with wisdom. Pray, the Holy Spirit will lead you.

I have heard so many people say to someone who just expressed pain over being abused, "You know you just need to forgive" and in most circumstances that's true. If someone tripped you on the bus or if someone broke into your car and stole your phone, you release them and give it to the Lord. But that doesn't mean when you remember it you will have fond, loving feelings about falling or the car theft. You hopefully will be able to pray and truly have God's heart for them, but you will never feel great about spitting sand out of your mouth and your skinned-up hands or the thief taking your credit card out of the center hatch and buying a $1200 computer with it, or having to replace your phone that had all your favorite photos on it.

The deeper the wound, the more healing that needs to take place. Let me say that it will be so much harder for our victims to heal if the family ignores or embraces the perp while continually reprimanding the victim with, "You need to forgive" every time the victim needs to express the loss. And I am certain about this: just because someone *never* talks about it, doesn't mean they have forgiven it.

These victims sense that as they speak about what happened to them, others are uncomfortable with their grief (sometimes because of the subject matter) and just want to slap a solution on the table. "Here, you just need to forgive... then all will be well! Forgive and forget...put it behind you! Move on!"

Is that how it works for a parent who has lost a child to a drunk driver? We just tell them to forgive that drunk driver and the pain will vanish? Then we don't have to talk about it anymore? No! Again, we totally can imagine the pain of the loss of a child ripped away. You see, it is the loss people don't comprehend! Even if it had been a hundred years, you would never think to tell a parent to just forgive the person responsible for their child's death. We might see pictures of the lost child on the mantle or coffee table. That would seem perfectly normal. We would understand it if the grieving parent posted pictures of the lost child on social media. In fact, we would expect it. But you can't take a photo of someone's lost self-esteem or their ruined childhood. You can't frame their inability to receive love or their inability to trust, but it remains a devastatingly painful loss just the same, except we can't physically see it. Most child abuse victims live in their own private hell and have been misunderstood for way too long.

That's why I wrote this book. If through Travis's and Suzie's testimonies we have grown and can now start to have a better understanding of the loss, we can allow victims of sexual molestation to cry if they need to and comfort them, even if it's been fifty years.

Sometimes people tell a victim to forgive in order to hush them, not out of malice, but because they want peace in their family. Peace is a good thing to want, but not at the victim's expense. Check your motives and make sure you are dealing with unforgiveness and that you really have the best interest of the victim in mind before you tell them to forgive. Don't use it as a quick fix. Love them and be as patient as you would with any other trauma victim.

One more point on what forgiveness is not: the assumption that because the victim doesn't want to be exposed to the perpetrator is evidence that the victim has not forgiven is an ignorant and extremely harsh attitude. It is incorrect, presumptuous, short-sighted, and hurtful. For one moment, try to put yourself in the victim's place. Telling a victim that they haven't forgiven if they refuse to sit next to the perpetrator at the Thanksgiving table is cruel. Especially if the perpetrator is your child. Remember, the victim knows things about that perpetrator you will probably never know or could ever guess. If they need space, give it to them. If you are caught between the victim you dearly love, and a perpetrator you dearly love… you need (good) professional help. Get it! My plan is to write about this specifically in the future. Hopefully there will be a second and third book continuing this subject.

Any family members protecting a perpetrator are involved in criminal negligence, not forgiveness. Please don't confuse justice and forgiveness; they are two totally different things. You can totally forgive and still do the right thing and report the offender or at least (if it is too late to prosecute or if they are a minor) put them at a distance and make absolutely sure that children are never exposed to them. Remember, the perpetrator needs help. Covering theircrime will only enable them to harm others, making you an accomplice. It can also break and destroy the victim's heart. It is a horrible position to be in, but remember the next time you are blaming God for not stepping in and stopping a crime. You can be the answer to some poor child's prayer by doing what's right and getting the perpetrators the professional intervention they need.

Covering up the crime of sexual abuse within families happens so often and is always damaging to a victim's soul and spirit. The only reason that I can think of to not tell would be if the perpetrator was dead and telling could only harm the family. Then I would leave it up to the victim. They need our support.

The best thing you can do for a person who has been hurt by sexual abuse is to reassure them that what happened to them is not their fault, that it was wrong on every level, and that you care about what they went through. Let them talk. Do not hurry or hush them. Don't try to fix them with a quick solution on your part. I have made that mistake, and it is so hurtful to the victim. Sign on for the loving long haul by committing in your spirit to pray for them, and then support them by helping them to maintain appropriate boundaries from the offender if they need to and seek professional help. They may need you to go to the authorities with them, as there is never a case of rape or child abuse when the authorities should not be involved. Never!

Travis's and Suzie's stories will continue in my next book, *Arrowhead*. Unfortunately, their troubles are not nearly over. I was advised by several people to resolve their stories to some cheerful end quickly as some readers are not patient, but I kept thinking that life just doesn't work that way. Not just that, but the truth is the truth, and Travis and Suzie suffered long. The truth is that the worst heartbreak is yet to come and writing it differently than it is doesn't seem fair to them. If you can continue to take their hands and walk their stories with them, you will grow, cry, learn and laugh with them.

What Forgiveness Is

Just last week I saw the report of a ten-year-old girl who was brutally murdered after being raped. Her mother watched and participated. How ghastly!

In my mind, I acknowledged how that horrible act had to grieve God's Holy Spirit. I tried, at a feeble level, to set my mind on God and spend a moment letting myself care about how it makes Him feel for a child to be treated so perversely, instead of just letting my feelings go unchecked. This time, I had the full knowledge of the "millstone" Scriptures in my mind. I let myself try to feel His heart. How does God hurt for that innocent child? How does He feel about the perpetrator he created, His own creation choosing (free will) such debauchery?

How painful would it be for me to have to sentence my own creation for that crime, especially after I had lived a sinless life and died to make it possible for them to choose (free will) to be clean? I can't understand it, but (if those involved are not 100 percent brokenhearted over their horrendous actions) God will do it. I can't really put myself in His place to feel His feelings because I didn't leave my place of Glory to submit myself to ridicule and shame becoming the actual sin I detest. No wonder God is so angry at them. "God hates sin and God abhors the wicked". (Psalms 11:15 KJV). How can God both love and hate? Well, He is God. He is both Love and a God of wrath. It may seem complex or contradicting to us, but God is both. Did God know some people would choose debauchery? Yes. Does God plan, or force them or want them to do those things...certainly not.

Do you know how I know it is not God's will that all these evil things happen?

"For the children of Judah have done evil in My sight," says the Lord; "they have set their disgusting and shamefully vile things in the house which called by My Name, to defile it. They have built the high places of Topheth, which is in the Valley of Ben-hinnom (son of Hinnom), to burn their sons and their daughters in the fire [to honor Molech, the fire god] which I did not command, nor did it come into My heart (mind)." (Jeremiah 7:30-31 KJV)

In Jeremiah 7:30-31, God's people were burning their sons and daughters in a fire to sacrifice them to a false god, and God says, "...which I did not command them to do, neither did it come into my heart or mind." He's saying He didn't ask them to do this, neither did it ever "enter into his mind to ask them to do this," meaning they were committing a sin (murdering children) that, of course, was not God's will or intention. Yet God did not immediately start regulating their free will and stop them from murdering their children.

The devastating events that have happened so far in Travis and Suzie's young lives are, without a doubt, not God's will. But yes, just like He allowed those parents to throw their babies in the fires of Molech, He allows free will today. If God Almighty chooses to wait and judge the perpetrators (2 Timothy 4:1) instead of stopping them now, that is His choice; and He promises us that He will deal with them. He is God and He will do what He says.

Sometimes God does step in. When you read these next two examples, where God did step in, think about our society today and compare it to our TV shows, movies, streets, schools, and homes.

"The Lord saw that the wickedness (depravity) of man was great on the earth, and that every imagination or intent of the thoughts of his heart were only evil continually. The Lord regretted that He had made mankind on the earth, and He was [deeply] grieved in His heart. So, the Lord said, "I will destroy (annihilate) mankind whom I have created from the surface of the earth not only man, but the animals and the crawling things and the birds of the air—because it [deeply] grieves Me [to see mankind's sin] and I regret that I have made them."

The [population of the] earth was corrupt [absolutely depraved—spiritually and morally putrid] in God's sight, and the land was filled with violence [desecration, infringement, outrage, assault, and lust for power]. God looked on the earth and saw how debased and degenerate it was, for all humanity had corrupted their way on the earth and lost their true direction." (Genesis 6:5-7:11-13 AMP).

Note the words "deeply grieved." God is grievously hurt to see men sin. Yet we now have the knowledge of good and evil, so we can judge God for allowing us to hurt one another.

I have changed since I had the dream. Now, (as I read about the young girl raped on her birthday and killed by her mom's boyfriend while her own mother participated) I cried in my spirit with His Spirit instead of accusing Him of not caring. I now realize that He cares so much more than I ever could. I will never lose sight of that again.

Can someone ever really grasp the weight of such a heinous crime and truly repent? I think that some are incapable of sorrow or true repentance. And, I'm not talking about them crying because they got caught or are in danger of going to jail. I'm not talking about them crying because they lost their family or are publically humiliated either. God knows our hearts and our motives. Here is the big question… If the person or persons who have hurt you or your loved ones acknowledged and admitted they were responsible and wrong—totally renouncing their sin, completely brokenhearted and humbled, grasping in its entirety the weight and awfulness of their reckless sin, turning themselves into the authorities, without lessening or lying about what happened and were willing to make restitution in any way possible—would you be able to forgive them?

Consider that one of two things will definitely happen to this offender: they will "fully" repent (feel the crushing guilt and condemnation) of their sin or they will face the wrath of God described in Matthew 18. These facts should make it at least easier to forgive, let it go, and trust in Jesus Christ. Forgiveness is a matter of trust in the faithfulness of God. He keeps His Word. If God said it, He will do it.

Please take a minute and watch a video about "one" out of the "over a hundred" young women who were molested by an Olympic doctor. who was supposed to be treating them all for injuries or pain. Google https://youtu.be/DHyxPHZ- j2l by Wretched Radio & TV. Listen as Rachael Denhollander speaks directly to her abuser. She speaks of repentance. Wow...it is heart wrenching and true. Just seven years after she was abused by this man she says this.

"You have become a man ruled by selfish and perverted desires. A man defined by his daily choices over and over again...to feed that selfishness and perversion. You chose to pursue your wickedness no matter what it cost others. If you have read the Bible you carry, you know that the definition of love portrayed is of God himself loving so sacrificially that He gave up everything to pay a penalty for the sin He did not commit. By His grace I too choose to love this way. You spoke of praying for forgiveness, but Larry if you have read the Bible you carry, you know that forgiveness does not come from doing good things, as if good deeds can erase what you have done. It comes from repentance which requires facing and acknowledging the truth about what you have done in all of its utter depravity and horror without mitigation... without excuse, without acting as if good deeds can erase what you have done." Rachael then shares the "millstone" scripture and reminds him of how many he has wounded. She then adds, "The Bible you speak of carries a final judgement where all of God's wrath and His eternal terror is poured out on men like you... Should you ever reach the point of truly facing what you have done... the quilt will be crushing, and that is what makes the gospel of Christ so sweet...because it extends grace and hope and mercy where none should be found. I pray you experience the soul-crushing weight of guilt so that you may someday experience true repentance and true forgiveness from God. Which you need far more than forgiveness from me."

Wow…that women should have been on the front of every magazine cover on the supermarket shelves that month.

I want to leave you with a question. Can you ask God to open your heart to how He might love the thieves, liars, rapists, cheaters, murderers, gang members, blind guides, wolves and yes…even the pedophiles and yet hold them accountable too? Just like Rachael Denhollander held her abuser accountable (got him off the street so others were protected) yet extended forgiveness and hoped for him to truly come to a place of understanding and sorrow over his actions. Forgiveness is not letting the offender walk free. Forgiveness is important, but so is justice. Walking through stern consequences for an offense is often the very best thing for an offender.

We all know that God instructs us to forgive others for their willful and reckless sins so that we can be forgiven. (See Matthew 6:15). Still, there are some offenses that are terribly hard to forgive. It sometimes seems like more than I can bear to think about them, the perpetrators, I mean. When I do, I recall Jesus tenderly drawing the child into his arms and His warning about the millstone. Then I close my eyes and picture myself reaching up to take His hand. I remember His immense capacity to love the broken, and that He is the one who will hold His creation accountable for every single deed. I remember that Jesus is coming back soon, and He will bring His reward with Him, repaying everyone for what they have done in the body, good and bad. I acknowledge that He will deal with the depraved and unrepentant wicked and that brings me extreme comfort. I think about His mercy toward me even now in my sin. I remember that I'm here to glorify the Lord and choose to love my enemies because of Jesus Christ's finished work in me. I recall that His blood justifies me…I remember that the word justified reminds me that it is: "just-as-if-I'd-never-sinned" and "just-as if I'll never sin again." He calls me "righteous" while I am still in a sinning state. I carefully consider the price He paid to justify me and then I pray that these perpetrators will experience the crushing weight of guilt and come to Jesus.

"My little children, these things write I unto you, that ye sin not. And if any man sin, we have an advocate with the Father, Jesus Christ the righteous: And he is the propitiation for our sins: *__and not for ours only, but also for the sins of the whole world.__*" 1 John 2:1-2 KJV

Just like King David cried for his wayward son Absalom, I think about how I would feel if they (the perpetrator) were my child. I forgive them and trust God to deal with them, remembering that they are God's responsibility and (all sinners) are first His creation and potentially His children too. It is all in His capable hands, so I decide to trust Him.

Can you pray for those who have offended to experience the eye-opening revelation and heart-breaking crushing guilt that leads to repentance? Can you see them and pray for them as if they were your own loved ones gone astray?

God bless you, dear reader.

Please visit our website www.idomministries.com and check out the link… Good Enough For God.

REFERENCES

Childrens Rights. "If I could Have My Childhood Back." YouTube, YouTube, 24 Nov 2012. https://www.youtube.com/watch?v=Cbl0YD_ibgM

Desiring God Foundation. "This Illness is For the Glory of God - John Piper." YouTube, YouTube, 14 Sep 2011. https://www.desiringgod.org/messages/this-illness-is-for-the-glory-of-god

Hurnard, Hannah. *Hinds' Feet on High Places*. Wheaton, IL: Living Books, 1988.

McVey, Crystal. "Nine Minutes in Heaven." The 700 Club, YouTube, 24 June 2013. https://www.youtube.com/watch?v=GMN28qbWvmQ

Rudder, Randy. "A Crime of Passion." CBN.com, YouTube, 1 Mar 2008. http://youtu.be/Fn5G0uoSo1s

Ten Boom, Corrie; Elizabeth Sherrill, and John L. Sherrill. *The Hiding Place*. Peabody MA: Hendrickson Publishers, 2015.

Vujicic, Nick. "God Will Not Give Up On You." CBN.com, YouTube, 26 June 2009. https://www.youtube.com/watch?v=KJ1OEi2OhSU

Vujicic, Nick. "What's Your Excuse?" YouTube, YouTube, 20 Dec 2016. http://youtu.be/nknzSWDcUgA

About the Author

Linda Idom lives near Houston, Texas with her husband, Travis. After years of volunteering and working at foster centers, youth organizations, and shelters, where the effects of sexual abuse run rampant, Linda struggled to make sense of these abandoned children and the suffering they endured. As she cried out to God over the pain she witnessed, God showed her His heart toward these dearly loved young ones. Unexpectedly, God showed her way more than she ever could have imagined.

Idom Ministries was birthed as a result of the Holy Spirit's amazing power to heal both her heart and Travis' after suffering the anguish of childhood sexual abuse. Together they share the love and redemptive power of Jesus Christ with their community and those devastated by abuse. Travis and Linda have a blended family of seven children and nine grandchildren whom they love and adore. Linda also enjoys, reading, painting, Bible journaling, decorating, and anything creative. Travis enjoys great gospel music, metal detecting, listening to audiobooks, and most of all, he loves the Word of God. Travis and Linda can testify that God brings dry bones to life, makes beauty from ashes and produces streams in the desert.

Praise for Millstone

"I commend Linda Idom for her COURAGE. This is a very difficult subject to raise, especially among church folks. Linda is a great writer and teacher, and her wit shines through in this work. Millstone was very thoughtfully written, yet even after twenty-five years of working in the trenches counselling abuse victims, it was difficult to read the painful encounters in Millstone. I believe this will greatly help those victims who are willing to confront their pain. This is a necessary work and God is using Linda Idom's Millstone to spark some much-needed conversations."

—Dr. Nick Eno Minister,
Licensed Professional Counselor and
Therapist Author of *The Orphan Syndrome*

"This book is powerfully written, anointed with profound spiritual revelations, full of heartfelt passion, and splattered with "Linda Humor" that oftentimes had me smiling and laughing just in the nick of time! Without question this was a hard read for me. But, this book opened my eyes to an evil epidemic that has been hidden for way too long. More than anything, I appreciate Linda Idom for having the courage to tell a real story that the world needs to know."

—Eileen Cornelsen,
Writer *The Forgotten People Ministry* Newsletter

"I grew up sheltered from the world and find it easiest to plant my head in the sand rather than acknowledge the darkness we live in. Millstone has helped me see the real, often horrific effects of childhood abuse and a biblical way to respond to such atrocities. Linda's love and gentle heart are poured into her work here and it shines. Of the many books coming out this year, this one needs a priority spot on your list."

—Rose McQuillin
Home school mother of five.

"Ms. Idom successfully informs the reader about the psychological effects on the victims of such atrocities. You will see how and why silence and rage become the unfortunate companions of those held captive. Millstone offers fresh insight and tools to help the victim release the person or persons who hurt them in their past. In Millstone, victims will find the courage to release their pain. I recommend this book to anyone who has suffered at the hands of an abuser or wishes to join the fight to end all sexual abuse. As a survivor, Ms. Idom is clearly qualified to share her insights with us.

Also, the reader is challenged to 'Make It Personal' by answering questions at the end of each chapter, making Millstone a workbook for individual or group study. Ms. Idom makes a clear, lasting impression, and this book is not soft on any person abusing a child. A victim of sexual abuse who has read Millstone could give this book to a family member and write a note or just say, 'Please read this so you can get an idea of what I've been through and how I feel, because I want you to understand, but it is too painful for me to talk about what happened.' This book will make a difference!"

—Marion E. Pietz,
Licensed professional Counselor, MA, PLLC, LPC-S, LMFT
25 years of professional counseling experience

"Millstone is incredible. It has given me a powerful, sobering look through the eyes of a child suffering abuse. Most children aren't talking, but Millstone speaks for them. It is tactful yet gravely honest. I cannot more highly recommend this book to victims and their families, also for people working with those effected by abuse. For someone like me who needed a reality check about the world we live in, it was really life changing. I am hoping that she is almost done with the sequel Arrowhead because the wait is probably going to kill me!

Do you know where you stand and what your thoughts are about sexual molestation? You may think you know, but Linda Idom answers questions that you didn't even realize you had and in a way that jumps at you, challenging your ideas, making you face off with questions that will heal your heart and grow you spiritually. Linda Idom has done an incredible job weaving these true testimonies and the biblical teaching together seamlessly! It was brutal, but I loved it. We need this on our bookshelves."

—Misti Bullen.
Executive Assistant

"It's about dang time! It needs to be broadcast to the world. Millstone is a radiant light just waiting to brighten the darkest corners of our society today. Warning...About the time you think that you can't continue reading it...persevere! Millstone, with God's guidance, will astound you. A must- read for victims of sexual abuse and for those who have committed sexual abuse, too. It couldn't hurt for the perpetrators to think about and understand what awful damage they are inflicting on their victims. Mothers and fathers, this book is for you. It will open your eyes to the world your children are growing up in and the dangers that seek to destroy them."

—Robin Parkin
–Park Ranger, Tx Parks and Wildlife Co-creator of wildlife education center materials Additional Duty Safety Officer for Sheldon Lake State Park

"Millstone is gut wrenching ... yet it gives an extraordinary peek into the heart of our heavenly Father. With delicate care, the author has skillfully woven together these victims' tragic experiences with heart-piercing spiritual reflections spotlighting the emotional aftermath and healing needed as a result of childhood sexual abuse."

-Anita Graves
Hospital Senior Administrative Assistant

"Millstone is eye-opening. The horrific subject of pedophilia has been swept under the rug for far too long! This book was thoughtfully arranged as the chapters alternate between gripping testimonies and biblical truths. The testimonies were tough for me to read, and I appreciated the much- needed respite during those in-between chapters. I gained staggering insight from the perspective of children who repeatedly suffer physically and emotionally at the hands of their abusers. The writing of such a sensitive subject was handled tactfully and without being too explicit. Millstone is an excellent read for those who were victimized as well as for those who were not. Linda's writing is powerful, honest, and anointed. I am anxiously waiting to read her second book, Arrowhead."

–Angela Kenney
Medical transcriptionist

Made in the USA
Coppell, TX
28 September 2020